# Alice 2.0
## Introductory Concepts and Techniques

**Gary B. Shelly**
**Thomas J. Cashman**
**Charles W. Herbert**

THOMSON COURSE TECHNOLOGY

25 THOMSON PLACE

BOSTON, MA 02210

SHELLY
CASHMAN
SERIES®

Australia • Canada • Denmark • Japan • Mexico • New Zealand • Philippines • Puerto Rico • Singapore
South Africa • Spain • United Kingdom • United States

**THOMSON**

**COURSE TECHNOLOGY**

# Alice 2.0:
# Introductory Concepts and Techniques

Gary B. Shelly

Thomas J. Cashman

Charles W. Herbert

**Executive Editor:**
Alexandra Arnold

**Senior Marketing Manager:**
Joy Stark-Vancs

**Senior Product Managers:**
Karen Stevens, Reed Curry

**Product Managers:**
Kim Crowley, Heather Hawkins

**Developmental Editor:**
John Bosco

**Associate Product Manger:**
Klenda Martinez

**Editorial Assistant:**
Jon Farnham

**Print Buyer:**
Julio Esperas

**Content Project Manager:**
Danielle Chouhan

**Copy Editor:**
Gary Michael Spahl

**Proofreader:**
Kathy Orrino

**QA Manuscript Reviewers:**
John Freitas, Peter S. Stefanis,
Susan Whalen

**Cover Artist:**
John Still

**Composition:**
GEX Publishing Services

**Alice 2.0**
Introductory Concepts
and Techniques

# Contents

# Preface

The Shelly Cashman Series® offers the finest textbooks in computer education. We are proud of the fact that our textbook series has been the most widely used in education. *Alice 2.0 Introductory Concepts and Techniques* continues with the innovation, quality, and reliability that you have come to expect from the Shelly Cashman Series.

Alice 2.0 is a software program designed to make it much easier for users to create computer programs. Alice uses a drag-and-drop interface to replace the need to correctly type commands according to obscure rules of syntax. This user interface ensures that programs are always well-formed. In addition, Alice clarifies object-based programming by providing animated, 3D virtual objects.

In this Alice 2.0 book, you will find an educationally sound and easy-to-follow pedagogy that combines a step-by-step approach with corresponding screens. All projects and exercises in this book are designed to introduce students to essential programming concepts through learning Alice 2.0. The Other Ways and More About features provide greater knowledge of Alice 2.0. The project material is developed carefully to ensure that students will see the importance of understanding programming concepts for future coursework in programming and computer science.

## Objectives of This Textbook

*Alice 2.0: Introductory Concepts and Techniques* is intended as a supplemental text for an introductory programming course, a computer concepts course, or an Office applications course. No programming experience is assumed, and no mathematics beyond the high school freshman level is required. The objectives of this book are:

- To teach the basics of Alice 2.0
- To teach fundamental concepts of computer programming and algorithm development
- To acquaint students with the proper procedures for planning and implementing a computer program
- To introduce students to modern object-oriented, event-driven programming
- To provide students with a foundation for further study of computer programming
- To develop an exercise-oriented approach that allows learning by doing
- To encourage independent study and help those who are working alone

## The Shelly Cashman Approach

Features of the Shelly Cashman Series *Alice 2.0* book include:

- **Project Orientation** Each project in the book presents a practical problem and complete solution using an easy-to-understand approach.
- **Step-by-Step, Screen-by-Screen Instructions** Each of the tasks required to complete a project is identified throughout the project. Full-color screens with callouts accompany the steps.
- **Thoroughly Tested Projects** Unparalleled quality is ensured because every screen in the book is produced by the author only after performing a step, and then each project must pass Thomson Course Technology's award-winning quality assurance program.
- **Other Ways Boxes** The Other Ways boxes displayed at the end of many of the step-by-step sequences specify alternative ways to do the task completed in the steps. Thus, the steps and the Other Ways box make a comprehensive reference unit.

- **More About and Q&A Features** These marginal annotations provide background information, tips, and answers to common questions that complement the topics covered, adding depth and perspective to the learning process.
- **Integration of the World Wide Web** The World Wide Web is integrated into the Alice 2.0 learning experience by More About annotations that send students to Web sites for up-to-date information and alternative approaches to tasks.

## Organization of This Textbook

*Alice 2.0: Introductory Concepts and Techniques* provides detailed instruction on how to use Alice 2.0. The material is divided into four projects.

**Project 1 — Exploring Alice and Object-Oriented Programming** In Project 1, students are introduced to the concept of object-oriented Programming (OOP). Students learn how to start Alice, and become familiar with the Alice drag-and-drop interface and its components. This project also has students load and play an existing Alice world, create and save a new Alice world, and print the code for Alice methods and events.

**Project 2 — Developing Software Methods** In Project 2, students are exposed to the notion of top-down design and modular development within the context of a program development cycle. The project explores the process and benefits of developing software as a collection of smaller modules that can be tested individually, then put together to form the overall program. They are guided through a step-by-step project in which they design, code, test, and debug an Alice world with several software methods.

**Project 3 — Programming with Logical Structures** In Project 3, students learn about the three major elements of logical structure found in algorithms — linear sequences, selection sequences, and repetition sequences — and how to implement these in Alice using built-in functions and methods. They learn to use Boolean AND, OR, and NOT operations along with the six logical comparison operations used in computer programming to create simple and compound Boolean expressions in Alice looping or branching instructions.

**Project 4 — Creating Event-Driven Software** In Project 4, students learn how to create interactive software using modern techniques of event-driven programming. They learn how event listeners detect event triggers and call event handlers into action. They also create their own events with Alice's easy-to-use event editor.

## End-of-Project Student Activities

A notable strength of the Shelly Cashman Series is the extensive student activities at the end of each project. Well-structured student activities can make the difference between students merely participating in a class and students retaining the information they learn. The activities in the Shelly Cashman Series *Alice 2.0* book include the following:

- **What You Should Know** A listing of the tasks completed within a project together with the pages on which the step-by-step, screen-by-screen explanations appear.
- **Apply Your Knowledge** This exercise usually requires students to open and manipulate a file that is provided in the Data Files for Students. To obtain a copy of the Data Files for Students, follow the instructions on the inside back cover of this textbook.
- **In the Lab** Three in-depth assignments per project require students to utilize the project concepts and techniques to create additional Web sites.
- **Cases and Places** Three unique, real-world, case-study situations, including one small-group activity.
- **Learning Exercises** Additional exercises covering Alice, programming and algorithm development, but do not require students to create any new code.

# Shelly Cashman Series Instructor Resources

The Shelly Cashman Series is dedicated to providing you with all of the tools you need to make your class a success. Information on all supplementary materials is available through your Thomson Course Technology representative or by calling one of the following telephone numbers: Colleges, Universities, Continuing Education Departments, and Post-Secondary Vocational Schools: 800-648-7450; Career Colleges, Business, Industry, Government, Trade, Retailer, Wholesaler, Library, and Resellers: 800-477-3692; K-12, Secondary Vocational Schools, Adult Education, and School Districts: 800-824-5179.

The Instructor Resources for this textbook include both teaching and testing aids. The contents of each item on the Instructor Resources CD-ROM (ISBN 1-4239-1223-3) are described below.

**INSTRUCTOR'S MANUAL**   The Instructor's Manual is made up of Microsoft Word files, which include detailed lesson plans with page number references, lecture notes, teaching tips, classroom activities, discussion topics, projects to assign, and transparency references. The transparencies are available through the Figure Files described below.

**SYLLABUS**   Sample syllabi, which can be customized easily to a course, are included. The syllabi cover policies, class and lab assignments and exams, and procedural information.

**FIGURE FILES**   Illustrations for every figure in the textbook are available in electronic form. Use this ancillary to present a slide show in lecture or to print transparencies for use in lecture with an overhead projector. If you have a personal computer and LCD device, this ancillary can be an effective tool for presenting lectures.

**POWERPOINT PRESENTATIONS**   PowerPoint Presentations is a multimedia lecture presentation system that provides slides for each project. Presentations are based on project objectives. Use this presentation system to present well-organized lectures that are both interesting and knowledge based. PowerPoint Presentations provides consistent coverage at schools that use multiple lecturers.

**SOLUTIONS TO EXERCISES**   Solutions are included for the end-of-project exercises, as well as the Project Reinforcement exercises.

**TEST BANK & TEST ENGINE**   The ExamView test bank includes 110 questions for every project (25 multiple-choice, 50 true/false, and 35 completion) with page number references, and when appropriate, figure references. A version of the test bank you can print also is included. The test bank comes with a copy of the test engine, ExamView, the ultimate tool for your objective-based testing needs. ExamView is a state-of-the-art test builder that is easy to use. ExamView enables you to create paper-, LAN-, or Web-based tests from test banks designed specifically for your Course Technology textbook. Utilize the ultra-efficient QuickTest Wizard to create tests in less than five minutes by taking advantage of Course Technology's question banks, or customize your own exams from scratch.

**DATA FILES FOR STUDENTS**   All the files that are required by students to complete the exercises are included. You can distribute the files on the Instructor Resources CD-ROM to your students over a network, or you can have them follow the instructions on the inside back cover of this book to obtain a copy of the Data Files for Students.

**ADDITIONAL ACTIVITIES FOR STUDENTS**   These additional activities consist of Project Reinforcement Exercises, which are true/false, multiple choice, and short answer questions that help students gain confidence in the material learned.

## Online Content

Thomson Course Technology offers textbook-based content for Blackboard, and WebCT.

**BLACKBOARD AND WEBCT**  As the leading provider of IT content for the Blackboard and WebCT platforms, Thomson Course Technology delivers rich content that enhances your textbook to give your students a unique learning experience. Thomson Course Technology has partnered with WebCT and Blackboard to deliver our market-leading content through these state-of-the-art online learning platforms.

## Obtaining Alice 2.0

The Alice software system is open source and provided as a free public service by Carnegie Mellon University. A CD-ROM containing Alice version 2.0 from Carnegie Mellon University is packaged into the back cover of this book.

You can also obtain Alice 2.0 by visiting the Alice Web site at www.alice.org. Click the Get Alice v2.0 link under the Free Stuff heading, and then following the instructions for your operating system.

The minimum system requirements for the version of Alice included on the CD-ROM packaged with this text are a 500 MHz Intel Pentium III processor (or equivalent) and later (1.0 GHz recommended); Windows ME, Windows 2000, or Windows XP; 128 MB RAM (256 MB recommended); VGA graphics card with 1024 × 768 resolution, 16-bit display (16 MB 3D video card recommended). Alice is also available for Apple iMac and Linux-based computer systems.

The material in this book is based upon work supported by the National Science Foundation under Grant No. ATE 0302542. Any opinions, findings, and conclusions or recommendations expressed in this material are those of the author and do not necessarily reflect the views of the National Science Foundation.

Alice 2.0

# Exploring Alice and Object-Oriented Programming

## CASE PERSPECTIVE

Dr. Carole Dodgson needs your help. She would like to use a sample virtual world to demonstrate some fundamental concepts of computer programming to students in her Information Technology course.

A virtual world is one that exists only in the memory of a computer, not in our real, physical world. Some virtual worlds have no user interaction and are similar to films or animated cartoons, while others are more like interactive video games with many mouse and keyboard controls.

Your task is to use Alice 2.0, a new easy-to-use programming system, to develop a sample virtual world for demonstrations in Dr. Dodgson's course. The new virtual world will contain an ice skater on a frozen lake. The overall project has been broken down into four smaller projects in which you will build the sample virtual world, then progressively add more sophisticated features to the world. When you have finished the fourth project, you will have a complete virtual world with programs to animate the ice skater and to let a user control what the skater does. Dr. Dodgson can then demonstrate concepts of computer programming in her course using your ice skater world.

# Alice 2.0

# Exploring Alice and Object-Oriented Programming

PROJECT

1

## Objectives

**You will have mastered the material in this project when you can:**

- Describe the concept of object-oriented programming (OOP)
- Start Alice
- Locate and describe the components of the Alice interface
- Load and play an existing Alice world
- Create and save a new Alice world
- Print the code for Alice methods and events

## What Is Alice?

**Alice** is a programming environment that allows users with little or no computer experience to program characters and objects in a virtual world, much like a modern animated film or video game. Like the real world, the virtual world of Alice has three-dimensional space (and time), and each object has properties just like physical objects, such as color, size, location, and so on. Alice has a camera that allows you to see its virtual world on a computer screen, so you can see what is happening in your virtual world as your programs run. Figure 1-1 shows an Alice virtual world.

A **computer program** is a step-by-step set of instructions telling a computer how to perform a specific task. Learning to write computer programs can be difficult because of two major problems faced by novice programmers: language and visualization. The language problem occurs when people trying to learn about programming concepts must also learn a new programming language at the same time. The visualization problem occurs when people have difficulty trying to visualize what will happen inside a computer when a program runs. Computer scientists and educators at Carnegie Mellon University and the University of Virginia have developed Alice to make programming easier to learn by minimizing the problems of language and visualization.

The graphic nature of Alice solves the visualization problem described above. For example, if you tried to program the skater in Figure 1-1 to skate around in a circle, and instead she simply stayed in one spot and spun around, you could see that happening on the screen, and correct your program accordingly.

The instructions in the language of Alice are contained on tiles, which you can drag and drop into place to write new programs. You can see the Alice instruction tiles in Figure 1-2, which shows a program under construction. Creating a program in this manner allows you to focus on the concepts of computer programming, especially the logic of your programs, instead of having to worry about the particular details of a new language, such as spelling and punctuation. This helps to solve the language problem faced by students who have traditionally had to create programs like that shown in Figure 1-3, which is from an introductory Java programming course.

**FIGURE 1-1**

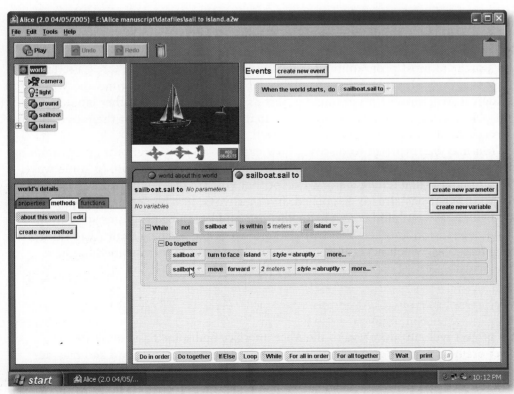

**FIGURE 1-2**

```
/*      This program demonstrates simple math.
        It takes user input and displays it.  */

import javax.swing.JOptionPane;
public class SimpleMath
{
        public static void main (String arg[] )
        {
                // declare variables
                double integer_one, integer_two;
                String number_one, number_two, sum;

                //get first of two integers
                number_one = JOptionPane.showInputDialog (null, "Please enter first number: ");
                integer_one = Integer.parseInt (number_one);

                number_two = JOptionPane.showInputDialog(null, "Please enter the second number");
                integer_two = Integer.parseInt (number_two);

                JOptionPane.showMessageDialog (null, number_one, "First Number", JOptionPane.OK_CANCEL_OPTION );
                JOptionPane.showMessageDialog (null, number_two, "Second Number", JOptionPane.OK_CANCEL_OPTION );

                JOptionPane.showMessageDialog (null, "Sum equals " + (integer_one + integer_two), "Sum of the numbers",
JOptionPane.PLAIN_MESSAGE);
                JOptionPane.showMessageDialog (null, "Difference equals " + (integer_one - integer_two), "Difference of two
Numbers", JOptionPane.PLAIN_MESSAGE);
                JOptionPane.showMessageDialog (null, "Product equals " + (integer_one * integer_two), "Integer Product",
JOptionPane.PLAIN_MESSAGE);
                JOptionPane.showMessageDialog(null, "Quotient equals " + (integer_one / integer_two), "Integer Division",
JOptionPane.OK_CANCEL_OPTION);

                System.exit(0);
        }

}
```

**FIGURE 1-3**

Although you will be working with Alice throughout this book, your ultimate goal is not to learn about Alice itself, but rather to use Alice to learn some of the fundamental concepts of modern computer programming. In many ways, Alice is very similar to most programming languages in use today, such as C#, C++, Java, and Visual Basic. It requires you to plan your programs ahead of time and work with the logical structures of programming, just as you must do with other languages. It is both object-oriented and event-driven, so that you can learn about these two important aspects of modern programming as well.

You may be surprised to discover how easy it is to learn computer programming once you get past the two big hurdles of language and visualization. In some ways, programming is like telling a story, except that you are describing what *will* happen instead of what has already happened. In other ways, it is like creating your own video game, as you build controls for the user and organize programs so that one action depends on another. You will also discover that working with Alice can be fun and interesting, which never hurts when you are trying to learn something new.

## More About

### Virtual Worlds

Alice is one of the programs used in the Building Virtual Worlds course for third-year students offered by the Entertainment Technology Center at Carnegie Mellon University. For more information on the course and for a look at some of the worlds created by students, visit www.etc.cmu.edu/curriculum/bvw/.

## Project One — Creating an Alice World

This project will introduce you to the Alice interface and some basic ideas about object-oriented programming. You will explore the Alice interface, load and play an existing Alice world, and then create a short Alice world of your own, in which an ice skater will perform a few short moves and then say "Hello, World!" as shown in Figure 1-4. Discussions of object-oriented programming are included within the project.

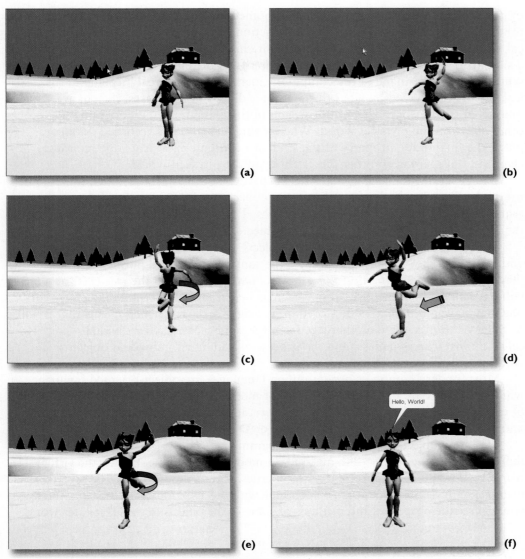

(a)  (b)

(c)  (d)

(e)  (f)

**FIGURE 1-4**

# Objects and Object-Oriented Programming

An object is anything that can be represented by data in the memory of a computer and manipulated by a computer program. An object can be a tangible item in the physical world or just an abstract idea. For example, most large airplanes have a computer, called an autopilot, that can fly the plane. The autopilot is a computer that manipulates an object in the physical world.

Most objects that computers manipulate, however, are not physical objects. Payroll information, student records, bank accounts, and the characters in a video game are all examples of objects that are not physical objects, but simply concepts or ideas represented in the memory of the computer. Whether an object actually exists in the physical world does not matter much in terms of what happens inside a computer. To a computer, an object is simply something that can be represented by data in the computer's memory and manipulated by computer programs.

The data that represents an object is organized into a set of **properties**. Each property describes the object in some way. For example, the weight of an airplane, its location, and the direction in which the plane is facing are all properties of the airplane. A computer manipulates an object by changing some of its properties or some of the properties of the object's subparts. Sometimes the hardware in a computer can translate these changes in properties into actions that affect real objects in the physical world. For example, the autopilot might change the angle of a wing flap, which is a subpart of the airplane, and that, in turn, affects the entire airplane. Both the representation of the airplane in the computer's memory and the real airplane in the physical world are affected by what the computer does. In other cases, the changes to an object's properties only affect information in the computer's memory and have no other effect on the physical world. When a student's grade is recorded on a computer, the final grade property of the student's computerized academic record is changed, but there is no other direct effect on the physical world.

The programs that manipulate the properties of an object are called the object's **methods**. You can think of an object as a collection of properties and the methods that are used to manipulate those properties. The values stored in the properties of the object at any one time are called the **state** of the object.

A **class of objects** is a set of similar objects that each have the same properties and methods. They usually do not have the same values stored in their properties, but they have the same properties. For example, two objects from the tree class of object will have all of the same properties—such as height, age, and trunk diameter—but one may have a different value stored in its height property, which means that it will be taller or shorter than another tree from the same class. Each individual object is called an **instance** of a class, and the process of adding an individual object to a world is called **instantiation**.

Most modern computer programming languages are object-oriented languages, in which programs are organized into a set of methods that manipulate the properties of objects stored in a computer. This modern approach to computer programming is known as **object-oriented programming**, or **OOP** for short.

Alice is an object-oriented system of programming. The objects in Alice exist in a three-dimensional virtual world, much like a modern video game. In fact, the virtual world itself is an object in Alice; it has properties, and methods that can be used to manipulate those properties. As you continue with this exploration of the Alice interface, you will see the properties and methods of some of the objects in the lakeSkater world.

## Starting Alice

Before starting, you should have a computer system with Alice properly installed. The software is available free of charge from Carnegie Mellon University via the Alice Web site at www.alice.org. Alice has been designed so that it is easy to install, and so that it will not interfere with other software on your computer system. It does use a lot of memory, though, so generally it is not a good idea to run Alice and other programs at the same time. The following steps show how to start Alice.

*More About*

### Clicking and Dragging

Many Alice tiles contain white parameter boxes, such as the **1 second** box in the **Wait 1 second** instruction tile. When clicking and dragging such tiles you should be careful to click an open background area on the tile, not a parameter box.

*More About*

### Slow and Steady Alice

You may notice that there is a Slow and Steady Alice icon in addition to the standard Alice icon. The standard version of Alice uses video hardware for screen graphics. On computers with older video cards, especially older notebook computers, this may not work well. The Slow and Steady version of Alice uses software video acceleration to avoid this problem, but runs a bit slower than the standard version of Alice. More information about different versions of Alice for various computers, including hardware requirements, is available on the Web at: www.alice.org/downloads/authoringtool/.

## To Start Alice

**1**

• **Navigate to the location where the Alice.exe program has been installed on your computer, or where a shortcut to the Alice.exe program has been placed. Often this will be on the desktop as in Figure 1-5, but your instructor or systems administrator may direct you to a different location.**

**FIGURE 1-5**

**2**

• **Double-click** the Alice **icon. If file extensions are visible on your system it will be named Alice.exe.**

*The Alice title box appears while Alice is loading, as shown in Figure 1-6. Note that Alice is a large program, so it may take up to a minute to load.*

**FIGURE 1-6**

*The Welcome to Alice! dialog box appears (Figure 1-7). You may return to this dialog box at any time while using Alice by clicking File on the menu bar, and then clicking New World or Open World.*

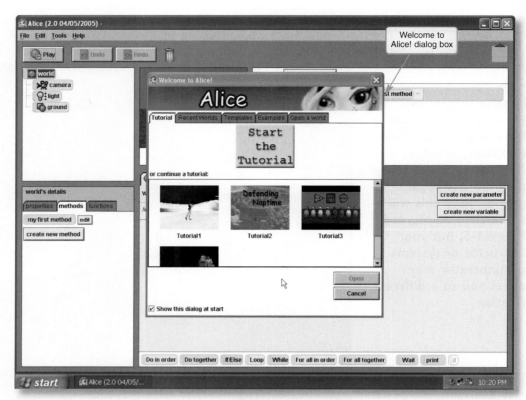

**FIGURE 1-7**

# The Alice Interface

Users interact with Alice through the Alice Integrated Development Environment (IDE). An **IDE** is a computer program that is used to facilitate the writing of other computer programs. Specialized IDEs exist for most modern programming languages and often contain everything programmers need to create and run computer programs. A typical IDE may contain a text editor for entering code, a debugger for finding and fixing errors, and an object library to store modules of prewritten code. Alice contains similar features, but its IDE is simpler than most. The Alice IDE is often called the **Alice interface**.

## The Welcome to Alice! Dialog Box

The first item the user sees when the Alice interface opens is the Welcome to Alice! dialog box (Figure 1-8), which contains several tabs: Tutorial, Recent Worlds, Templates, Examples, and Open a world. The following section describes the items in this dialog box:

- Tutorial: You will not use the tutorials now, but you may want to come back to them later as an exercise on your own. When you are ready to use the tutorials, either click the tutorial you would like to run, or click the large Start the Tutorial button to follow them in order. They were created by the developers of Alice to help people learn the system and are quite easy to follow.
- Recent Worlds: The Recent Worlds tab contains thumbnail sketches of the most recently saved Alice worlds.

- Templates: Alice has six blank templates for starting a new virtual world: dirt, grass, sand, snow, space, and water. Each template includes a texture for the ground and a background color for the sky.
- Examples: Several example worlds are included with Alice. This tab is used later in the project to run one of the example worlds.
- Open a world: This tab is used to open other Alice worlds saved on your computer and is similar to the Open dialog boxes seen in other programs, such as Microsoft Word. Navigation icons appear across the top, a list of folders and Alice worlds from the current folder appear in the middle, and some controls to view and open files appear at the bottom of the dialog box.

In the following steps, you explore the Welcome to Alice! dialog box.

**Q&A**

**Q:** How can I prevent the Welcome to Alice! dialog box from being displayed?

**A:** Click the **Show this dialog at start** check box in the Welcome to Alice! dialog box to deselect it. After this, Alice will open to a new world with a blank grass template instead of the Welcome to Alice! window.

## To Explore the Welcome to Alice! Dialog Box

**1**

• **Click the** Tutorial **tab (if it is not already selected).**

*Four Alice tutorials appear, as shown in Figure 1-8.*

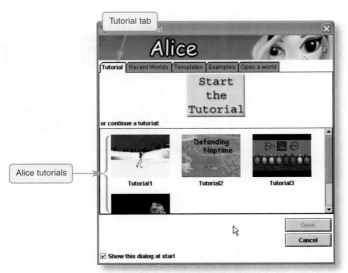

FIGURE 1-8

**2**

• **Click the** Recent Worlds **tab.**

*A typical Recent Worlds tab is shown in Figure 1-9, but if no worlds have been saved since Alice was installed on your system, the message "No recent worlds." appears.*

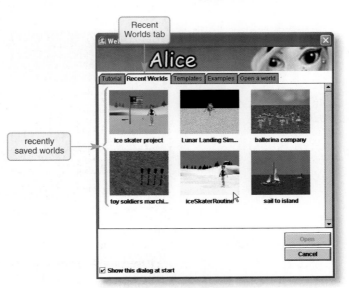

FIGURE 1-9

Alice 2.0

**3**

• **Click the** Templates **tab.**

*The six default templates are displayed, as shown in Figure 1-10.*

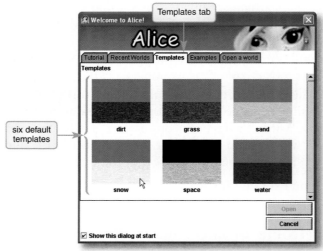

six default templates

**FIGURE 1-10**

**4**

• **Click the** Examples **tab.**

*Thumbnail sketches of example worlds are visible on the Examples tab, as shown in Figure 1-11.*

thumbnails of example worlds

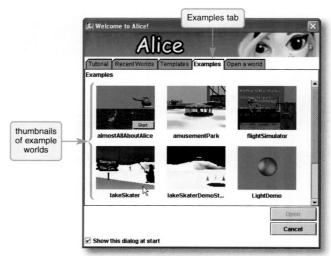

**FIGURE 1-11**

**5**

• **Click the** Open a world **tab.**

*The Open a world tab appears (Figure 1-12). Notice that Alice world files end with the extension .a2w. These files were created with version 2.0 of Alice, the most recent version.*

.a2w extensions identify Alice world files

**FIGURE 1-12**

While you are viewing or editing an Alice world, a save warning window will appear every 15 minutes, warning you that you have not saved your Alice world (Figure 1-13). If this happens while you are simply viewing an Alice world, such as in this section of the project, then it is probably safe to ignore the warning. If it happens while you are creating or editing your own Alice world, then it is a good idea to save your world.

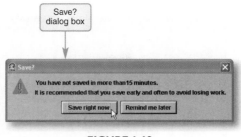

**FIGURE 1-13**

## The Main Work Areas of the Alice Interface

The Alice interface has five main work areas: the World window, the Object tree, the Details area, the Editor area, and the Events area. In the following set of steps, you will open and manipulate a sample world in order to explore and become familiar with the Alice interface.

### To Open the lakeSkater World and Explore the Alice Interface

**1**

• **Click the** Examples **tab in the Welcome to Alice! dialog box.**

*The Examples tab is displayed (Figure 1-14).*

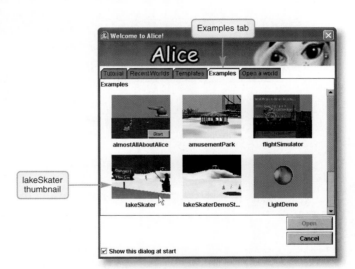

**FIGURE 1-14**

**2**

• **Click the** lakeSkater **thumbnail, and then click the** Open **button to open the** lakeSkater **Alice world.**

*It takes a few seconds for Alice to load all of the elements of the world. The names of the elements flash past in a small window in the center of the screen while this happens. When Alice is finished loading, the standard interface will appear as shown in Figure 1-15.*

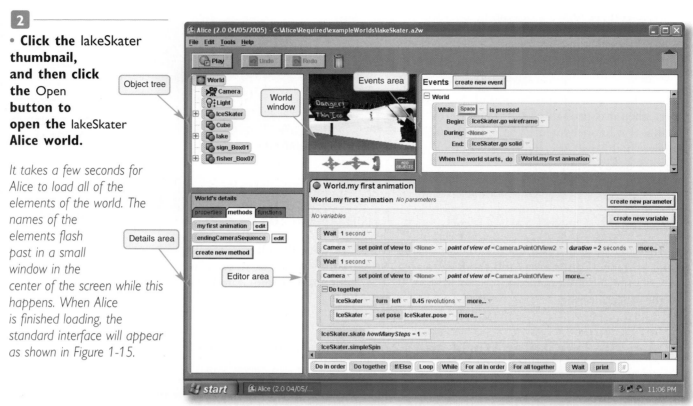

**FIGURE 1-15**

## The World Window

The **World window** contains a view of the current Alice world, as shown in Figure 1-16.

You can pan, tilt, zoom, and move the Alice camera using the blue arrows below the World window. The curved arrow on the right is the camera's **tilt control**. It is used to tilt the camera up or down, similar to the way that you might tilt your head up or down. The center control is a mixed control, to **zoom** and **pan** the camera. A camera can zoom in and zoom out, and pan left and pan right. Zooming in means the camera is moved in closer to get a tighter shot of an item, so that it fills more of the screen. Zooming out means the camera is moved out further to get a longer shot of an item, so that it becomes smaller on the screen. Panning means to turn the camera left or right without moving the position of the camera, although it is possible that you could pan and move at the same time. The left set of arrows at the bottom of the world window is the **move control**, which provides controls to move the camera left and right, and up and down.

The large green ADD OBJECTS button, located to the right of the camera control arrows, switches the interface from the standard mode to Scene Editor mode, which is used to add and position objects in an Alice world before playing the world. You will work with Scene Editor mode later in this project.

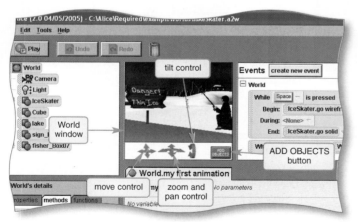

**FIGURE 1-16**

# The Object Tree

The **Object tree** is to the left of the World window. It shows the objects in the current Alice world organized as a tree of **tiles**, with a tile for each object (Figure 1-17). Four object tiles — World, Camera, Light, and ground — appear in every new Alice world, although the creator of this lakeSkater world has deleted the ground object from the world. The plus sign next to an object shows that it has subparts, which may be seen by clicking the plus sign.

In the steps on the next page, you view the subparts of the IceSkater object.

**FIGURE 1-17**

## To View the Subparts of the IceSkater Object

**1**

• **Click the plus sign next to the** IceSkater **tile in the Object tree**.

*Tiles for each subpart of the IceSkater, such as left and right thighs (ThighL and ThighR), are displayed (Figure 1-18). These parts are actually objects themselves, which together compose the IceSkater object. Notice that some of these parts have plus signs, indicating that they also have subparts.*

**2**

• **Click the minus sign next to the IceSkater tile.**

*The IceSkater tile's subparts are hidden.*

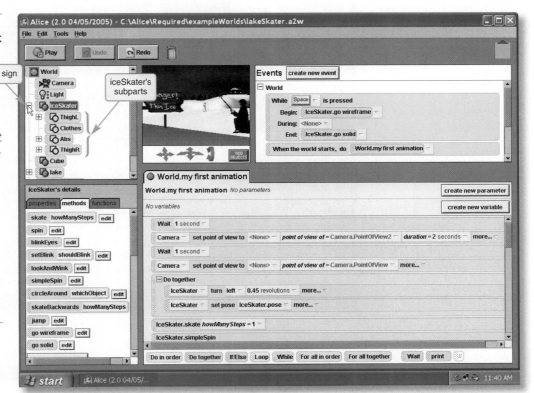

**FIGURE 1-18**

# The Details Area

The **Details area** of the Alice interface is located below the Object tree. It has tabs to show properties, methods, and functions for an Alice object. Figure 1-19 shows the methods tab in the Details area for the IceSkater object. As described above, properties contain information about an object, such as its color and position in the world, and methods are programs that manipulate an object, such as the set of instructions used to make an **IceSkater** turn. A **function** is simply a method that computes and returns a value, such as the distance between two objects. The values that functions return can sometimes be used like properties, but while a property is a stored value that describes an object, the value returned by a function must be calculated by the computer.

Information about the currently selected object is displayed in the Details area. You may select an object by clicking that object in the World window or by clicking its tile in the Object tree. When you do so, that object's properties, methods, and functions will appear on the tabs in the Details area. In the following steps, you explore the Details area to view the details of an object.

## To View the Details of an Object

**1**

• **Click the** IceSkater **tile in the Object tree. If necessary, click the** methods **tab to display the** IceSkater **object's methods.**

*The IceSkater's methods are displayed in the Details area (Figure 1-19).*

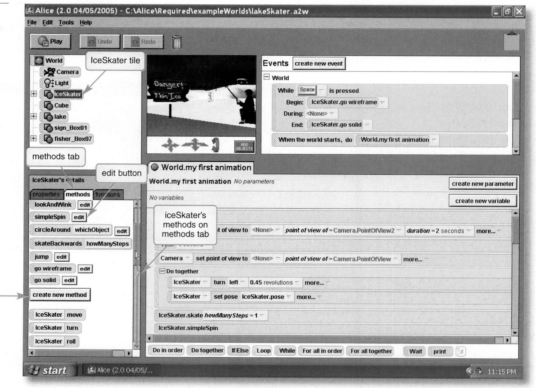

**FIGURE 1-19**

**2**

• **Click the** properties **tab.**

*The IceSkater's properties tab is displayed in the Details area (Figure 1-20).*

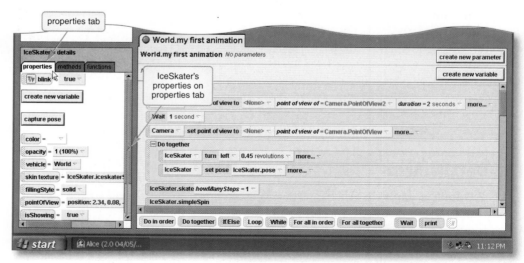

**FIGURE 1-20**

**3**

• **Click the** functions **tab.**

*The IceSkater's functions are displayed in the Details area (Figure 1-21).*

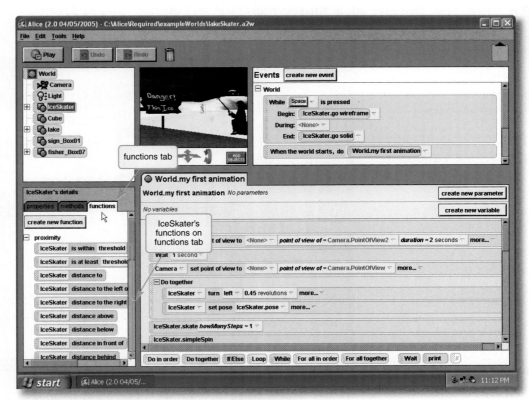

**FIGURE 1-21**

Even though a function is a method, functions are placed on a separate tab in the Details area because of the special nature of functions. None of the objects in this lakeSkater sample world has any user-created functions; they are all primitive functions, similar to the primitive methods described in the next section.

## Primitive and User-Defined Methods

In Figure 1-19 on page AL 14, you can see a create new method button. Note that an edit button appears next to the method tiles above this button, and there is no edit button next to the method tiles below the button. The tiles that have an edit button are for user-created methods; the tiles that do not have an edit button are for primitive methods. **Primitive methods** provide basic behaviors for objects, such as turning and moving, and are examples of encapsulated methods. The details of an encapsulated method are hidden from the user. **Encapsulated methods** can be used within other programs, but they cannot be changed or edited because their details are hidden. Encapsulation is an important part of object-oriented programming.

Later in this project, you will begin working with methods. For now, it is enough to see where methods are located on the Alice interface. In the following steps, you view the details of a user-created method.

## To View the Details of a Method

**1**

• **Click the** edit **button next to the** spin **tile on the** methods **tab.**

*The details of the spin method appear in the Editor area, as shown in Figure 1-22. This is an example of a user-created method that is not encapsulated.*

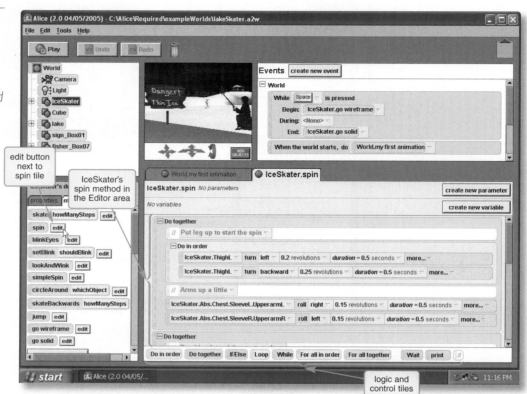

**FIGURE 1-22**

## The Editor Area

The largest area of the Alice interface is the **Editor area**, which is located below the World window, as shown in Figure 1-22 above. Methods are assembled here by clicking and dragging tiles from other parts of the interface. The bottom of the Editor area has a row of logic and control tiles that can be used to put branching, looping, and other logical structures into Alice methods. Later in this project, you will build your first method. Project 3 contains more information about logic in Alice methods and using the logic and control tiles.

## The Events Area

The **Events area** in Alice is located above the Editor area, as shown in Figure 1-23. This part of the interface shows existing events and is used to create new events. An **event** consists of a condition, called an event trigger, and the name of a method, called an event handler. The event handler runs whenever the event trigger occurs. For example, you could create an event to make the ice skater spin whenever the user presses the s key. Pressing the s key would be the event trigger, and the method that makes the ice skater spin would be the event handler.

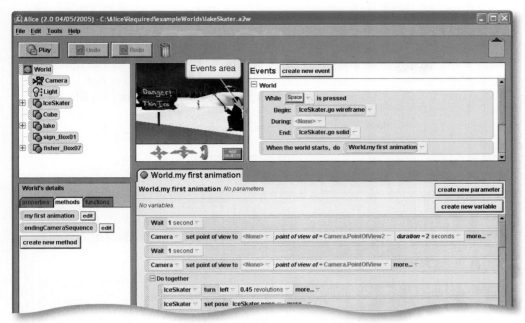

**FIGURE 1-23**

Software with events is called **event-driven software**. Operating systems that allow the user to manipulate the computer by using the mouse and keyboard shortcuts, such as Microsoft Windows, contain event-driven software. Events are covered in detail in Project 4.

## Other Elements of the Alice Interface

In addition to the main work areas that you have just explored, the Alice interface has two icons, three buttons, and a menu bar near the top of the screen, as shown in Figure 1-24. These are discussed in the following sections.

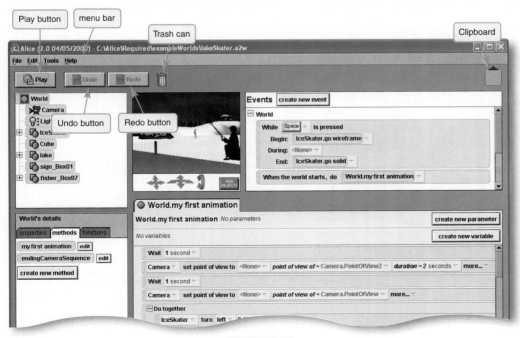

**FIGURE 1-24**

Q & A

**Q:** How can I tell where an item that is being dragged may be dropped?

**A:** The color of the border around an Alice tile, and around other elements of the interface, will indicate where an object that is being dragged may be dropped. When you begin to drag an object, yellow borders will appear around places where the object may be dropped. When an object is correctly in place over a location where it could be dropped, then the border of the target location and of the item being dragged will both turn green. A red border indicates that the item being dragged cannot be dropped in its current location.

## The Clipboard

The **Clipboard** icon is used for copying instruction tiles in Alice methods. You can copy a tile by dragging and dropping it on the Clipboard icon in the upper-right corner of the interface, and then dragging it from the Clipboard icon and dropping it in its new location. The following steps illustrate copying an instruction tile.

## To Copy an Instruction Tile

**1**

• **Click the** World.my first animation **tab in the Editor area.**

*The instructions in* World.my first animation *appear in the Editor area (Figure 1-25).*

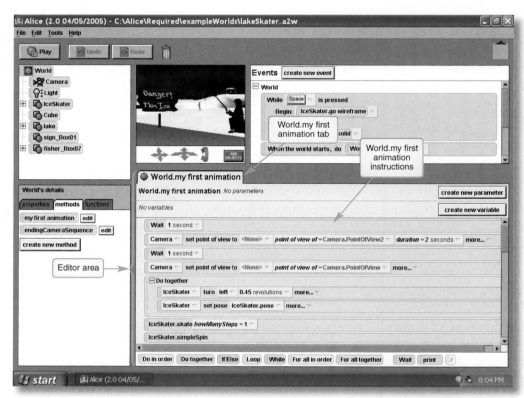

FIGURE 1-25

**2**

• **Drag the** Wait 1 second **instruction tile from the** World.my first animation **tab in the Editor area and drop it on the Clipboard.**

*The instruction is stored in the Clipboard's memory. A white paper appears on the Clipboard whenever there is something in the Clipboard's memory, as shown in Figure 1-26.*

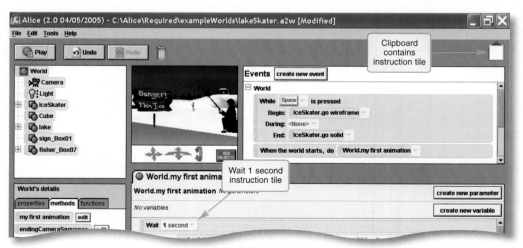

FIGURE 1-26

**3**

• **Drag the Clipboard and drop it on the** World.my first animation **tab, just below the first** Wait 1 second **instruction tile.**

*A new copy of the Wait 1 second instruction tile appears just below the first one, as shown in Figure 1-27.*

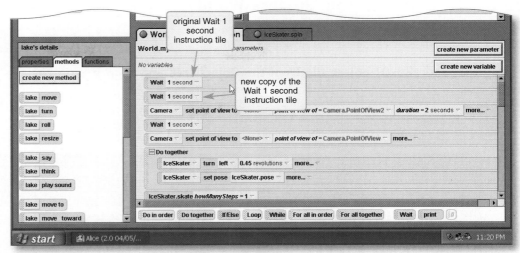

**FIGURE 1-27**

You can also duplicate a method tile by right-clicking it and selecting make copy on the menu that appears. This works only with methods and not with Alice objects.

## The Trash Can

The **Trash can** icon just below the menu bar is used for deleting both Alice objects and instruction tiles in Alice methods. You can delete an item by dragging and dropping it on the Trash can icon, as shown in the following step.

## To Delete an Instruction Tile from a Method

**1**

• **Drag the second instance of the** Wait 1 second **instruction tile from** World.my first animation **in the Editor area and drop it on the Trash can.**

*The second copy of the Wait 1 second instruction tile is removed from the Editor area (Figure 1-28).*

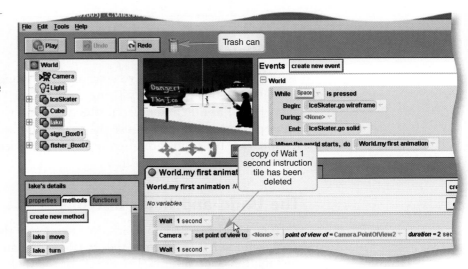

**FIGURE 1-28**

You can also use the Trash can to delete an object from the Alice World, as shown in the following steps.

## To Delete an Object from an Alice World

**1**

• **Drag the** fisher_Box07 **object tile from the Object tree and drop it onto the Trash can.**

*The fisherman sitting on the box disappears from the Alice World window (Figure 1-29).*

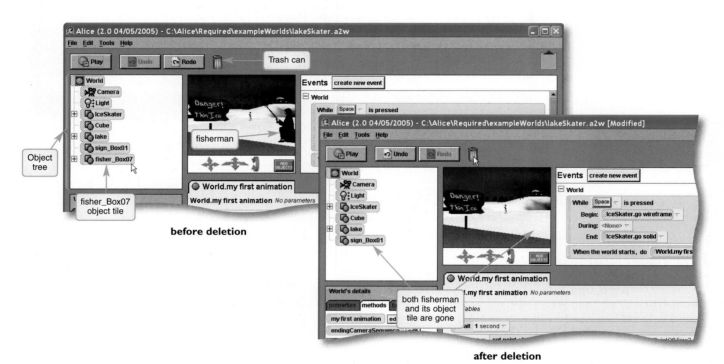

before deletion

after deletion

**FIGURE 1-29**

**Other Ways**

1. Right-click an object or tile, click delete

## The Play Button

The Play button is used to start an Alice world. In the terminology of virtual reality software, this is called "playing" a world or "running" a world. People with a background in film and video production tend to use the term "playing," while computer programmers tend to use the term "running," but in the world of virtual reality software the terms are often used interchangeably. You shortly will use the Play button to view a world in Alice.

## The Undo and Redo Buttons

The Undo and Redo buttons, located below the menu bar (see Figure 1-30), are also useful when editing an Alice world. You can undo the last change you made by clicking the Undo button. The effects of the Undo button can be reversed by clicking the Redo button. Alice can remember the last several dozen changes that you made. The following steps undo the deletion of the fisherman object.

## To Undo and Redo Changes to an Alice World

**1**

• **Click the** Undo **button.**

*The fisher_Box07 object tile reappears in the Object tree and the fisherman sitting on the box reappears in the Alice World window (Figure 1-30).*

**FIGURE 1-30**

**2**

• **Click the** Redo **button.**

*The fisherman sitting on the box and its fisher_Box07 object tile are deleted again, as you have just redone the instruction to delete it from the Object tree and the Alice World window (Figure 1-31).*

**FIGURE 1-31**

**3**

• **Click the** Undo **button again.**

*The fisher_Box07 object tile reappears in the Object tree and the fisherman sitting on the box reappears in the Alice World window.*

> **Other Ways**
>
> 1. Press CTRL+Z to undo a change and CTRL+Y to redo a change.

## The Menu Bar

The Alice interface has a menu bar at the top of the screen with four menus: File, Edit, Tools, and Help. The menus are used much less frequently in Alice than in most other computer programs. The following section describes the menus and their functions.

**FILE MENU** The Alice File menu, similar to the File menu found in other programs, has commands for opening, closing, and saving Alice worlds, as well as options to export an Alice world as a movie file or as an HTML Web page, as shown in Figure 1-32. It also has options to let you import saved objects into an Alice world, add 3-D text to your world, and to make a billboard (which is a graphical image, such as a photograph, that has been converted into an Alice object).

You will use these options throughout the projects in this book, except for the Export movie option, which has been disabled in the current version of Alice.

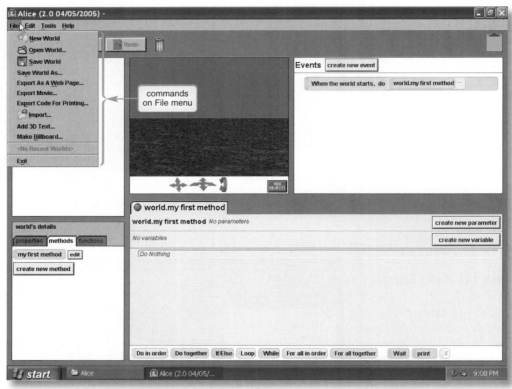

**FIGURE 1-32**

**EDIT MENU** Currently, the only option on the Alice Edit menu is Preferences, which is used to change settings for Alice. Appendix B describes these settings. The most important thing to know for now is that the Alice Edit menu is not used to edit Alice methods in the same way that, for example, the Edit menu in Microsoft Word can be used to edit elements in a document. Instead, Alice emphasizes the use of a drag-and-drop interface, which uses the editing icons and buttons described earlier in this project.

**TOOLS MENU** The Tools menu contains three options: World Statistics, Text Output, and Error Console. The World Statistics option allows you to see statistics, such as the number of objects in a world, the time the world has been open, and many other useful items.

The World Statistics window is shown in Figure 1-33. Only some of the information here will be meaningful to you until you learn more about Alice and computer graphics. You can use this feature, however, to see the amount of time the current world has been open, how many times it has been run, and how many times it has been saved. You can also see how much memory is used for the world's texture maps, which form the surfaces of objects, such as the **IceSkater**'s clothes. Generally, texture maps and sound files are the two items in an Alice world that consume the most memory.

**FIGURE 1-33**

The Text Output option allows you to see system messages generated as you play Alice worlds, and the Error Console can be used to look at detailed Alice error messages. Both of these tools are rather sophisticated, and are not very useful for novice programmers.

**HELP MENU**   The Help menu has three options: Tutorial, Example Worlds, and About Alice. The Help menu does not contain an option to look up the features of Alice, as you might expect. By not providing a way to look up features, the developers of Alice were hoping to encourage people to learn about Alice through experimentation.

Example Worlds and Tutorial both take you back to the Welcome to Alice! dialog box that you saw earlier in this project. The About Alice option provides general information about the development of Alice and displays the URL for the Alice Web site, www.alice.org, where you can find out more about Alice.

The About Alice version 2.0 04/05/2005 dialog box is shown in Figure 1-34. Take a moment to read the text in the dialog box before continuing.

**Q:** What is a texture map?

**A:** A texture map is a graphic image that is used to paint the surface of an object. It can be a simple pattern that is repeated on a flat surface such as a grass or snow ground object in Alice, or a more complicated image that is wrapped around a 3-D object, such as the image of the IceSkater's costume, face, and hair.

**FIGURE 1-34**

# Playing an Existing Alice World

You can play an open Alice world at any time by clicking the Play button on the standard Alice interface. In this part of the project, you will play the lakeSkater world to see how this works. Some Alice worlds are interactive in the way a video game is, with mouse and keyboard controls that work while the world plays; others are simply played and viewed like an animated film. The lakeSkater world is an example of a film-like world. When the world runs, you will see the skater perform a figure skating routine. As you will see, virtual worlds without user interaction still can be quite complex, especially when camera movements are included in the world.

*More About*

### Error Messages

Occasionally you may see the Alice error message window appear. It contains a button to submit a bug report to the Alice development team at Carnegie Mellon University. Reporting any errors that occur will help to improve future versions of Alice, and in some cases a member of the team may contact you directly. You may also submit bugs and suggestions about Alice through the Alice web site at www.alice.org.

The window in which an Alice virtual world runs has a speed slider control and five buttons across the top of the window: Pause, Resume, Restart, Stop, and Take Picture. The speed slider control is used to change the speed of the world while it is playing. The Pause and Resume buttons work like the pause and play buttons on a VCR or DVD, pausing a world and then resuming it from the point at which it was paused. The Restart button is used to begin playing the current world again from the beginning. The Stop button stops the world that is currently playing and returns you to the standard Alice interface. Once the Stop button is clicked, you will need to click the standard interface's Play button to replay the world. Finally, the Take Picture button captures an image of the currently playing world and saves it in a data file. The stored image file can be viewed and used like any other computer image file. Appendix B has more information on changing the settings for Alice's screen capture function. (Note that the world continues to play while the Image captured and stored window is on the screen. In many cases, it is probably best to pause the playing world before taking a picture.)

The following steps show how to play, pause, stop, and restart an Alice world, and how to capture and save an image of the world.

## To Play the lakeSkater World

**1**

• **Click the** Play **button.**

*An Alice virtual world plays in a new window called the World Running window, shown in Figure 1-35. When the skater stops moving, her routine is finished.*

**FIGURE 1-35**

**2**

• **Click the** Restart **button in the World Running window.**

*The world plays again from the beginning.*

**3**

• **Click the** Restart **button in the World Running window again to restart the** lakeSkater **world, and then experiment with the** Pause **and** Resume **buttons.**

• **Restart the world, and experiment with the speed slider control.**

• **Restart the world, let it play for about 3 or 4 seconds, and then click the** Take Picture **button to take a picture of the world.**

*An Image captured and stored dialog box is displayed, showing you the full path name of the file that was saved (Figure 1-36).*

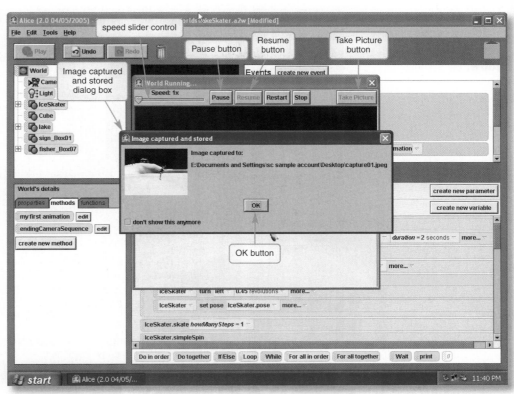

**FIGURE 1-36**

**4**

• **Click the** OK **button in the Image captured and stored dialog box.**

*The Image captured and stored dialog box closes, and you are returned to the World Running window, where the Alice world is still playing (Figure 1-37).*

**FIGURE 1-37**

**5**

• **Click the** Stop **button in the World Running window.**

*The world stops playing and you are returned to the standard Alice interface, as shown in Figure 1-38.*

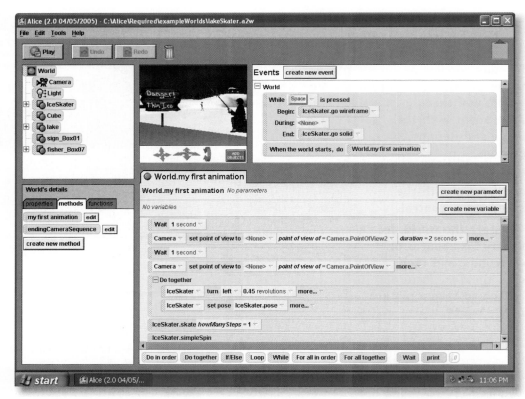

**FIGURE 1-38**

You have finished exploring the Alice interface and now know how to load and play an existing world. In the next section of this tutorial, you will create, save, and play a world of your own that is similar to the lakeSkater world.

## Creating a New Alice World

In this section of Project 1, you create and save a simple Alice world that looks something like the lakeSkater example world you previously saw. You start with a blank Alice world, add the skater and the lake scenery, and write a simple method to make the skater perform a few simple actions. In the projects that follow, you add events and additional methods to the world to build an interactive ice skater world while learning about fundamental concepts of computer programming. As you continue, remember that your ultimate goal is not to build an Alice world, nor to learn about all of the features of Alice, but to use Alice to learn about some fundamental concepts of computer programming.

Before continuing, it is a good idea to exit Alice and restart it. Alice worlds are rather large and can fill a great deal of a computer's internal memory. Alice doesn't always empty a world completely from its memory when a new world is loaded, but it does clear the memory when you quit Alice. If too much of the computer's memory is filled, then the computer will run more slowly and could even stop running. The following steps exit and then restart Alice.

## To Exit and Restart Alice

**1** **Click** File **on the Menu bar to display the File menu, and then click** Exit **on the File menu to exit Alice. Click** No **if asked to save the Alice world.**

**2** **Start the Alice program again by double-clicking the Alice icon on the desktop, or in the same way that you were directed to do so by your instructor at the beginning of this project.**

Once the program is loaded you will see the Welcome to Alice! dialog box over the front of the Alice interface, just as you saw when you first started the program earlier in this project (and as shown previously in Figure 1-7). The Examples tab should be visible in the window.

In the following steps, you select a template for a new Alice world, add some objects to the world, position them, and then begin to write methods to animate one of the objects.

## To Create a New Ice Skater World

**1**

• **Click the** Templates **tab on the Welcome to Alice! dialog box, as shown in Figure 1-39.**

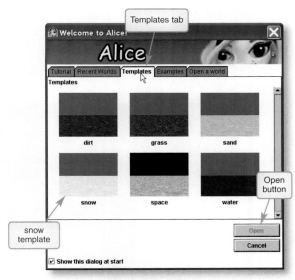

**FIGURE 1-39**

**2**

• **Click the** snow **template and then click the** Open **button.**

*A new Alice world opens with a snow texture for the ground. Figure 1-40 shows the World window for this new world.*

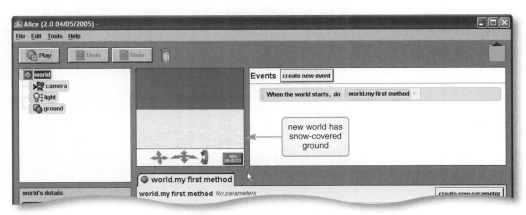

**FIGURE 1-40**

You now have a new Alice world as the basis for your work, but it only has the four default objects: camera, light, ground, and the world itself. You need to add a few more objects using Scene Editor mode and position them in their starting positions. The large green **ADD OBJECTS** button in the lower-right corner of the World window will take you into Scene Editor mode.

Once you are in Scene Editor mode you will be able to add objects from Alice's object galleries and move things around to set the scene for your new world. There are two object galleries: a Local Gallery that has been installed on your computer as part of Alice, and a more extensive Web Gallery at Carnegie Mellon University that can be accessed from Alice whenever your computer has a live Internet connection. The projects in this book do not require you to use the Web Gallery, but you may choose to do so as part of the end-of-project exercises if your Internet connection is fast enough.

You will use the same lake scene that you saw in the lakeSkater example world earlier in this project. This scene has many objects in it, including a cabin and more than 100 trees. Fortunately, the scene has already been assembled and saved in one of the object galleries so that you can load it from there instead of having to load and position all of the objects individually. Creating a scene by positioning objects in a virtual world can be a very tedious process that often takes longer than writing all of the methods and events for the new world. The following step allows you to enter Scene Editor mode.

## To Enter Scene Editor Mode

**1**

• **Click the** ADD OBJECTS **button in the lower-right corner of the World window.**

*Alice enters Scene Editor mode, as shown in Figure 1-41. Notice that the Events area and Editor area from the standard Alice interface are not visible. The World window is now larger, with object manipulation tools appearing to the right of the window, and the Local Gallery visible at the bottom of the screen. The Local Gallery has tiles for folders that contain Alice objects, such as the Amusement Park folder, the Beach folder, and so on.*

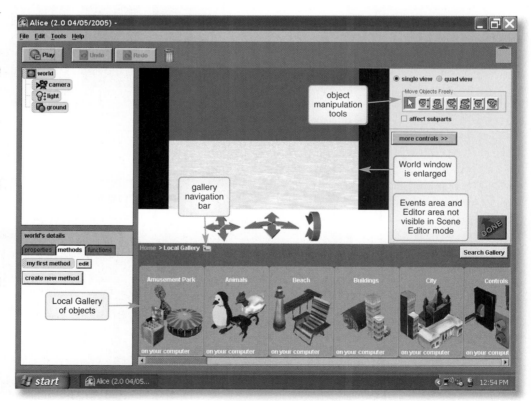

**FIGURE 1-41**

The galleries are organized as a tree of folders containing related objects. You can navigate the tree of galleries by clicking a gallery folder to enter that gallery, or by using the gallery navigation bar, which is just above the galleries. You may wish to come back to the Local Gallery later on your own to explore some of the folders, but for now you will simply use the gallery to add objects to the ice skater world you are building. You need to add the **lake** object and the **iceSkater** object to the world. The lake is in the Environments folder, and the ice skater is in the People folder. Note that the object you need is not the one named Frozen Lake, but simply Lake.

The Environments folder has a subfolder for Skies and tiles for other Alice classes of environment objects, as shown below in Figure 1-42. You should recall that a class of objects is a set of similar objects that each have the same properties and methods, and that the process of adding an individual object to a world is called instantiation. You are now about to instantiate an object from the Lake class in your Alice world.

## To Add the Lake Object to the World

**1**

• **Using the horizontal scroll bar at the bottom of the screen, scroll to the right until you can see the** Environments **tile. Click the tile to enter the** Environments **folder.**

*The Environments folder opens, as shown in Figure 1-42.*

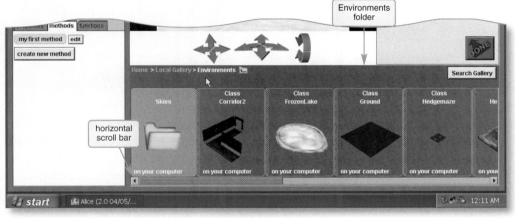

**FIGURE 1-42**

**2**

• **Scroll to the right until you can see the** Lake **tile, then click the tile once.**

*The Lake class information dialog box appears in the Alice interface, as shown in Figure 1-43. The window shows the size of the object and the number of parts that it has. Notice that this is a rather large object, with 127 parts that consume more than 2 megabytes of memory.*

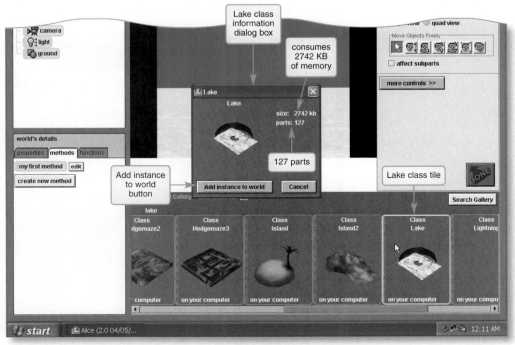

**FIGURE 1-43**

**3**

• **Click the** Add instance to world **button to add an instance of the Lake class to your world. It will take a few seconds for Alice to finish adding the object and all of its subparts to your world.**

*Part of the lake object is now visible in the World window. Also notice that a lake tile has been added to the Object tree for your world. Both can be seen in Figure 1-44.*

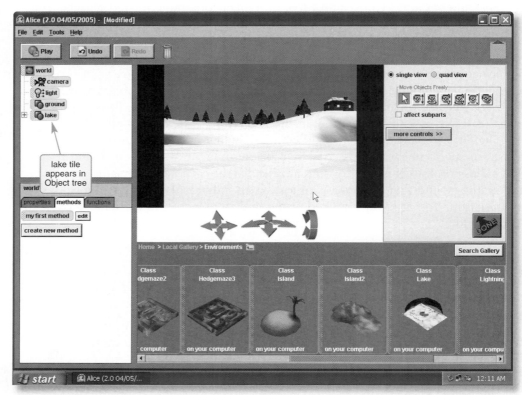

FIGURE 1-44

Next you need to add the ice skater to your world, as shown in the following steps. The ice skater object class is named IceSkater and is stored in the People folder.

## To Add the Ice Skater to the World

**1**

• **Click the** Move Up a Level **button, shown in Figure 1-45, to go up one level in the** Local Gallery's **tree of folders.**

*The main level of the Local Gallery is now shown.*

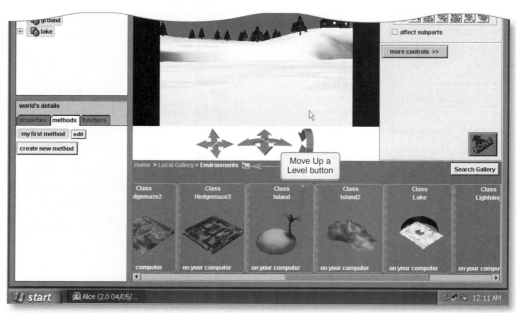

FIGURE 1-45

**2**

• **Scroll to the right until the** People **folder tile is visible, then click the** People **folder tile to enter the folder.**

*The People folder is now visible on the screen (Figure 1-46).*

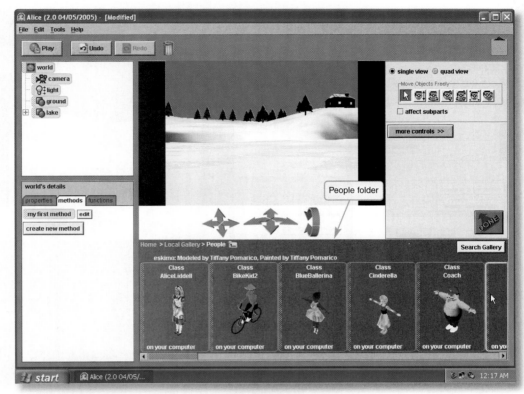

**FIGURE 1-46**

**3**

• **Take a moment to scroll back and forth through the folder and see some of the many characters that you can add to Alice worlds, then find and click the IceSkater class tile.**

*The IceSkater information dialog box is displayed. Notice that an instance of this object has 32 parts and will consume 493 kilobytes of memory, as shown in Figure 1-47.*

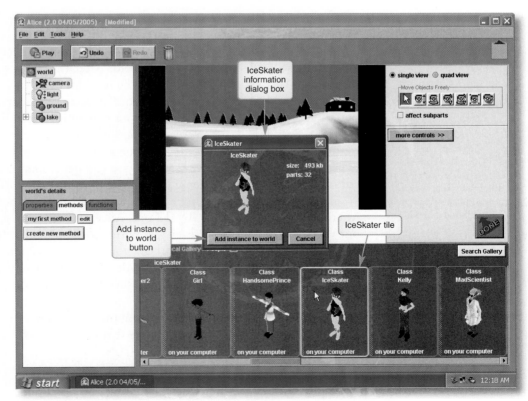

**FIGURE 1-47**

**4**

• **Click the** Add instance to world **button to add an instance of the** IceSkater **class to your world.**

*Your screen should now look something like Figure 1-48. It may look slightly different, depending on your computer's screen size and screen resolution.*

**FIGURE 1-48**

You now have a blank world with the objects you need in place. Before doing anything else, you should save the world. After that, you will create your first method in Alice, which will animate the iceSkater.

You should expect to make mistakes as you create computer software, so it is a good idea to know how to recover from your mistakes. Alice's Undo button is one feature that will help when this occurs, but you can protect yourself even more by frequently saving your work. Each time you finish setting the scene for a new Alice world, you should save that scene so you can get it back if problems occur during editing. In the following steps, you save the new Alice world.

The Save World As dialog box has features similar to Save As dialog boxes for Microsoft Office programs. By default, Alice saves files on the Windows desktop, but you may save files wherever you wish. Ask your instructor where you should save your files, as this may depend on how your classroom computers are configured. If you are working on your own, you should decide where to save your Alice worlds, and remember (or write down) where you saved them. Choose a folder that will be easy to find.

The Save World As dialog box contains a File name text box for you to enter the name of the world. You will name this world skaterHello.a2w, as shown in the following steps.

## To Save the Alice World

**1**

• **Click** File **on the menu bar to display the File menu, then click** Save World **on the File menu.**

*Because this is the first time you have saved this world, a Save World As dialog box is displayed (Figure 1-49).*

**2**

• **In the Save World As dialog box, navigate to the folder in which you wish to save your world, type** skaterHello **in the File name text box, and then click the** Save **button.**

*A file named, skaterHello.a2w, has been saved in the folder you selected. This world uses more than 3 megabytes of storage space, so you may have to wait a few seconds while the world saves.*

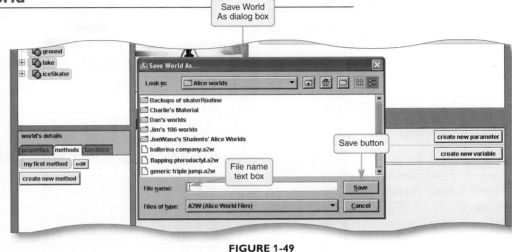

**FIGURE 1-49**

## Positioning the iceSkater in the New World

Once the necessary objects have been added to a new world, they need to be properly positioned. You can do this by using the seven object manipulation tools to the right of the Scene Editor World window. The functions of these tools are summarized in Table 1-1.

**Table 1-1    The Object Manipulation Tools**

| BUTTON | NAME | FUNCTION |
|---|---|---|
| | Pointer tool | Selects an object and moves the object parallel to the ground. (X-Y plane movement) |
| | Vertical tool | Moves an object up or down. (Z-axis movement) |
| | Turn tool | Turns an object parallel to the ground. (X-Y plane rotate) |
| | Rotate tool | Rotates an object forward or backward (Z-axis rotate). |
| | Tumble tool | Freely turns and rotates an object in any direction. |
| | Resize tool | Changes the size of an object. |
| | Duplicate tool | Creates a new instance of the same object. |

You only need to position the IceSkater in this world. She should be between the center and the right side of the screen, and she should be pushed back from her original location. She should also be in a three-quarter view, turned so that she is facing about halfway between looking directly at the camera and directly off to the left side. The following steps position the iceSkater object.

## To Position the iceSkater

**1**

• **If you are not already in Scene Editor mode, click the** ADD OBJECTS **button to enter Scene Editor mode.**

• **The** Pointer **tool is already selected. Click and drag the** iceSkater **back and to the right so that she is in the location shown in Figure 1-50.**

*The iceSkater is now positioned.*

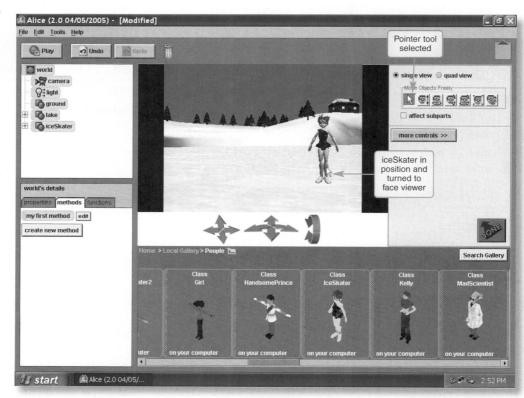

FIGURE 1-50

**2**

• **Select the** Turn **tool and turn the object so that she is facing as shown in Figure 1-51.**

*The iceSkater is facing the correct direction.*

FIGURE 1-51

**3**

• **The** iceSkater **is now in place. Click the** DONE **button to close Scene Editor mode and return to the standard Alice interface.**

*The standard Alice interface is restored (Figure 1-52).*

**4**

• **Click** File **on the menu bar, then click** Save World **on the File menu to save the world again with the skater in position.**

*Since you have already saved the world once, it will be saved this time without asking you for a file name.*

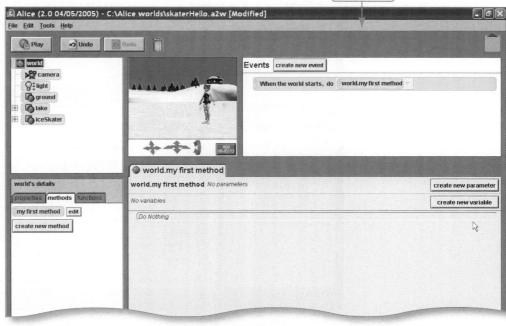

standard Alice interface restored

**FIGURE 1-52**

# Creating a Method to Animate the iceSkater

Next, you will create a method to animate the iceSkater. To be precise, you will add instructions to the default method, world.my first method, that appears in each new Alice world. The full name of each Alice method has two parts separated by a period. The name of the object with which the method is associated comes before the period, and the specific name of the method comes after the period. In this case, world is the object and my first method is the specific name of the method. world.my first method should be visible in the Editor area and a my first method tile should be visible on the methods tab in the Details area.

Currently, world.my first method has no instructions. The finished method will look like Figure 1-53. It is a simple sequence of instructions with no looping or branching. The method contains ten tiles — eight instruction tiles and two Do together control tiles that function as follows:

- The first instruction sets a pose for the skater. A pose is a position that an object can assume. The person who created the iceSkater object also took the time to create several poses and store them as properties of the object, which you will see shortly.
- The second instruction causes the ice skater to spin around twice.
- The third and fourth instructions are in a Do together tile. The skater will assume a new pose while moving forward 2 meters.
- The fifth instruction causes the iceSkater to spin around twice again.
- The sixth and seventh instructions, in a Do Together tile, will cause the skater to go back to her original pose while also turning to face the camera.
- The last instruction (not visible in Figure 1-53) causes the iceSkater to say "Hello, World!"

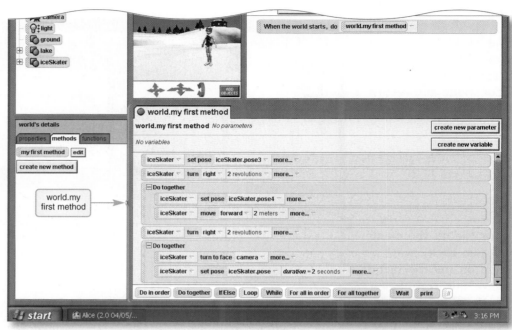

**FIGURE 1-53**

Notice that there is an Event in the Event area that says, When the world starts, do world.my first method. This is Alice's default event, which will cause world.my first method to play whenever the world starts playing. Later, you will create events of your own. For now, you will simply add the instructions described above to world.my first method to animate your first Alice world, as shown in the following series of steps.

## To Start Coding world.my first method

**1**

• **Click the** iceSkater **tile in the Object tree and then click the** properties **tab in the Details area.**

*The iceSkater's properties are visible in the Details area. Notice that four different saved poses for the iceSkater appear on the properties tab above the capture pose button: pose, pose2, pose3, and pose4 (Figure 1-54).*

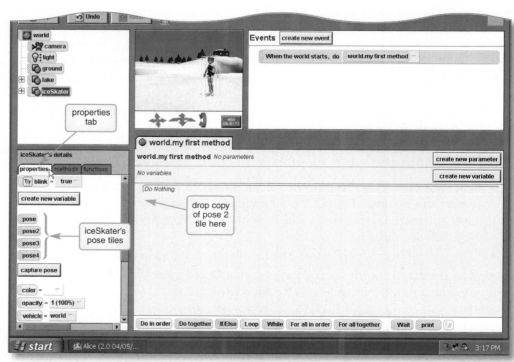

**FIGURE 1-54**

**2**

• **Drag a copy of the** pose2 **tile from the** properties **tab and drop it in the blank area below** Do Nothing **in the Editor area.**

*An instruction tile to set the iceSkater's pose to pose2 appears (Figure 1-55).*

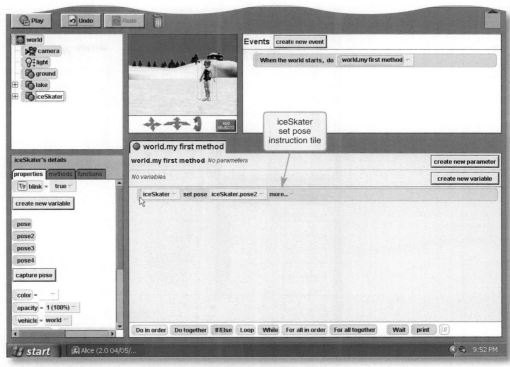

**FIGURE 1-55**

## To Add an Instruction to Make the iceSkater Spin

**1**

• **Click the** methods **tab in the Details area, then drag a copy of the** iceSkater turn **tile from the** methods **tab and drop it in the Editor area below the** iceSkater set pose **instruction.**

*A short menu appears, prompting you to specify the turn's direction, as shown in Figure 1-56.*

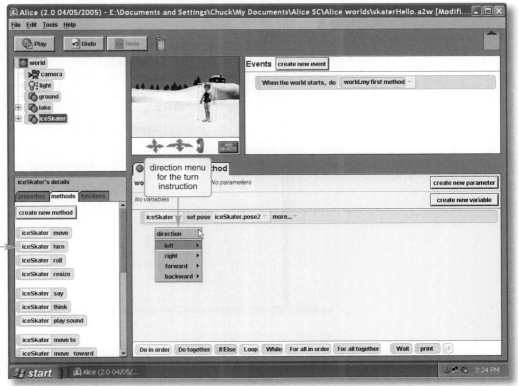

**FIGURE 1-56**

**2**

• **Point to** right **on the** direction **menu.**

*Another short menu appears, as shown in Figure 1-57, allowing you to set the amount for the turn instruction.*

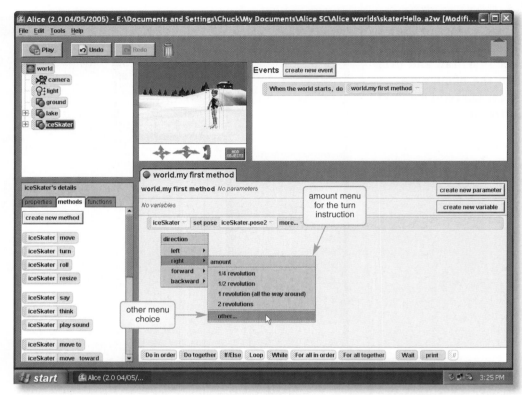

**FIGURE 1-57**

**3**

• **Click** other **on the** amount **menu.**

*The Custom Number dialog box, which looks like a calculator, appears (Figure 1-58).*

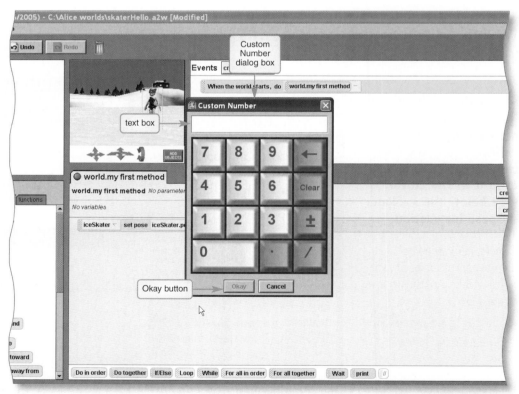

**FIGURE 1-58**

**4**

• **Type** 2 **in the text box and then click the** Okay **button.**

*An iceSkater turn right 2 revolutions instruction tile appears in the Editor area (Figure 1-59).*

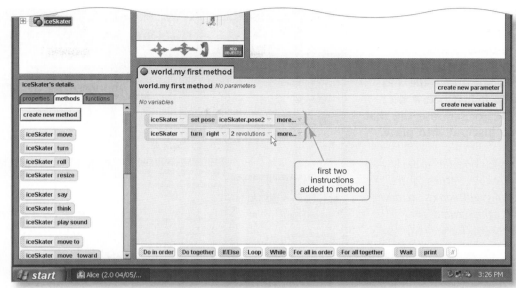

**FIGURE 1-59**

*Other Ways*

1. Click appropriate buttons on calculator-style keypad in Custom Number dialog box

The next two instructions, to again change the iceSkater's pose and move the iceSkater forward, should happen at the same time, so they should be in a Do together tile. The Do together tile is one of several logic and control tiles at the bottom of the Editor area, as shown in Figure 1-60.

## To Add Instructions to Make the iceSkater Change Poses While Moving

**1**

• **Drag a copy of the** Do together **tile from the bottom of the Editor area and drop it in the Editor area below the first two instructions.**

*A blank Do together tile appears in the method (Figure 1-60).*

**2**

• **Click the** properties **tab in the Details area, then drag a copy of the** pose4 **tile and drop it in place of** Do Nothing **in the** Do together **tile.**

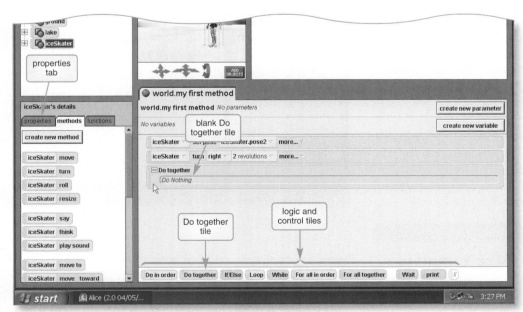

**FIGURE 1-60**

*The Do together tile now contains an instruction to set the iceSkater's pose to pose4.*

**3**

• **Click the** methods **tab in the Details area, then drag a copy of the** iceSkater move **tile and drop it just below the** iceSkater set pose **tile that you just put into place.**

*A menu appears, allowing you to set the direction for the move instruction as up, down, left, right, forward, or backward. These are the six major directions in three-dimensional space.*

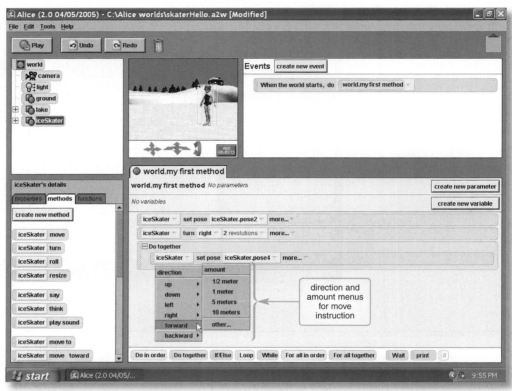

**FIGURE 1-61**

**4**

• **Point to** forward **on the** direction **menu, then click** 2 meters **on the** amount **menu, as shown in Figure 1-61. If** 2 meters **is not an option on the** amount **menu, click** other..., **type** 2 **in the Custom Number window, and then click the** Okay **button.**

*An iceSkater move forward 2 meters instruction tile appears in the Do together tile below the iceSkater set pose tile (Figure 1-62).*

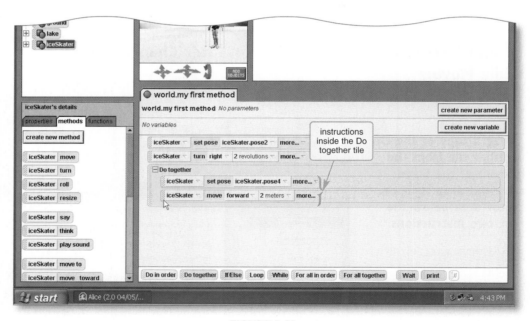

**FIGURE 1-62**

*More About*

**Alice Parameters**

Distance parameters in Alice are in meters because the development of Alice was funded in part by the National Science Foundation, which requires the use of the metric system in educational projects.

Next, you need an instruction to make the ice skater spin around. In this case, the iceSkater will turn right 2 revolutions. The direction and number of revolutions are parameters for the turn method, just as direction and amount were parameters for the move method above. The following steps add an instruction to make the skater spin again.

## To Add an Instruction to Make the iceSkater Spin Again

**1**

• **Drag a copy of the** iceSkater turn **tile from the Details area and drop it below the** Do together **tile in the Editor area.**

*A menu appears asking for the direction for the turn instruction.*

**2**

• **Point to** right **on the** direction **menu, and then select** 2 revolutions **on the** amount **menu.**

*An iceSkater turn right 2 revolutions instruction appears in the method (Figure 1-63).*

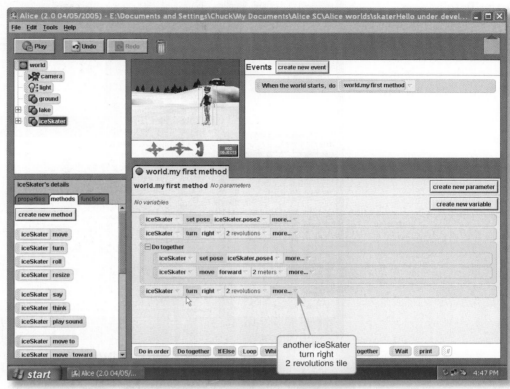

**FIGURE 1-63**

After the iceSkater spins around twice, the sixth and seventh instructions in the method should cause her to go back to her original position while turning to face the camera. These two instructions will happen at the same time, so they should be placed in a Do together tile, as shown in the following steps.

## To Make the iceSkater Pose and Face the Camera at the Same Time

**1**

• **Drag a copy of the** Do together **tile from the bottom of the Editor area and drop it in** world.my first method, **below all of the existing instruction tiles.**

*A blank Do together tile appears at the bottom of the method (Figure 1-64).*

**FIGURE 1-64**

**2**

• **Click the** methods **tab in the Details area, scroll down if necessary, and then drag a copy of the** iceSkater turn to face **tile and drop it in the lower** Do together **tile.**

*The target menu appears (Figure 1-65).*

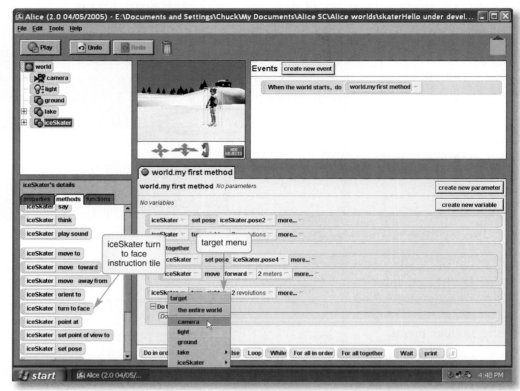

FIGURE 1-65

**3**

• **Click** camera **to select it as the target that the ice skater should turn to face.**

*An iceSkater turn to face camera instruction appears in the Do Together tile (Figure 1-66).*

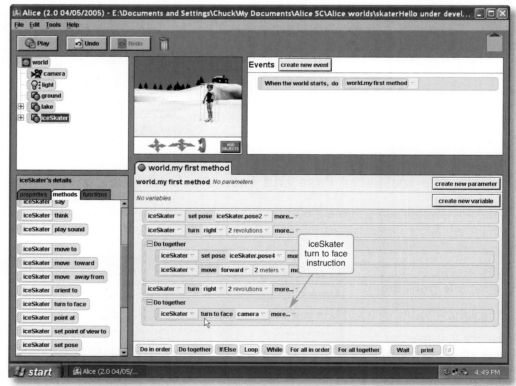

FIGURE 1-66

**4**

• **Click the** properties **tab in the Details area, then drag a copy of the** pose **tile and drop it in the** Do together **tile below the** iceSkater turn to face camera **instruction.**

*The Do together tile now contains an instruction to set the iceSkater's pose to pose (Figure 1-67).*

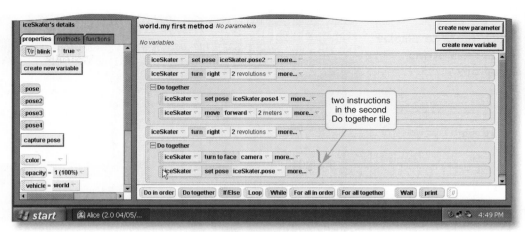

**FIGURE 1-67**

You only need one more instruction to finish the method. The iceSkater should say "Hello, World!" when she has finished her routine. By default, messages from the **say** command only stay on the screen for one second, so it will be necessary to adjust the instruction's **duration** parameter to make it stay on the screen longer. Parameters like **distance** and **amount** for the **move** and **turn** commands are almost always set by the programmer. Other parameters that exist but which are not often used are hidden and can be accessed using the **more** button, following the instruction's other parameters. Figure 1-68 shows the additional parameters for the **say** method that can be accessed with the **more** button. For now, you will change the **duration** to three seconds and ignore the other parameters. After you put the say instruction in place, you will check the world and save it. The following steps illustrate adding an instruction to make the ice skater say "Hello, World!"

**FIGURE 1-68**

## To Add an Instruction to Make the iceSkater Say "Hello, World!

**1**

• **Click the** methods **tab in the Details area, then drag a copy of the** iceSkater say **tile and drop it onto** world.my first method **in the Editor area, below all of the existing instruction tiles.**

*The what menu appears, asking you what the iceSkater should say (Figure 1-69).*

**FIGURE 1-69**

**2**

• **Click** other **to display the Enter a string dialog box.**

*The Enter a string dialog box appears, as shown in Figure 1-70.*

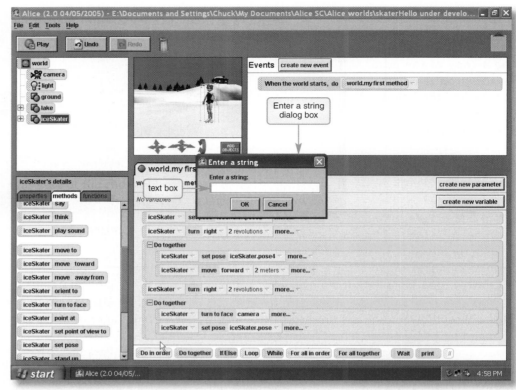

**FIGURE 1-70**

**3**

• **Type** Hello, World! **in the text box and then click the** OK **button to continue.**

*An instruction to make the iceSkater say "Hello, World!" appears in the method. (Figure 1-71).*

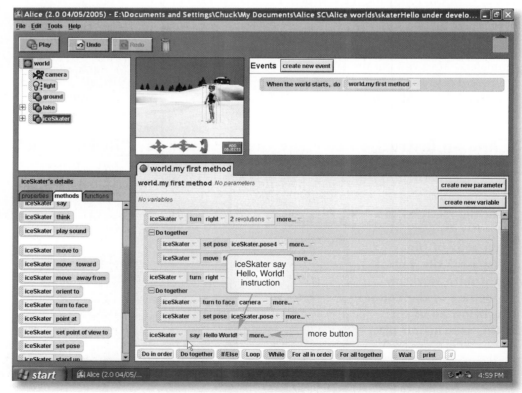

**FIGURE 1-71**

**4**

• **Click** more **on the IceSkater say Hello, World!** instruction tile.

*A menu of additional parameters is displayed, as shown in Figure 1-72.*

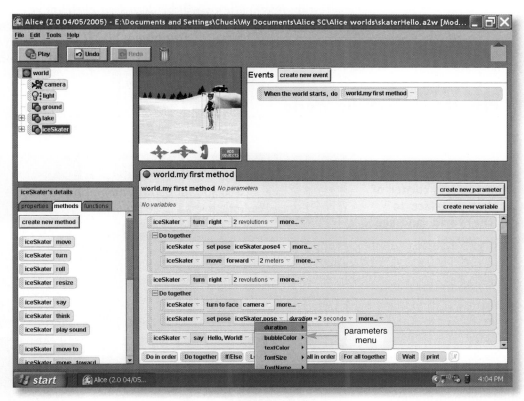

**FIGURE 1-72**

**5**

• **Point to** duration **to open the** duration **menu. If 3 seconds is not an option on the menu, then click** other **and use the calculator-style keypad to enter** 3 **as the amount. Click the** Okay **button.**

*world.my first method is now complete, as shown in Figure 1-73. Before performing any other tasks, you should save your world.*

**6**

• **Click** File **on the menu bar, and then click** Save World **on the File menu to save your world with its existing file name, skaterHello. As before, it will take a few seconds for Alice to save the world.**

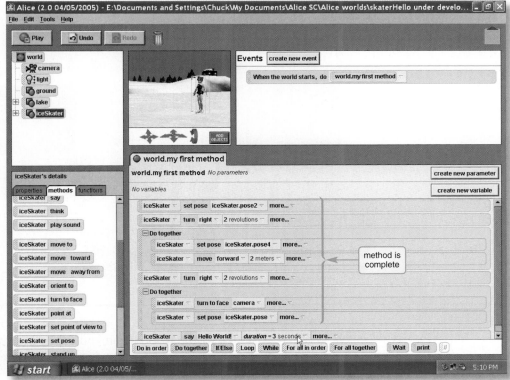

**FIGURE 1-73**

Testing new methods will be discussed in the next project, so for now, simply check to see that your new method matches the one shown in Figure 1-73 and save the world again before continuing if you make any changes.

In the following steps, you try the new method to see how it works.

## To Play the skaterHello World

**1**

• **Click the** Play **button in the top left corner of the Alice interface to play the world, and see how it works.**

*When the world is played, the skater's actions should follow the sequence of those shown in Figure 1-74.*

**2**

• **Click the** Stop **button when finished playing the world.**

*The world stops playing and the World Running window closes.*

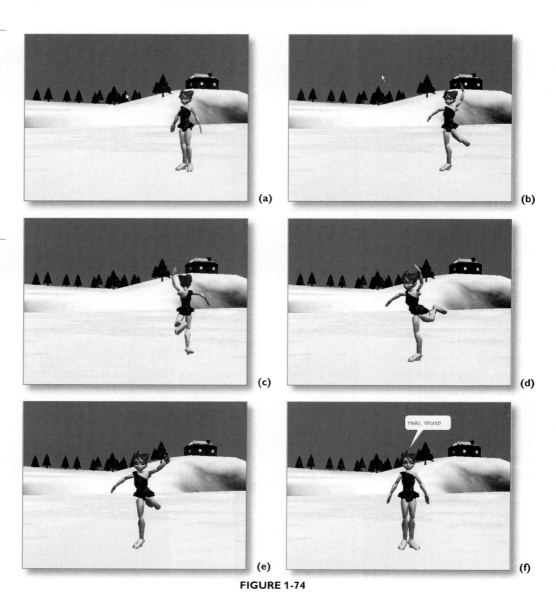

(a) (b) (c) (d) (e) (f)

**FIGURE 1-74**

You may wish to play the world again and experiment with the Restart, Pause, and Resume buttons. See if you can match the actions on the screen with the instructions in world.my first method.

# Printing the Code for an Alice World

The code for methods and events in Alice worlds can be exported to a Web page, using the Export Code for Printing feature on Alice's File menu. The resulting Web page can then be viewed and printed using any standard HTML Web browser, such as Internet Explorer, Mozilla Firefox, or Apple Safari. In addition, the HTML file with code from an Alice world can easily be sent to someone as an e-mail attachment, or used in almost any other way that an HTML page can be used. Figure 1-75 shows a Web page with the code from world.my first method in the world created during the previous section of this project.

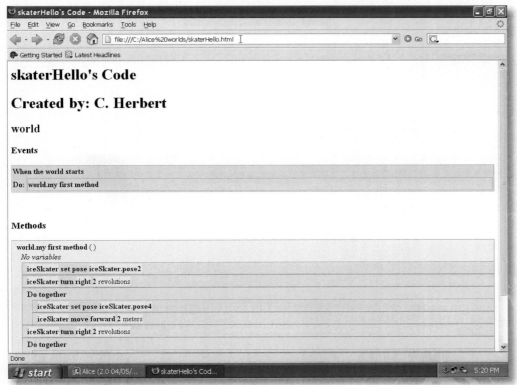

**FIGURE 1-75**

The Export to HTML dialog box will appear as you start to export your code to an HTML page, as shown in Figure 1-76. Most of the items in the Export to HTML dialog box are straightforward and easy to understand. You need to tell Alice what to export, where to export it, and the name of the author of the Alice world.

In the **What to export** section of the Export to HTML dialog box, you select what elements to export for printing. You can click the check boxes individually, or use the Select All or Deselect All buttons when selecting what methods and events to include on the Web page. By default, all methods and events will be selected. In skaterHello, the only method is world.my first method, and the only event is the default event. You will leave both selected in the steps below.

The Export to text box contains the full path name of the HTML file to be saved. By default, this will save your new Web page to the desktop, and the Web page will have the same name as the world, but with .html instead of .a2w as the file extension. Unless you have a good reason to do so, you should probably leave this as is. The Browse button can be used to select a different folder when you need to do so, or the new folder and file name can be entered in the Export to text box. You should leave the folder and file name as is in the following steps, unless your instructor tells you differently.

The Author's name text box is used to enter a name that will be displayed on the resulting Web page, as can be seen in Figure 1-75. In this case, you will type your own name, export the code to a Web page, then view and print the resulting page.

## To Export Code from skaterHello.a2w to a Web Page

**1**

• **Code can be exported only from the currently open Alice world. If you have not closed the world since the steps above, then it should be ready to export. If it is not open,** use the Open World **command on the File menu to locate and open the world named** skaterHello.

• **Click** File **on the menu bar, and then click** Export Code For Printing.

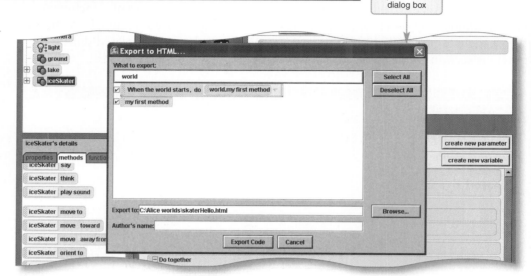

FIGURE 1-76

*The Export to HTML dialog box opens, as shown in Figure 1-76.*

**2**

• **In the** Author's name **text box, type your name as you would like it to appear on the Web page that will be created.**

*Your name should be in the Author's name text box, as shown in Figure 1-77.*

• **Leave the** Export to **text box as it is, unless your instructor has directed you to change the location for the resulting Web page. In either case, write down or remember the full path name that appears in the** Export to **text box.**

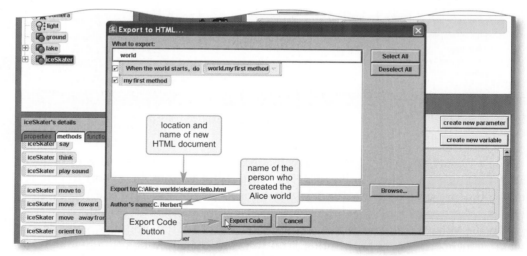

FIGURE 1-77

*The full path name of the folder in which the new Web page will be stored is in the Export to text box (Figure 1-77).*

**3**

• **Click the** Export Code **button to create a new Web page.**

*A new Web page, containing the code shown in Figure 1-78, is saved in the folder you specified.*

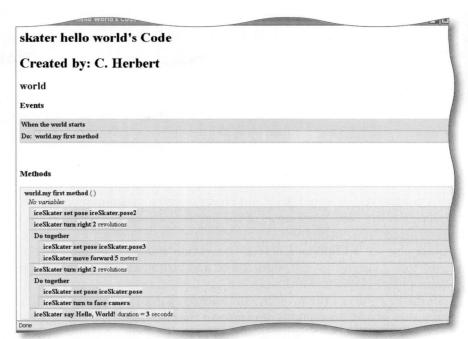

**FIGURE 1-78**

The following steps illustrate opening the HTML file for viewing and printing.

## To Print the Code from the skaterHello Web Page

**1**

• **Close Alice, and then, using Windows Explorer, open the folder that contains the HTML file that was just created.**

*The folder containing the HTML file, similar to the one in Figure 1-79, should be visible on your screen.*

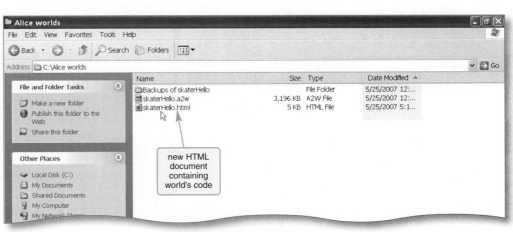

**FIGURE 1-79**

**2**

• **Double-click the** skaterHello.html **file to open it in your computer's default browser.**

*The Web page with the code for skaterHello is visible on your screen.*

**3**

• **Use the Print command on your browser's File menu to print the page that shows the code for your new Alice world.**

*The Web page with the code for skaterHello prints at the printer.*

## Project Summary

In this project, you explored Alice and object-oriented programming. You started by exploring the Alice interface, including the five main work areas of the interface: the World window; the Object tree; the Details area, which contains the properties, methods, and functions tabs; the Editor area; and the Events area. You learned that the Alice Interface also has a Clipboard, a Trash can, Undo and Redo buttons, and a button to play an Alice world. You visited the four Alice menus: File, Edit, Tools, and Help, but learned that not all of them are used the way menus are in programs like Microsoft Word.

In the first part of the project, you learned that an object is a collection of properties and methods. You learned that properties contain information that describes an object, and that methods are computer programs to manipulate an object by changing its properties. The values stored in the properties of the object at any one time are called the state of the object. This modern approach to programming is called object-oriented programming.

You learned how to open and play an existing world, and how to start a new world using Alice's Scene Editor mode to add and position objects in the world. You also learned how to create code for methods in the new world. In the last part of the project, you learned to export the code from an Alice world to a Web page for printing.

## What You Should Know

Having completed this project you should know how to:

1. Start Alice (AL 7)
2. Explore the Welcome to Alice! Dialog Box (AL 9)
3. Open the lakeSkater World and Explore the Alice Interface (AL 11)
4. View the Subparts of the iceSkater Object (AL 13)
5. View the Details of an Object (AL 14)
6. View the Details of a Method (AL 16)
7. Copy an Instruction Tile (AL 18)
8. Delete an Instruction Tile from a Method (AL 19)
9. Delete an Object (AL 20)
10. Undo and Redo Changes to an Alice World (AL 21)
11. Play the lakeSkater World (AL 24)
12. Exit and Restart Alice (AL 27)
13. Create a New Ice Skater World (AL 27)
14. Enter Scene Editor Mode (AL 28)
15. Add the Lake Object to the World (AL 29)
16. Add the iceSkater to the World (AL 30)
17. Save the Alice World (AL 33)
18. Position the iceSkater (AL 34)
19. Start Coding world.my first method (AL 36)
20. Add an Instruction to Make the iceSkater Spin (AL 37)
21. Add Instructions to Make the iceSkater Change Poses while Moving (AL 39)
22. Add an Instruction to Make the iceSkater Spin Again (AL 41)
23. Make the iceSkater Pose and Face the Camera at the Same Time (AL 41)
24. Add an Instruction to Make the iceSkater say "Hello, World!" (AL 43)
25. Play the skaterHello World (AL 46)
26. Export Code from an Alice World to a Web Page for Printing (AL 48)
27. Print the Code from the skaterHello Web Page (AL 49)

# Apply Your Knowledge

## 1 An Animated Hello World Program

In this exercise you will apply the skills that you have learned to modify an existing world. The world already contains the word "Hello" as a 3-D text object in Alice. It spins faster and faster while rising off the screen. Your task is to add a bunny who will move onto the screen from the side and make a few comments.

**Instructions:** Start Alice. Open the file, Apply 1 Hello.a2w, from the Data Files for Students. See the inside back cover of this book for instructions for downloading the Data Files for Students or see your instructor for information about accessing the files required in this book. The word "Hello" is visible as 3-D text in the World window (Figure 1-80).

**FIGURE 1-80**

1. Click the Play button to see what happens in the existing world before continuing with the exercise. After the word "Hello" has left the screen, click the Stop button to return to the standard Alice interface.
2. Click the ADD OBJECTS button to enter Scene Editor mode.
3. Click the tile for the Animals folder, which will then open in the Alice gallery.
4. Click the Class Bunny tile to open the Bunny information dialog box, shown in Figure 1-81, then click the Add instance to world button to add a bunny object to the world.
5. You will now run three methods, one after the other, to position the bunny. First, right-click the bunny tile in the Object tree, point to methods on the menu that appears, point to bunny turn to face, and then click camera.

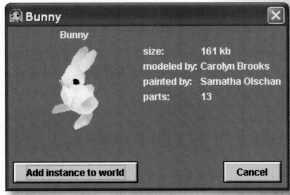

**FIGURE 1-81**

*(continued)*

## An Animated Hello World Program *(continued)*

6. Right-click the bunny tile in the Object tree, point to **methods** on the menu that appears, point to **bunny turn**, point to **right**, and then click **1/4 revolution**.

7. Right-click the bunny tile in the Object tree once more, point to **methods** on the menu that appears, point to **bunny move**, point to **backward**, and then click **10 meters**. The bunny is now off screen.

8. Using the **Save World As** command on the File menu, save the world with the file name, Apply 1 animatedHello.a2w.

9. Click the **DONE** button to return to the standard Alice interface. World.my first method is visible in the Editor area with the single instruction, Hello.whirled, in the method.

10. Click the bunny tile in the Object tree. Drag a copy of the **bunny move** instruction tile from the Details area and drop it into the method below the **Hello.whirled** tile. Select **forward** on the menu that appears, then click **10 meters**.

11. Click the **more** parameter in the **bunny move forward** tile, point to **duration**, and then select **2 seconds** as the value for **duration**.

12. Drag a copy of the **bunny turn** instruction tile from the Details area and drop it into the method below the **bunny move forward** tile. Select **left** on the menu that appears, and then click **1/4 revolution**.

13. Drag a copy of the **bunny say** instruction tile from the Details area and drop it into the method below the **bunny turn** tile. Select **other** on the menu that appears, type `That was the famous "Hello Whirled" program.` in the **Enter a string** dialog box that appears, and then click the **OK** button.

14. Click the **more** parameter in the **bunny say** instruction tile, point to **duration**, and then click **other** on the menu that appears. Type the value 4 in the **Custom Number** dialog box, then click **Okay**.

15. Click the **Hello** tile in the Object tree, then drag a copy of the **Hello move to** instruction tile from the Details area and drop it into the method below the **bunny say** instruction tile. Make sure to drag the **move to** instruction and not the **move** instruction. Select **bunny**, and then select **the entire bunny** from the menus that appear.

16. Click the **more** parameter in the **Hello move to bunny** tile, point to **duration**, and then click **0.25 seconds** on the menu that appears.

17. Click the **bunny** tile in the Object tree, then drag a copy of the **bunny turn** instruction tile from the Details area and drop it into the method below the **Hello move to bunny** instruction tile. Select **backward** on the menu that appears, then click **1/4 revolution**.

18. Click the **more** parameter in the **bunny turn backward** tile, point to **duration**, then click the value **0.25 seconds** on the menu that appears.

19. Drag a copy of the **bunny say** instruction tile from the Details area and drop it into the method below the **bunny turn backward** tile. Select **other** on the menu that appears, type `I don't write this stuff, I just work here.` in the **Enter a string** dialog box that appears, and then click the **OK** button.

20. Click the **more** parameter in the **bunny say** tile, point to **duration** on the menu that appears, and then select **4 seconds** as the value for **duration**.

21. Your new world is now complete. Save it again with the **Save World** command on the File menu before playing the world.

# In the Lab

## 1 Greetings from a Japanese Fan Dancer

Your task is to create a world in which a Japanese fan dancer will perform a short routine and then say "Welcome to the world of Alice."

**Instructions:**

1. Open an Alice world with a grass template.
2. Click the ADD OBJECTS button to enter Scene Editor mode.
3. Find and click the Japan tile in the Alice object gallery.
4. Find and click the Class Dojo tile, and then click the Add instance to world button to add a Dojo object to your world as a background for the dancer.
5. Find and click the Class FanDancer tile, and then click the Add instance to world button to add a fanDancer to your world.
6. Use the pointer tool to move the fanDancer back and to the right so that she is in the location shown in Figure 1-82, about halfway between the center and right edge of the World window.

**FIGURE 1-82**

7. Use the Turn tool to turn the fanDancer so that she is facing diagonally to her right, as shown in Figure 1-82.
8. Click the DONE button to exit Scene Editor mode.
9. Use Save World As on the File menu to save the world with the filename, Lab 1-1 fanDancer greeting.
10. Make sure that the fanDancer is selected in the Object tree and that the methods tab is selected in the Details area.
11. Drag a copy of the fanDancer turn tile from the methods tab and drop it in world.my first method in the Editor area.
12. Point to left on the direction menu that appears, then click 2 revolutions on the amount menu.
13. Drag a Do together tile from the bottom of the Editor area and drop it in world.my first method below the fanDancer turn instruction.

*(continued)*

## Greetings from a Japanese Fan Dancer *(continued)*

14. Drag a copy of the fanDancer move tile from the methods tab and drop it in the Do together tile in place of Do Nothing.

15. Point to right on the direction menu that appears, then click other on the amount menu.

16. Use the Custom Number dialog box to enter the number 3 as the amount, and then click the Okay button.

17. Drag a copy of the fanDancer turn to face tile from the methods tab and drop it in the Do together tile below the move instruction.

18. Select camera on the target menu that appears.

19. Drag a copy of the fanDancer turn tile from the methods tab and drop it in world.my first method below the Do together tile.

20. Point to left on the direction menu that appears, then click 2 revolutions on the amount menu.

21. Click the plus sign next to the fanDancer tile in the Object tree, and then click the upperBody tile that appears.

22. Drag a copy of the upperBody turn tile from the methods tab and drop it in world.my first method below the Do together tile.

23. Select forward and ¼ revolution on the menus that appear.

24. Right-click the fanDancer.upperBody turn instruction in world.my first method and select make copy on the menu that appears. Be sure to right-click the tile and not one of the white parameter boxes in the tile.

25. There are now two copies of the fanDancer.upperBody turn instruction. Click the forward parameter in the bottom copy and select backward on the menu that appears.

26. Click the fanDancer tile in the Object tree to re-select the fanDancer.

27. Drag a copy of the fanDancer say tile from the methods tab and drop it into world.my first method below all of the existing instruction tiles.

28. Select other on the menu that appears.

29. Type "Welcome to the world of Alice." in the Enter a string dialog box, then click the OK button.

30. Click more on the fanDancer say instruction tile and then select duration and 2 seconds on the menus that appear.

31. Your new fanDancer world is now complete. Save the world again before continuing. You may now play the world to see the fanDancer perform her routine.

## 2 A Penguin Demonstration

**Problem:** The penguin class of objects in the Local Gallery has built-in methods to make a penguin walk, jump up and down, flap its wings, and so on. Your task is to create a world that can be used to show people what some of the more useful built-in methods do. You should create a new Alice world in which a penguin will announce what action it is going to perform, and then perform the action. For example, the penguin would say "I am now going to flap my wings," then it would flap its wings, as shown in Figure 1-83.

(a)                                                                 (b)

**FIGURE 1-83**

**Instructions:**

1. Start Alice and begin a new world with a snow template.
2. Enter Scene Editor mode and add a penguin to the world from the Animals folder. The tile for the penguin class of objects is shown in Figure 1-84.

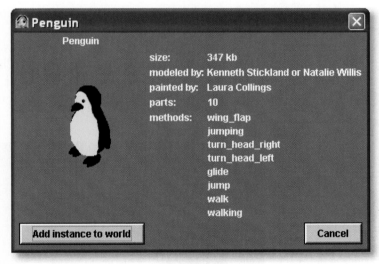

**FIGURE 1-84**

3. Place the penguin in the middle of the screen, facing the camera. Click the DONE button to exit Scene Editor mode.
4. Click the penguin tile in the object tree. You will see several user-defined methods on the methods tab in the Details area. You will start with the wing_flap method.
5. First, make the penguin say "I am now going to flap my wings." The duration for the instruction should be 2 seconds.
6. Next, the penguin should actually flap its wings. Use the wing_flap tile from the methods tab to create an instruction to make the penguin flap its wings two times.

*(continued)*

## In the Lab

### A Penguin Demonstration *(continued)*

7. Following this pattern, have the penguin demonstrate some of the other things that it can do. The Penguin class built-in user methods are shown on the Penguin class tile in Figure 1-84.

8. By changing the penguin's color property in a manner similar to the way you changed the IceSkater's pose property during Project 1, you can make the penguin demonstrate that he can change color. For example, he could say "I am now going to turn blue," then do so.

9. The penguin should also execute several moves together at the same time. For example, the penguin could say "I am now going to jump up and down, flap my wings, and spin around all at the same time." You will need to use a Do together tile and adjust the instructions' parameters to coordinate such actions.

10. Finally, the penguin should turn to face the camera, say "Now, I'm leaving," and then turn to the side and glide out of the scene. You can use the penguin glide method to make the penguin glide out of the scene.

11. When you are finished creating the code for the world, save your world with the filename, Lab 1-2 penguin methods.a2w before playing the world.

## 3 American Chicken Farmers Association

**Problem:** The American Chicken Farmers Association needs your help. For several months, the Amalgamated Beef Producers of America have been running a television advertising campaign that has been cutting into the profits of chicken farmers. They want you to create an animated advertisement to respond to the Beef Producers' ads. Their catch phrase is "Don't even think beef."

The American Chicken Farmers Association advertisement will feature a cow that walks to the middle of the screen, turns its head to face the camera, and then says the following, one at a time: "Chicken is healthy.", "Real healthy.", "And tasty, too." The cow will then turn its head to face forward, start to walk off the screen, then stop, look at the camera again, and say "Don't even think beef." Finally, it will turn its head to face forward again and continue to walk off the screen.

### Instructions:

1. Start Alice and begin a new world with a grass template.

2. Enter Scene Editor mode and add a cow to the world from the Animals folder.

3. Turn the cow so that it is perpendicular to the camera, facing to the left as seen by the camera, as shown in Figure 1-85.

4. Using the blue camera control arrows, move the camera to the left just enough so that the cow is off screen on the right, then exit Scene Editor mode and return to the standard Alice interface.

**FIGURE 1-85**

# In the Lab

5. Click the cow tile in the Object tree to select the cow. Several user-defined methods are visible for the cow in the Details area, including walk, walkTowards, and tailSwish.

6. You will need to create the animation sequence by dragging instruction tiles from the methods tab into world.my first method in the Editor area. You will need the following 15 instructions:

   cow.walk times = 10 speed = 2

   cow.tailSwish times = 2 speed = 2

   cow.neck turn left 1/4 revolution

   cow say "Chicken is healthy." duration = 2 seconds

   cow say "Real healthy." duration = 2 seconds

   cow say "And tasty, too." duration = 2 seconds

   cow.neck turn right 1/4 revolution

   cow.tailSwish times = 2 speed = 2

   cow.walk times = 2 speed = 2

   cow.tailSwish times = 2 speed = 2

   cow.neck turn left 1/4 revolution

   cow say "Don't even think beef." duration = 2 seconds

   cow.neck turn right 1/4 revolution

   cow.tailSwish times = 2 speed = 2

   cow.walk times = 11 speed = 2

   Most of the instructions use the walk, say, or tailSwish tiles found on the cow's methods tab, so you simply need to drag those instructions into world.my first method in the proper order and set the parameters as indicated. Four of the instructions are turn instructions for the cow's neck, which is a subpart of the cow. For each of these, you will need to click the plus sign next to the cow tile in the Object tree to see the neck tile, then you can drag the neck turn instruction from the methods tab into world.my first method.

7. When you are finished creating the code, save your world with the file name, Lab 1-3 chicken is tasty.a2w, before playing the world.

# Cases and Places

**1** The Caribbean School of Computer Programming would like a 10-second video advertisement in the form of an animated virtual world. They wish to show a beach scene with a lighthouse, two beach houses, a pier, a sailboat, and several palm trees, as shown in Figure 1-86.

**FIGURE 1-86**

When the advertisement starts, the sailboat sails away, then two messages appear on the screen one at a time. One of the beach houses should say "Come to the Caribbean School of Computer Programming." Then the other should say "Where the summer semester never ends." Each message should stay on the screen for several seconds.

Your task is to add the necessary objects to an existing beach scene and then create the advertisement. You can find most of the items you will need in the **Beach** folder in Alice's local object gallery. The sailboat is in the **Vehicles** gallery and the palm tree is in the Nature folder. You can resize, turn, and rotate copies of the palm tree so that they do not all look the same.

You should begin by starting Alice and opening the file, Case 1-1 beach scene.a2w, from the Data Files for Students. See the inside back cover of this book for instructions for downloading the Data Files for Students or see your instructor for information about accessing the files required in this book. Once you have a properly working world, save it with the file name, Case 1-1 Caribbean School of Computer Programming.a2w.

# Cases and Places

**2** Daphne Belle, the Director of the Shelly Cashman Drama Society, has been trying to create an animation to show students the movement and dialogue for their upcoming production of the 1970's revival "Joe Cool!". Scene II, Act III opens with Mary standing in a room between classes. The door opens, Joe enters the room and, trying to be cool, says in French, "Ehhh! Mon Ami. Je t'adore." To which Mary says "Shut the door? Shut it yourself." She then walks away.

The problem is that a director like Daphne often is quite busy, and she hasn't finished creating the Alice animation to show her actors what to do. Your task is to finish working on the animation so that it functions as described above.

Start Alice and open the world Case 1-2 Joe Cool.a2w from the Data Files for Students. See the inside back cover of this book for instructions for downloading the Data Files for Students or see your instructor for information about accessing the files required in this book. Play the world to see how far Daphne got, decide what changes need to be made, then complete the world. When you are finished, save the world with the file name, Case 1-2 Joe Cool Revival.a2w.

**3** Alice has two tools that you can use to build characters of your own for an Alice virtual world: the **hebuilder** and **shebuilder** classes of objects found in the **People** folder in the Alice Local Gallery. The new characters created with **hebuilder** and **shebuilder** have built-in, user-defined methods to walk, move, and show various emotions. Working together with several other students, create a simple Alice world with two characters created using **hebuilder** and **shebuilder** that engage in a short dialogue.

You should experiment with **hebuilder** and **shebuilder** before you start on your final world to become familiar with the different options available for new characters. You should also experiment with the various methods for the new characters to see how they function. Once you are familiar with the **hebuilder** and **shebuilder** characters, you can work as a team to plan and build your new world. You might want to start the planning process by sketching the sequence of events in your new world, either with a series of storyboards or with an outline. Storyboards can often give you a better feel for the movement and placement of objects, as well as camera angles, when planning a new Alice world.

Keep in mind McGinley's Rule for new programmers: K.I.S.S. – Keep It Short and Simple. Do not get too carried away planning a world that will be difficult and time consuming to implement. Start with just two characters, perhaps a few background objects, and a short and simple sequence of events.

When you are finished, save the new world with the file name, Case 1-3 new characters.a2w.

# Learning Exercises

**1** The URL for the official Alice Website is www.alice.org. The page contains links to many items about Alice. Visit the site and try the links to these or other features:

- **Alice Gallery.** An online gallery of objects that can be saved as data files with the extension "a2c" and then later imported into an Alice world. To save an object, click on the link for the desired object and save it to disk. Do not change its file name. To import a saved character, start Alice and open an existing world, or create a new world and then select Import from the Alice File menu.
- **Alice FAQ.** A large collection of answers to the most frequently asked questions by Alice users.
- **Export as a webpage tutorial.** A short tutorial on saving an Alice world as an interactive Web page.
- **Alice community.** A link to the Alice Community Forums, where users of Alice exchange questions, information, and ideas. You may read the messages posted on the forum without joining, but to post questions or comments to the site you will need to join. The forum is free, and is operated by faculty, staff, and students at Carnegie Mellon University. There are sections on the forum for announcements, students, and educators, and for sharing Alice objects and worlds.

**2** The Alice software includes a set of built-in tutorials to introduce you to Alice. Open the Alice software and complete the first two tutorials. The third tutorial involves music, which requires a computer with a sound card.

**3** Briefly describe how to complete each of the following Alice tasks:

A. view the subparts of an Alice object

B. view the properties of an Alice object

C. add an instance of an object to an Alice world

D. delete an object from an Alice world

E. delete an instruction tile from an Alice method

F. print the code for an Alice world

Alice 2.0

# Developing Software Methods

## CASE PERSPECTIVE

After seeing your first virtual world, Dr. Dodgson is pleased with the potential for using Alice to demonstrate computer programming. She wishes to show her students a more complex world composed of several different software methods, so that she can demonstrate good modular design. She would like you to you to develop a more elaborate routine for the skater composed of several parts. Each of these parts will appear in the Alice world as separate methods for the ice skater.

ater World

Opening Sequence

A.   iceSkater Say "Hello, World."

B.   Camera move back 5 meters

Skating Routine

A.   Skate around two cones in a fig

B.   Jump and spin while skating fro

C.   Jump and spin while skating fro

Closing Sequence

A.   iceSkater

B.   iceSkater

C.   The camera                    kater

# Developing Software Methods

## Objectives

**You will have mastered the material in this project when you can:**

- Understand the software development cycle and its four phases
- Describe the different types of software documentation and their appropriate uses
- Understand modular development and its benefits
- Understand top-down software design and bottom-up software development
- Perform unit testing and integration testing

## Introduction

An algorithm is a step-by-step process that can be clearly defined. When you create a computer program, you are implementing an algorithm. Long and complex algorithms can be broken down into a collection of smaller algorithms that are easier to understand and manage. Likewise, software developers often break down complex programs into a collection of simpler programs, called modules, which are each developed independently, then assembled to make up the overall program. In modern object-oriented computer programming, they implement these modules as methods for specific objects.

## Project Two — Developing the Ice Skater Routine

In Project 1 you created a simple one-method program, in which an ice skater performs a short routine and then says "Hello, World!" In this project, you will create a more elaborate routine for the ice skater, shown in Figure 2-1. In doing so, you will learn about a process known as the software development cycle, which programmers use to design and implement computer programs. You will also begin to document your work.

The new performance routine that you will create is an example of an algorithm. As described above, you will take this algorithm and break it down into smaller algorithms, which will be implemented as a series of methods for the ice skater object. When assembled, these methods will make up the overall routine. Figure 2-2 shows an outline of the skater's routine.

**FIGURE 2-1**

## Skater World

I. Opening Sequence
  A. iceSkater Say "Hello, World."
  B. Camera move back 5 meters

II. Skating Routine
  A. Skate around two cones in a figure 8
  B. Jump and spin while skating from left to right across the screen
  C. Jump and spin while skating from right to left across the screen

III. Closing Sequence
  A. iceSkater turn to face the camera
  B. iceSkater raise her right arm
  C. The camera circles the skater

**FIGURE 2-2**

## The Software Development Cycle

The process of designing and building computer software fits into a general four-phase pattern known as the **software development cycle**, in which developers design, implement, test, and debug software. This process is shown in Figure 2-3. Different software developers use variations of the software development cycle, but they all basically follow a general pattern similar to the one described below.

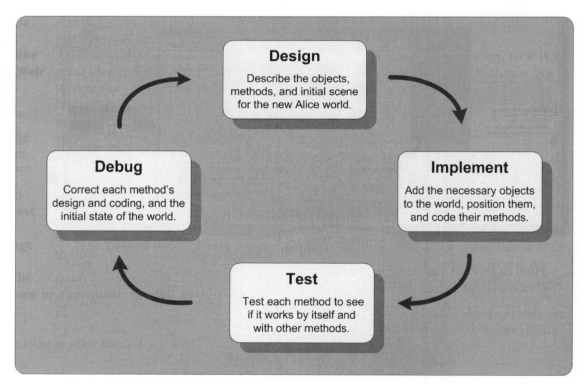

**FIGURE 2-3**

## The Design Phase

The cycle starts when the developers begin to design the software. The person, company, or organization for whom the software is being developed is referred to as the client. Usually the software design is based on **specifications** from the client, which describe what the program should do. Sometimes the client provides complete specifications, and sometimes the software developers work with the client to create the necessary specifications.

Modern object-oriented software specifications include descriptions of the objects needed for the software and the methods associated with those objects. Designers select existing objects to be used in the software, describe any new objects that need to be created, and describe the methods needed for each object as algorithms that perform specific tasks. In this project you will use existing objects found in Alice's object galleries; you will not create any new objects. However, you will create new methods for the existing objects.

The collection of step-by-step tasks performed by the objects' methods forms the overall algorithm for the software. Designers break a complex algorithm down into a collection of smaller algorithms, called modules, which usually correspond to individual methods performing specific tasks within a larger software package.

When creating virtual worlds, such as with Alice or with video game software, the designers must also develop specifications for the starting scene for the world— describing the initial position of objects within the world and the placement and orientation of the world's camera. The design for a virtual world should include descriptions of:

- the necessary objects
- the methods associated with each object
- the initial state of the world

## The Implementation Phase

Once a satisfactory design for the software exists, it needs to be implemented. For virtual world software this includes adding the necessary objects to the world, setting the initial scene, and coding the methods for the world.

The process of coding includes translation of each method's algorithm into a particular programming language as well as actually entering the instructions into a computer system. Coding can be the most tedious part of programming, and coding specialists must have patience and must pay attention to seemingly minor details, such as spelling, capitalization, and punctuation in their code. For example, inserting a semicolon at the end of a while clause when setting up a loop in a Java program can change the entire meaning of the program. Such a simple mistake could take hours to find and correct.

## The Testing Phase

After each software method is coded and ready to use, it needs to be tested to see if it works properly and meets its specifications. Software testing is one of many highly specialized and important jobs in software development. People who obtain graduate degrees in Computer Science or in Software Engineering often need to complete at least one course in software testing.

Several different types of software tests exist, including unit tests and integration tests, as shown in Figure 2-4. A **unit test** checks an individual software method to see if it works all by itself. An **integration test** checks to see if a method works when it is mixed in with other methods to form an overall software package. Typically, unit tests focus on the algorithmic correctness and efficiency of an individual method, while integration tests focus on side effects. An individual method is algorithmically correct if it does what it is supposed to do. A **side effect** is an unwanted or unexpected result, usually caused by one method interfering with another. For example, if one method instructs an Alice object to move forward 10 meters, and another method is turning the object when the move instruction starts, then you may end up with some unexpected results.

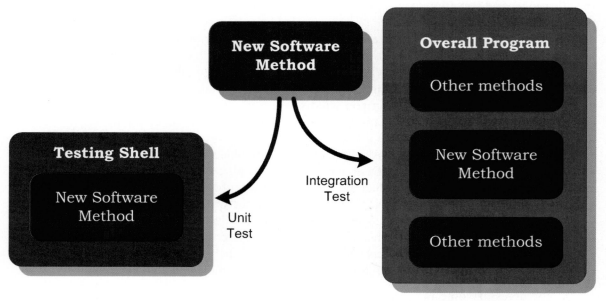

A new software method can be unit tested by itself, or inside a testing shell that simulates the environment in which it will run. Once it passes unit testing, the new method can be put in place in the overall program for integration testing.

**FIGURE 2-4**

## The Debugging Phase

In **debugging**, the last phase of the software development cycle, developers attempt to correct mistakes that have been found in the testing phase. Debugging is what leads the development process to become a cycle, because it is often necessary to go back to the earlier phases when debugging software methods.

Software developers may need to correct errors in the design of methods, in their coding, or in the initial setup of the software, such as the initial values of object's properties or the initial placement of an object in an Alice world.

In summary, there are four phases in the software development cycle: design, implement, test, and debug. The process starts with the development of specifications for the software, and is complete when the software meets those specifications.

## Software Documentation

**Software documentation** includes written text and visual material, such as charts, diagrams, and drawings, that describe computer software. Good computer software requires good documentation, starting with the specifications for the new software. While the project is in progress, the documentation serves as a guide and working tool for the programmers. Once the project is finished, the documentation will describe what the program does and how the software works.

The three different types of software documentation are:

- comments that appear in the code itself
- notes that appear while the program is running
- user notes or an instruction manual supplied with the software

*More About*

### Software Efficiency

New software needs to be tested for its efficiency as well as its correctness. Software developers can determine both the time efficiency and space efficiency of new software through testing and a mathematical analysis of the program's algorithms. Time efficiency refers to the amount of time a program needs to complete a particular task. Space efficiency refers to the amount of memory the program uses. For example, if one program can sort a list of names in three seconds, and another program takes three minutes to sort the same list, the second program would probably be sent back to the designers because of its poor time efficiency.

Software developers are often responsible for creating the messages that appear when the program runs and for comments in the body of the code itself. Together these are referred to as the program's internal documentation. Messages that appear when the program runs are intended to make the program easier to use. Comments placed in the body of the code are intended to provide guidance for anyone who reads the code. They usually describe:

- who created the method
- when it was created
- what purpose the method serves
- the purpose and function of any variables or parameters used in the method
- notes about any special techniques that are used in the method, especially any new or unusual techniques the programmer used

Figure 2-5 shows an Alice method with comments in the code. In this project, you will document your work by placing identifying comments in the body of the Alice world's main method, world.my first method.

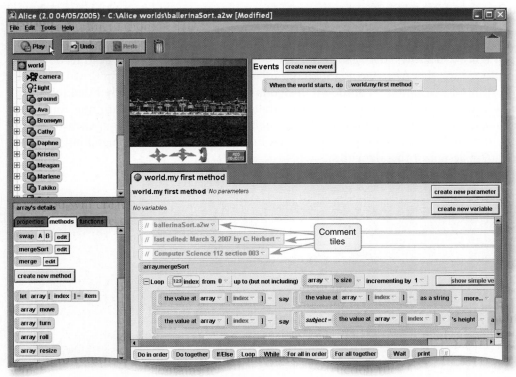

**FIGURE 2-5**

You will not be responsible for creating a user manual, which is often referred to as external software documentation. In a professional project, external documentation is often developed by technical writers and editors working with the software developers.

## A Modular Design for the Ice Skater World

The world you created in Project 1 was named skaterHello.a2w. The Alice world to be created in this project will be called skaterRoutine.a2w. The skaterHello.a2w world will be modified to create the new world.

A good developer begins by breaking a task down into smaller tasks called modules. Each module is a logically independent unit that handles a well-defined task.

*More About*

## Documentation

A different form of documentation, called project documentation, includes information about the actual process followed by developers in creating computer software. **Project documentation** includes the software documentation, along with schedules, budgets, and any other notes or correspondence written by the development team. This material creates a historical record of the development process itself, which can be studied to reduce errors and increase the efficiency of the overall process.

*More About*

## Camel Case Names

The names of classes, objects, methods, and worlds in this book generally follow a pattern called the **camel case** naming convention, which is used with most programming languages and is recommended by many software developers, including Microsoft. Camel case is the practice of writing compound names without using blank spaces, but capitalizing the first letter of each name that forms the compound name, as in "CamelCase." In a general discussion of the world, one might refer to the "ice skater" but the correct name of the object in the Alice gallery is "IceSkater". You will also notice that object class names usually begin with capital letters, whereas the names of instances of a class begin with lowercase letters. The class name is IceSkater, with a capital "I"; the first instance of the class is named iceSkater with a lowercase "i."

The developer then builds software methods that correspond to each module in the algorithm. Modular development provides many benefits to computer programming:

- It makes a large project more manageable, since a collection of smaller and less complex tasks is easier to understand than one large and complex task.
- It speeds up a project, because different people can work on different modules at the same time, and then combine their work.
- It leads to a higher quality product, because programmers with knowledge and skills in a specific area, such as graphics, accounting, or data communications, can be assigned to parts of the project that require those skills.
- It simplifies correcting errors in programs, because it is easier to isolate the part of the software that is causing each error.
- It increases the reusability of software, because smaller modules are more likely to be useful elsewhere as part of other large programs.

This last point is an important one. Software developers can save methods created as part of one project for use in future projects. Software developers often specialize in a particular kind of software, such as educational software or accounting software, so it is very likely that a method created for one project could be reused in another. Object-oriented programming, by its very nature, encourages such reusability, since entire classes of special-purpose objects can be reused in many similar projects.

Figure 2-6 shows an organizational chart with the modules that need to be developed for this Alice world. Such organizational charts show a top-down view of algorithm development. **Top-down design** is the process of repeatedly breaking large algorithms down into several smaller modules, starting at the top with one concept or big idea, and continuing until the design includes a set of modules that each represent an individual task. The programmers then build software methods matching the modular design of the algorithm.

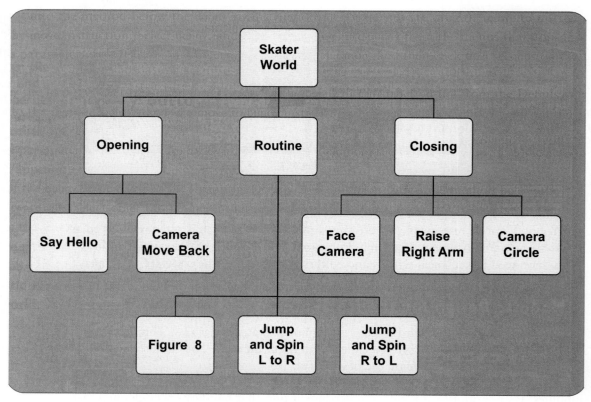

**FIGURE 2-6**

Notice that the jump-and-spin module appears twice: once while moving from left to right and once while moving from right to left. You only need to build one jump-and-spin method, which can be used twice within the program. This is an example of software reusability *within* a program.

## Implementing the Ice Skater World — Setting the Scene

Before creating the actual code for a new Alice world, you need to insert the required objects and position them in the world. The Alice world that you will create in this project will be called skaterRoutine.a2w. You will start by opening the skater-Hello.a2w world from Project 1, and using the objects that are already in that world. You will modify the opening scene by adding two cones to the world, and making sure that the skater, cones, and camera are in the proper position. This setup work must be completed before you begin to work on the code for the world.

Initially, the skater should be standing near the center of the screen, with one cone a few meters to the skater's left, and the other cone a few meters to the skater's right.

Before attempting the following steps, you need to know where you saved the original skaterHello.a2w world from Project 1.

## To Start the New World from the Old World

**1**

• **Start Alice as described in Project 1.**

*After a few seconds, the Welcome to Alice! dialog box appears (Figure 2-7).*

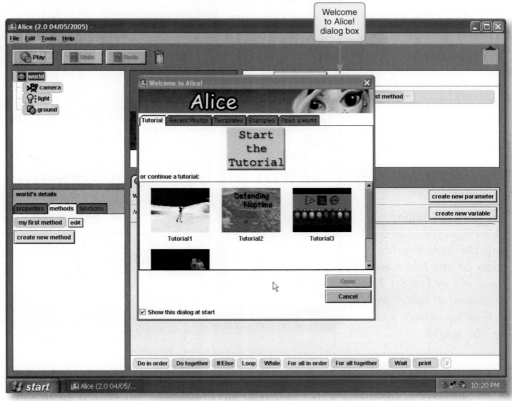

**FIGURE 2-7**

**2**

• **Click the** Open a world **tab.**

*The Open a world tab appears (Figure 2-8).*

**FIGURE 2-8**

**3**

• **Navigate to the folder that contains the Alice file, skaterHello.a2w, and open the file by selecting it and clicking the** Open **button.**

*world.my first method from the skaterHello.a2w world appears in the standard Alice interface (Figure 2-9).*

**4**

• **Save the file with the new name** skaterRoutine.a2w **by using the** Save World As **option on the File menu, as you did in Project 1. Remember or write down the location where you save the world.**

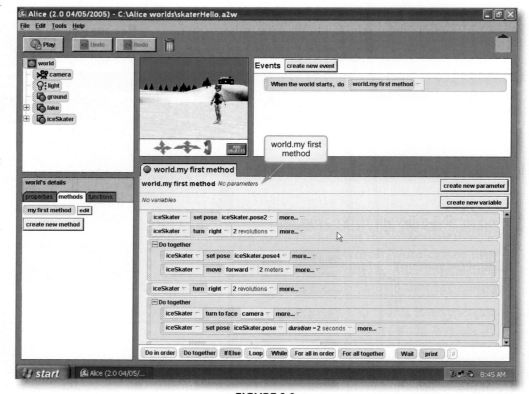

**FIGURE 2-9**

## More About

### Recent Worlds

Often, a world that you previously created or modified will appear on the Recent Worlds tab. If so, you can open the world by clicking the Recent Worlds tab and then double-clicking the icon for that world. Note that this may not work as expected in a classroom environment where many people use the same computer.

Next you will reposition the ice skater in the new world.

## To Position the iceSkater in the New World

**1**

• **Click the green** ADD OBJECTS **button to enter Scene Editor mode.**

*The Events area and Editor area disappear. The World window is now larger, with Scene Editor controls appearing to the right of the window and the Local Gallery visible at the bottom of the screen (Figure 2-10).*

**FIGURE 2-10**

**2**

• **Click the** iceSkater **in the World window and drag her to the center of the window and back (away from the camera), as shown in Figure 2-11.**

*The iceSkater is now in the correct location.*

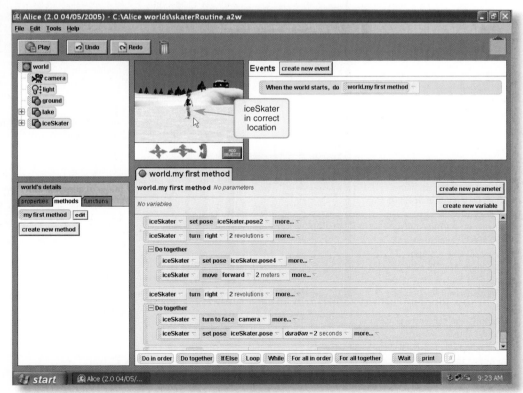

**FIGURE 2-11**

**3**

• **Right-click the** iceSkater **tile in the Object tree and point to** methods **on the shortcut menu.**

• **Point to** iceSkater turn to face **and then click** camera **on the** target menu, **as shown in Figure 2-12.**

*The iceSkater is positioned in the middle of the screen, facing the camera. (Figure 2-13).*

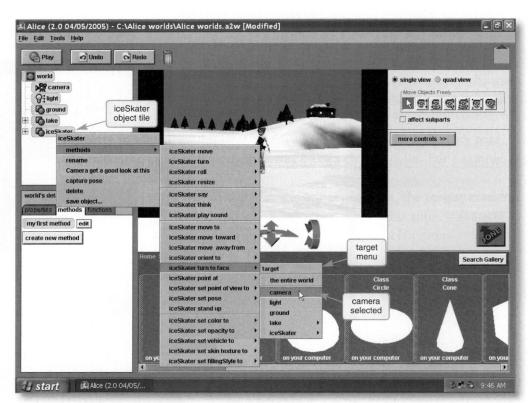

**FIGURE 2-12**

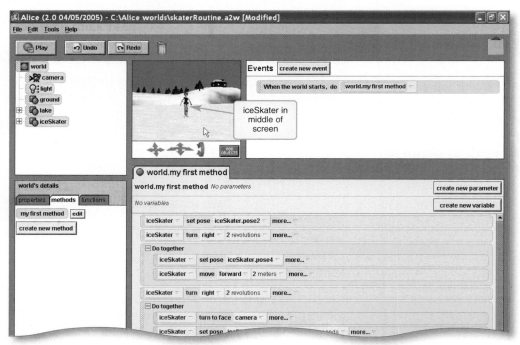

**FIGURE 2-13**

Two cones need to be added to the world, as shown previously in Figure 2-1: one red cone to the skater's left and one blue cone to the skater's right. You will first add and position the red cone, then add and position the blue cone.

## To Add a Red Cone to the World

**1**

• **Using the horizontal scroll bar at the bottom of the object galleries, scroll to the right until you can see the** Shapes **tile. Click the tile to enter the** Shapes **folder.**

*The Shapes folder appears on the screen (Figure 2-14).*

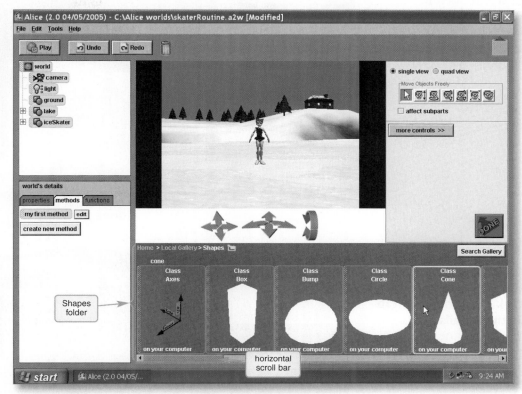

**FIGURE 2-14**

**2**

• **Find and click the** Cone **class tile in the** Shapes **folder.**

*A Cone information dialog box appears on the screen (Figure 2-15).*

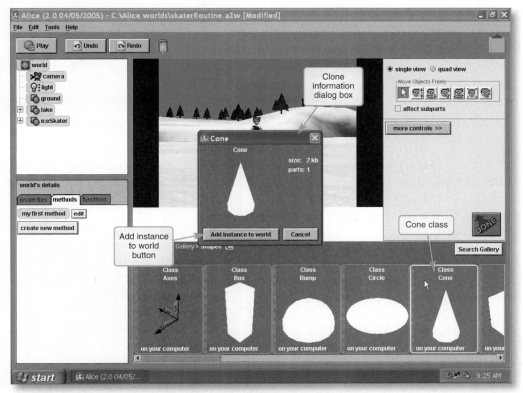

**FIGURE 2-15**

**3**

• **Click the** Add instance to world **button.**

*A white cone appears in the World window and a cone tile appears in the Object tree (Figure 2-16).*

**FIGURE 2-16**

**4**

• **Click the** cone **tile in the Object tree and then click the** Properties **tab in the Details area.**

*The cone's properties appear in the Details area. Thin, yellow lines appear around the red cone. These are the edges of the cone's bounding box, a rectangular solid that outlines the three-dimensional space filled by the cone (Figure 2-17).*

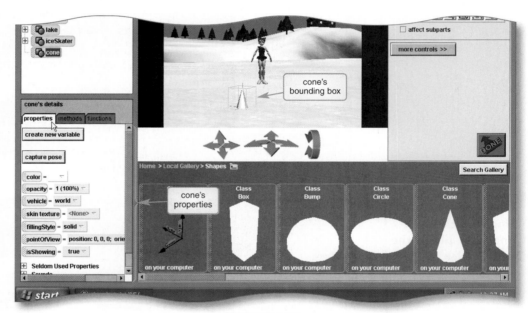

**FIGURE 2-17**

**5**

• **Click the selection box next to the** color **property tab in the Details area to open the** color **menu.**

*The color menu appears, from which you can choose a color for the cone (Figure 2-18).*

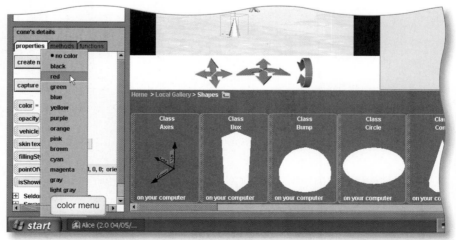

**FIGURE 2-18**

**6**

• **Click** red **on the** color **menu.**

*The cone in the World window and the color property on the properties tab both turn red (Figure 2-19).*

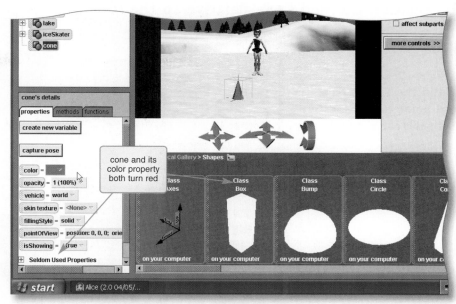

**FIGURE 2-19**

**7**

• **Right-click the** cone **tile in the Object tree, and click** rename **on the shortcut menu.**

• **Change the text for the** cone's **name from** cone **to** redCone, **then press the ENTER key.**

*The tile in the Object tree now has the name redCone (Figure 2-20).*

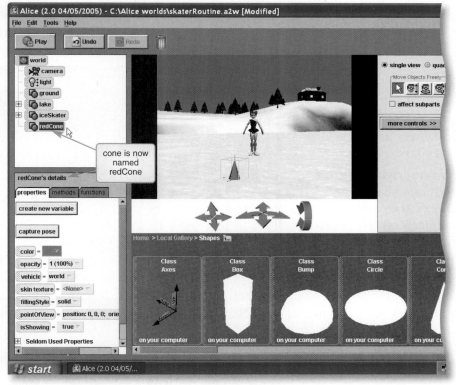

**FIGURE 2-20**

The following steps show how to position the red cone.

# To Position the Red Cone Relative to the iceSkater

**1**

• **Right-click the** redCone **tile in the Object tree and point to** methods **on the shortcut menu.**

*A menu of the redCone's primitive methods appears (Figure 2-21).*

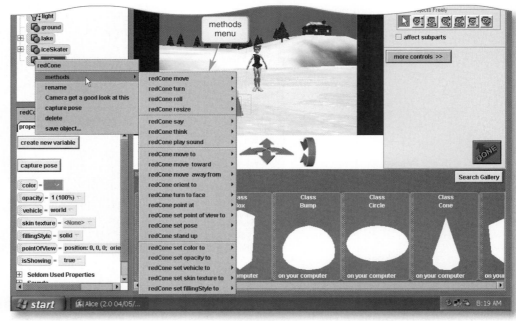

**FIGURE 2-21**

**2**

• **Point to** redCone move to **on the** methods **menu, point to** iceSkater, **and then click** the entire iceSkater.

• **Again, right-click the** redCone **tile in the Object tree and point to** methods **on the shortcut menu. This time, point to** redCone turn to face, **and then click** camera **on the** target **menu.**

*The red cone moves to the ice skater's position. The two objects overlap each other and are pointing in the same direction (Figure 2-22).*

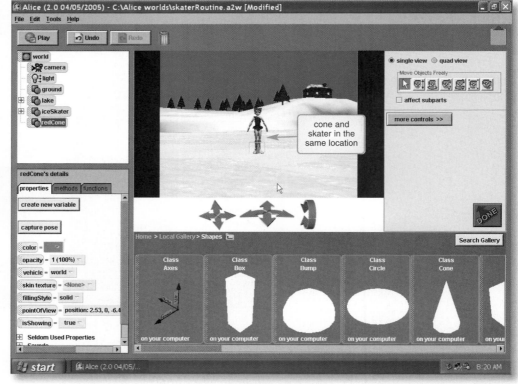

**FIGURE 2-22**

**3**

• **Right-click the** redCone **tile in the Object tree, point to** methods **on the shortcut menu, point to** redCone move, **point to** left **on the** direction **menu, and then click** 2 meters **on the** amount **menu. If 2 meters is not an option on the** amount **menu, then click** other, **and use the Custom Number dialog box to enter the number** 2.

*The redCone is now 2 meters to the iceSkater's left, as shown in Figure 2-23.*

**FIGURE 2-23**

The red cone is in the correct position. The following steps show how to add a blue cone to the world and position it just as you did the red cone.

## To Add a Blue Cone to the World

**1** **Click the** Cone **class tile in the Shapes folder, and then click the** Add instance to world **button.**

**2** **Click the** cone **tile in the Object tree and then click the** properties **tab in the Details area.**

**3** **Click the selection box next to the** color **property tab in the Details area and select** blue **on the menu that appears.**

**4** **Right-click the** cone **tile in the Object tree, click** rename **on the shortcut menu, change the text for the cone's name from** cone **to** blueCone, **and then press the ENTER key.**

*Now there is a blue cone, named blueCone, in the world (Figure 2-24).*

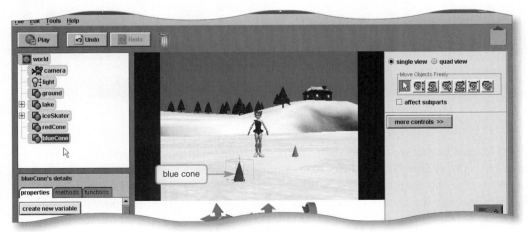

**FIGURE 2-24**

*More About*

## Adding Objects

An Object can also be added to an Alice world by dragging the object's tile into the world from one of the object galleries in Scene Editor mode. However, the object would then be in the world at the spot where the cursor was when the person placing the object let go of the mouse button. The method described in the text, using the "Add instance to world" button, always places the object in the same spot in the world—the (0,0,0) center point of the world's (x,y,z) coordinate system.

*Q & A*

**Q:** Why do the values available on parameter menus, such as the amount for the move instruction, change?

**A:** Alice "remembers" values that were previously used, so they will show up as options on menus, such as the amount menu for the move instruction. However, the menus are sometimes reset to their default values when Alice is restarted, so recently used values may not always appear as additional options on menus.

In the following set of steps, you will place the blue cone in its proper starting position.

## To Position the Blue Cone Relative to the iceSkater

**1** **Right-click the** blueCone **tile in the Object tree and point to** methods **on the shortcut menu.**

**2** **Point to** blueCone move to **on the methods menu, point to** iceSkater **on the** asSeenBy **menu, and then click** the entire iceSkater.

**3** **Right-click the** blueCone **tile in the Object tree and point to** methods **on the shortcut menu. This time, point to** blueCone turn to face, **and then click** camera **on the** target **menu.**

**4** **Right-click the** blueCone **tile in the Object tree and point to** methods **on the shortcut menu. This time, point to** blueCone move, **point to** right **on the** direction **menu, and then click** 2 meters **as the amount.**

*The blue cone is now 2 meters to the iceSkater's right (Figure 2-25).*

**FIGURE 2-25**

The two cones are now in their correct starting positions: The red cone is two meters to the skater's left and the blue cone is two meters to the skater's right. In other words, the skater is halfway between the two cones, and all three objects are facing the same direction. You can now put the camera in its initial position, and then save the world before continuing. The camera should be pointing at the ice skater, and just far enough away so that each cone is near the edge of the World window.

## To Place the Camera in Its Initial Position

**1**

• **Right-click the** camera **tile in the Object tree and then point to** methods **on the shortcut menu.**

*A menu of the camera's primitive methods appears (Figure 2-26).*

**2**

• **Point to** camera point at **on the methods menu, point to** iceSkater **on the** target **menu, and then click** the entire iceSkater.

*The camera points directly at the iceSkater. You probably won't see much change in the World window, since the camera was already pointing almost at the ice skater.*

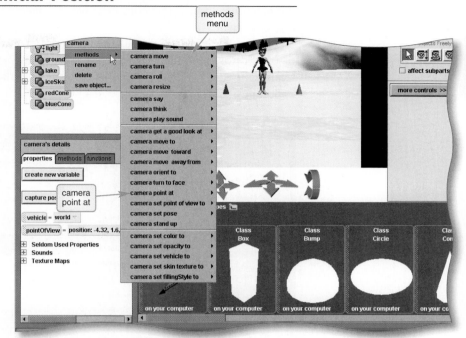

**FIGURE 2-26**

**3**

• **Using the camera's zoom control, position the camera so that each cone is near the edge of the World window, as shown in Figure 2-27.**

*The initial scene for the world is now in place.*

• **Click the green** DONE **button to exit Scene Editor mode and then save the world before continuing.**

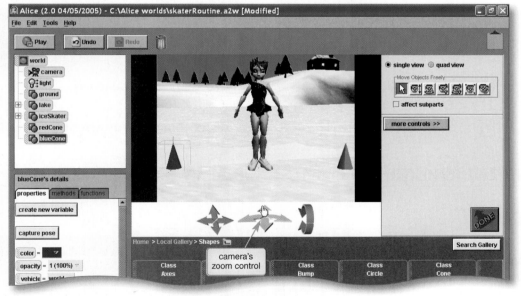

**FIGURE 2-27**

## Implementing the Ice Skater World — Documentation

You will now begin to document the program by adding some identifying comments to world.my first method. This is the world's main method, so it is a good place to add comments about the entire world, not just this particular method. You will add three identifying comments to the code: The first identifies the program by name; the second identifies the programmer and tells the reader when the code was last modified; and the third tells the purpose of the program, which, in this case, is for a project in a particular computer course. The third comment also has a very brief description of what the program does. If this comment were longer, it might be better to place it in a separate comment.

Note, in Figure 2-28, the small tile with two green slashes on it at the bottom-right of the Editor area. This tile is used to add new comments to an Alice method. Comments in Alice begin with two slashes, as they do in many programming languages.

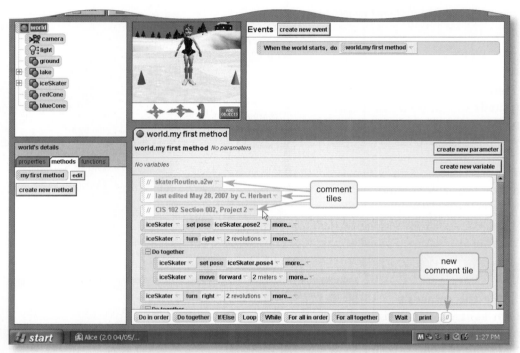

**FIGURE 2-28**

The next step is to add comments, as described in the following set of steps.

## To Add Identifying Comments to world.my first method

**1**

• **Drag a copy of the comment tile from the bottom of the Editor area and drop it into the body of the method, just above the first instruction.**

*A new comment tile with the comment No comment appears in the method (Figure 2-29).*

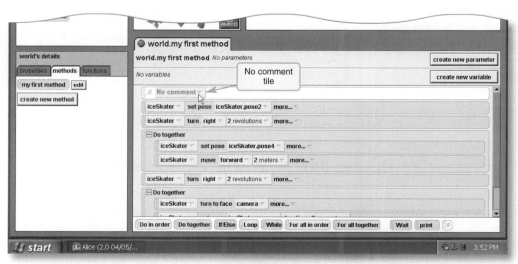

**FIGURE 2-29**

**2**

• **Click the phrase** No comment **in the new tile to open the comment tile for editing.**

*The tile opens for editing, with the existing text highlighted in blue (Figure 2-30).*

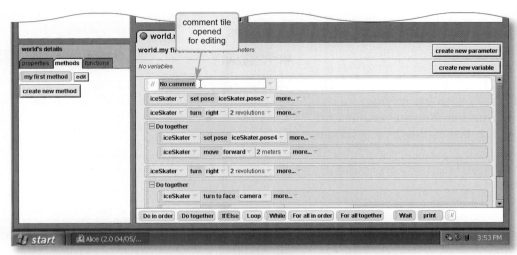

**FIGURE 2-30**

**3**

• **To replace the existing text with the name of the world, type** skaterRoutine.a2w **and then press the** ENTER **key.**

*The comment tile looks like the first comment tile shown in Figure 2-31.*

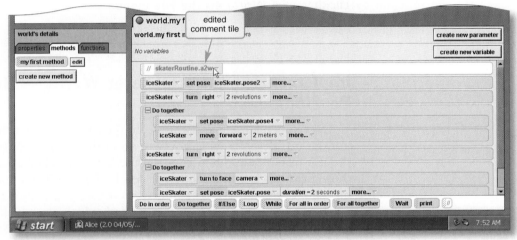

**FIGURE 2-31**

**4**

• **Repeat Steps 1 - 3 to add a second comment tile with the text** last edited <date> by <your name>, **with today's date and your own name inserted where indicated.**

*The comment tile looks like the second comment tile shown in Figure 2-32, but with your name and today's date appearing.*

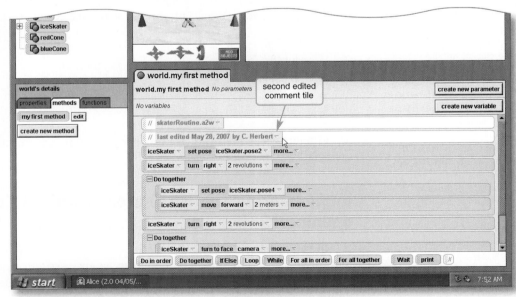

**FIGURE 2-32**

**5**

• **Add a third comment tile with the text** `<course and section >, Project 2 — a modular routine for an ice skater`**, with identifying information for your course and section inserted where described.**

*The comment tile looks like the third comment tile in Figure 2-33, but with your course and section information appearing. The world now contains all three comments.*

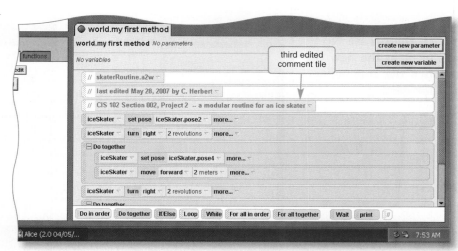

**FIGURE 2-33**

**6**

• **Save the world again by clicking** Save World **on the File menu.**

## Implementing the Ice Skater World — Bottom-Up Development

Developers design software from the top down, but they often build it from the bottom up, which is what you will do in this project. **Bottom-up development** is the process of building the methods at the lowest level of organization first, then using those methods to build the higher level methods. The organizational chart shown in Figure 2-6 on page AL 68 can help us see what methods to build first.

Before finishing world.my first method, which already exists, you will build the three methods that it calls: opening, routine, and closing. The opening method can be built from primitive methods without constructing any other methods first, but before building the routine method you will build the two methods that it calls: figure8 and jumpSpin. The closing method can be built from primitive methods. So, you will need to build five new methods for the iceSkater in the following sequence:

1. opening
2. figure8
3. jumpSpin
4. routine
5. closing

Once the five methods are finished, you will tie everything together through world.my first method.

## Implementing the Ice Skater World — Coding the opening Method

In the opening method, the skater will say "Hello, World!", and then the camera will move back 5 meters. There already is an instruction to make the skater do this, but the instruction is in world.my first method, so it needs to be moved to the new method. You'll create this method in the following set of steps.

## To Create a New iceSkater Method Named opening

**1**

• **Click the** iceSkater **tile in the Object tree and then click the** methods **tab in the Details area.**

*The iceSkater's methods are visible in the Details area, as is the create new method button (Figure 2-34).*

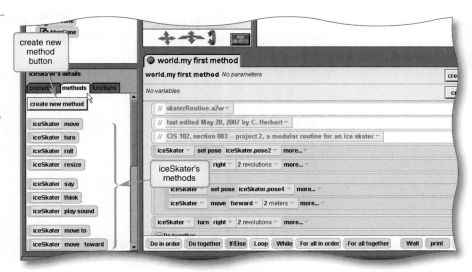

**FIGURE 2-34**

**2**

• **Click the** create new method **button to begin creating a new method.**

*The New Method dialog box opens, as shown in Figure 2-35.*

**FIGURE 2-35**

**3**

• **Type the name** opening, **then click** OK.

*The New Method dialog box disappears, and a new blank method tab with the title iceSkater.opening appears in the Editor area (Figure 2-36).*

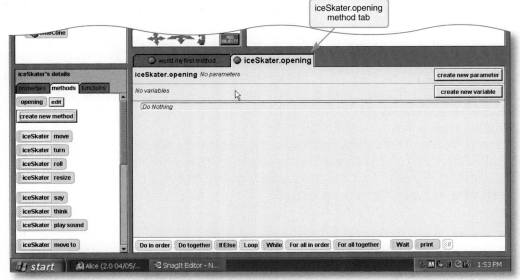

**FIGURE 2-36**

In the following steps, you add an instruction to the new method by copying an instruction from another method.

## To Copy the iceSkater say Hello, World! Instruction from Another Method

**1**

• **Click the** world **tile in the Object tree and then click the** edit **button next to** my first method **in the Details area.**

*world.my first method is visible in the Editor area (Figure 2-37).*

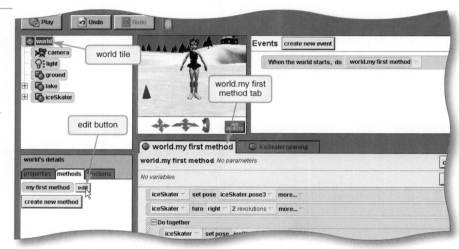

**FIGURE 2-37**

**2**

• **Drag the** iceSkater say Hello, World! **instruction tile from the bottom of the method and drop it onto the Clipboard in the upper-right corner of the Alice Interface. (You may need to scroll down to see the say Hello, World! instruction tile.)**

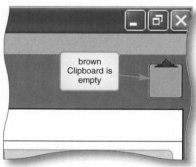

**(a) empty Clipboard**

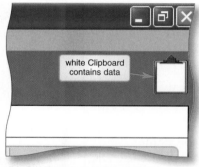

**(b) Clipboard containing data**

**FIGURE 2-38**

*The iceSkater say Hello, World! instruction is now in the Clipboard's memory. If nothing was previously on the Clipboard (as indicated by the Clipboard shown in Figure 2-38a), then a white page will now appear on it, and it will change to look like the Clipboard in Figure 2-38b. If something was already on the Clipboard, then the white page was already there, and you will not see any change.*

**3**

• **Click the** iceSkater **tile in the Object tree and then click the** edit **button next to** opening **in the Details area.**

*The opening method is now visible again in the Editor area, as shown previously in Figure 2-36.*

• **Drag the contents of the Clipboard and drop them onto the** opening **method in the Editor area in place of** Do nothing.

*The iceSkater say Hello, World! instruction is visible in the opening method (Figure 2-39).*

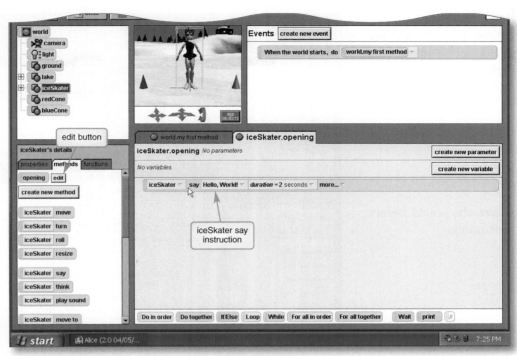

**FIGURE 2-39**

The first instruction is in place in the opening method. In the following steps, you will add an instruction to the method to move the camera back 5 meters.

## To Add an Instruction to Move the Camera Back 5 Meters

**1**

• **Click the** camera **tile in the Object tree and then click the** methods **tab in the Details area.**

• **Drag a copy of the** camera move **instruction tile from the Details area and drop it onto the** opening **method, below the existing instructions.**

*A menu asking for the parameters for the move instruction appears, as shown in Figure 2-40.*

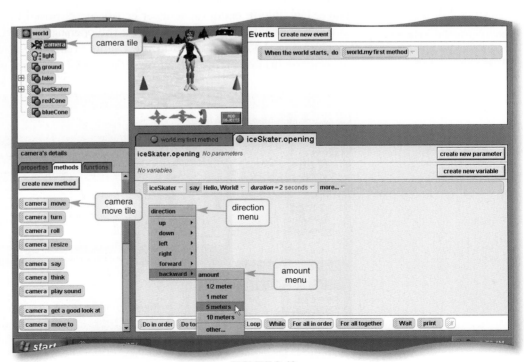

**FIGURE 2-40**

**2**

• **Point to** backward **on the** direction **menu, then click** 5 meters **on the** amount **menu.**

*The camera move backward 5 meters instruction appears in the method (Figure 2-41).*

**3**

• **Save the world before continuing.**

**FIGURE 2-41**

The **opening** method is now complete and ready for testing. Although testing and debugging follow implementation in the software development cycle, testing occurs in two parts. Each method is unit tested as it is developed to see if it works all by itself, and the entire software package is integration tested with the new method in place. Debugging occurs whenever errors are exposed in the testing process.

For now, you will simply unit test the **opening** method. This can be done in Alice by changing the default event in the Events area, shown in Figure 2-42, to run the **opening** method directly, instead of running **world.my first method.**

**FIGURE 2-42**

The iceSkater should say "Hello, World!" and then the camera should move back 5 meters, so that the World Running window looks like Figure 2-43 when the method is finished running. You'll unit test the opening method in the following set of steps.

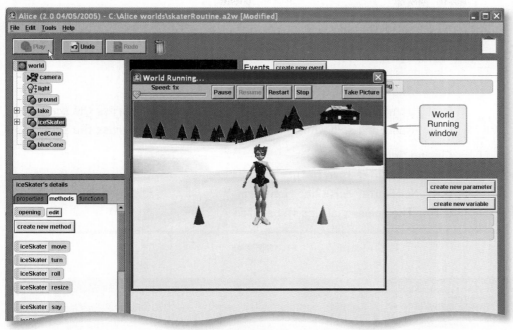

**FIGURE 2-43**

## To Unit Test the opening Method

**1**

• **Click the** iceSkater **tile in the Object tree and then click the** methods **tab in the Details area.**

• **Drag a copy of the** opening **method tile from the Details area and drop it in the Events area in the default event in place of** world.my first method.

*The default event now looks like Figure 2-44.*

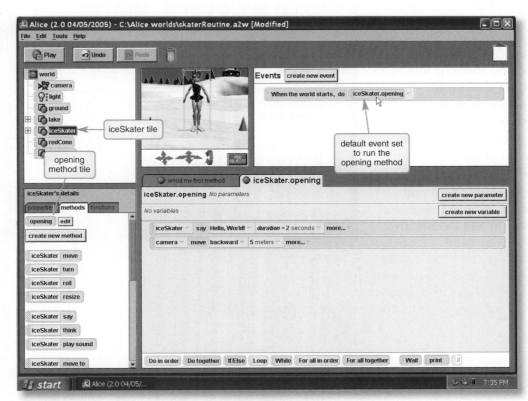

**FIGURE 2-44**

**2**

• **Click the** Play **button to see what happens when the world plays.**

*The Alice world should perform as in the original outline for the opening method (Figure 2-45).*

## Skater World

I.   Opening Sequence
    A.    iceSkater Say "Hello, World."
    B.    Camera move back 5 meters     }   specifications for the opening method

II.  Skating Routine
    A.    Skate around two cones in a figure 8
    B.    Jump and spin while skating from left to right across the screen
    C.    Jump and spin while skating from right to left across the screen

III. Closing Sequence
    A.    iceSkater turn to face the camera
    B.    iceSkater raise her right arm
    C.    The camera circles the skater

**FIGURE 2-45**

**3**

• **If the** opening **method does not perform as expected, then go back to page AL 83 and recheck the steps you followed to create the** opening **method. You can click the** Restart **button to see the world play again or the** Stop **button to close the World Running window. Once the world performs as expected, click the** Stop **button and move on to the next step.**

• **Click the** world **tile in the Object tree and then click the** methods **tab in the Details area.**

*The world's methods become visible in the Details area, as shown in Figure 2-46. There is only one world method at this time: world.my first method.*

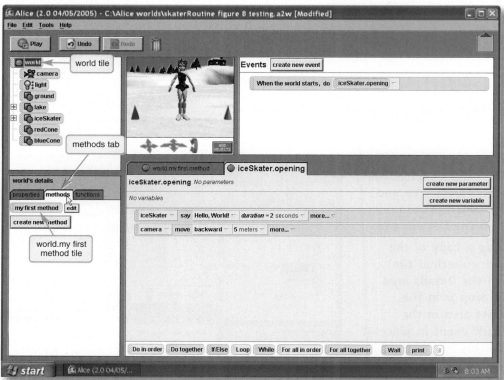

**FIGURE 2-46**

**4**

• **Drag a copy of the** world.my first method **tile from the Details area and drop it in the Events area in the default event in place of** iceSkater.opening.

*The default event should now be back to normal, as shown in Figure 2-47.*

**5**

• **Save the world again before continuing.**

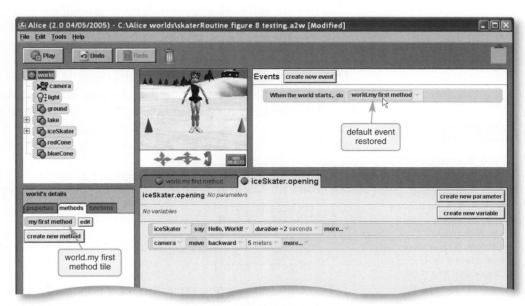

FIGURE 2-47

Throughout the rest of this project you will be instructed to test each method as it is completed. Follow the process described above to do so.

## Implementing the Ice Skater World — Coding the figure8 Method

An ice skater can form a figure eight by tracing two circles that touch each other, as shown in Figure 2-48.

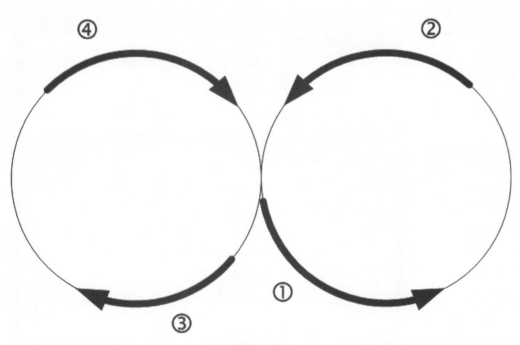

FIGURE 2-48

**More About**

**Entry and Exit Conditions**

Software developers usually describe entry and exit conditions for unit testing. The **entry conditions** describe the state of the software before a method is run, such as the values of variables, parameters, and the properties of objects. The **exit conditions** describe the state of the software after a method runs. Developers often create a testing shell (also called a testing hull) to create the necessary entry conditions and capture the exit conditions. In this project, you will test the methods using the default event without creating a testing shell. The exit condition for each method will be described within the project.

In this method the iceSkater will circle around the redCone and then around the blueCone to form a figure eight. Alice has an as seen by parameter for its turn and move instructions that will let an object move according to the point-of-view of another object. Adding the parameter as seen by the redCone to an iceSkater's turn instruction will cause the skater to move around in a circle, as if it were on a string attached to the red cone. This is exactly what needs to happen here. The skater needs to move around the cones in a circle; first around the red cone, then around the blue cone, to form a figure eight. The skater should also change positions while moving, to look more realistic. The following outline describes the algorithm for the figure 8 method:

> Do together
>> turn left 1 revolution as seen by the red cone style = begin gently
>> set pose to pose 4
> Do together
>> turn right 1 revolution as seen by the blue cone style = end gently
>> set pose to pose 2

This algorithm assumes that the skater is already in position halfway between the two cones and facing the correct direction when the figure8 method is called. This is how the skater and cones were positioned when the scene was set for the new world, so the figure8 algorithm should work.

Now you can begin to create the method. First you will create the new method, then you will add two do together sequences, one for each half of the figure eight, to the method. First the skater will circle the red cone, then the skater will circle the blue cone.

## More About

### Style Parameters

Notice that the algorithm on this page calls for the skater to begin the first circle gently and end the second circle gently. Alice action instructions, such as move and turn, have a style parameter that affects the way actions begin and end. There are four style settings: gently, begin gently, end gently, and abruptly. When the style is set to gently, an action will begin and end gently. This is the default setting for Alice action instructions.

## To Create the figure8 Method

**1**

• **Click the** iceSkater **tile in the Object tree, click the** methods **tab in the Details area, click the** create new method **button, type the name** figure8 **in the** New Method **dialog box that appears, and then press the** ENTER **key.**

*A new blank method tab with the title "iceSkater.figure8" appears in the Editor area (Figure 2-49).*

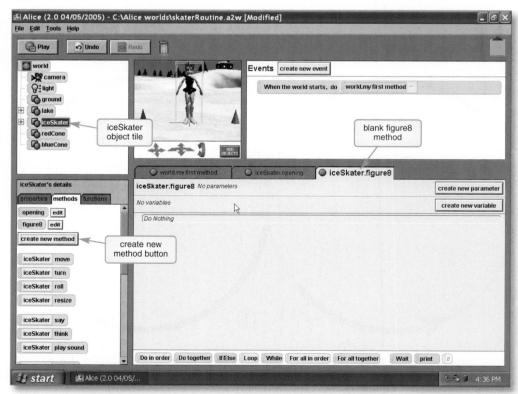

**FIGURE 2-49**

**2**

• **Drag a copy of the** Do together **tile from the bottom of the Editor area and drop it into the** figure8 **method in place of** Do Nothing.

*A Do together instruction tile appears in the method in the Editor area (Figure 2-50).*

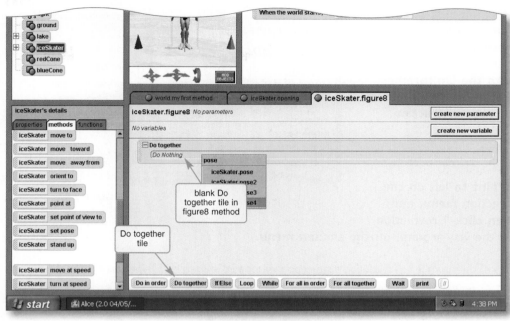

**FIGURE 2-50**

**3**

• **Drag an** iceSkater set pose **method tile from the** methods **tab and drop it onto the** Do together **tile in place of** Do Nothing.

*A menu appears, from which you can choose a pose (Figure 2-51).*

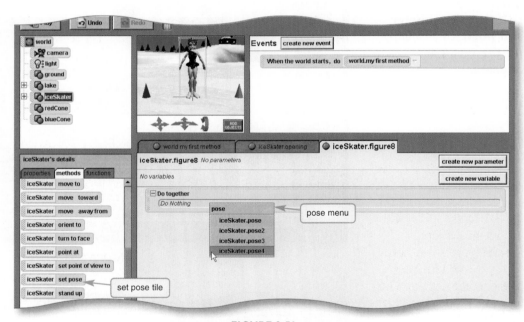

**FIGURE 2-51**

**4**

• **Select** iceSkater.pose4 **from the menu.**

*The Do together tile now contains an instruction to set the iceSkater's pose to iceSkater.pose4, as shown in Figure 2-52.*

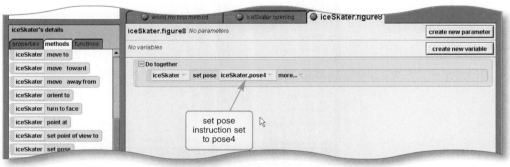

**FIGURE 2-52**

**5**

• **Drag an** iceSkater turn **method tile from the** methods **tab and drop it onto the** Do together **tile, below the** iceSkater set pose **instruction.**

*A menu appears, asking you for the direction of the turn.*

• **Point to** left **on the** direction **menu, and then click** 1 revolution (all the way around) **on the** amount **menu.**

*An iceSkater turn left 1 revolution instruction tile appears in the Do together tile (Figure 2-53).*

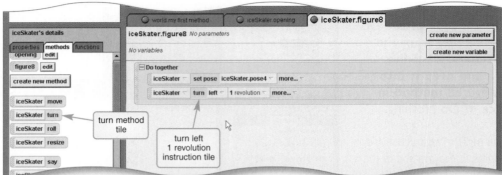

**FIGURE 2-53**

**6**

• **Click the** more... **button following the** 1 revolution **parameter and point to** asSeenBy **on the menu that appears.**

*A menu appears, from which you can choose a target object for the asSeenBy parmeter (Figure 2-54).*

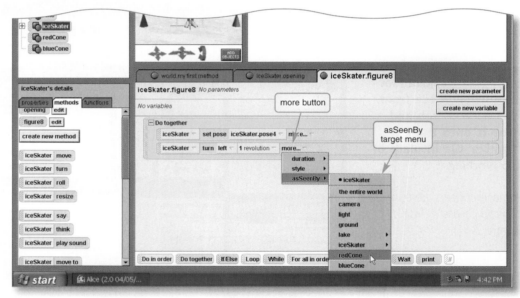

**FIGURE 2-54**

**7**

• **Click** redCone **to select the red cone as the target object.**

*The instruction now reads iceSkater turn left 1 revolution asSeenBy = redCone (Figure 2-55).*

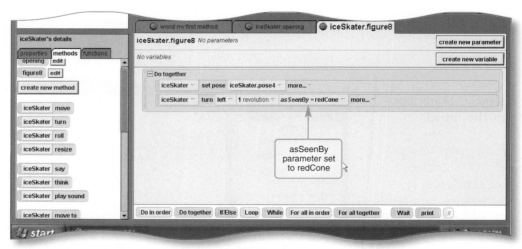

**FIGURE 2-55**

**8**

• **Click the** more... **button again, select** style **from the menu that appears, and then select** begin gently **as the style.**

*The instruction now reads iceSkater turn left 1 revolution asSeenBy = redCone style = begin gently (Figure 2-56).*

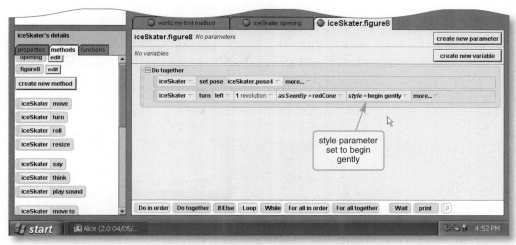

**FIGURE 2-56**

**9**

• **Click the** more... **button again, select** duration **from the menu that appears, and then select** 2 seconds **for the duration.**

*The instruction now reads iceSkater tun left 1 revolution asSeenBy = redCone style = begin gently duration = 2. The Do together tile should now match Figure 2-57.*

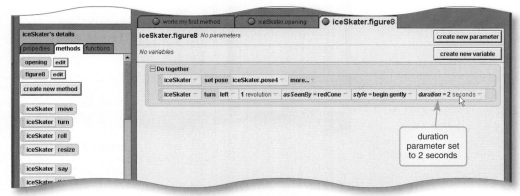

**FIGURE 2-57**

The first part of the figure eight is complete. Now you will add instructions to the method to make the skater circle around the blue cone.

## To Instruct the iceSkater to Circle Around the blueCone

**1** **Drag another copy of the** Do together **tile from the bottom of the Editor area and drop it onto the** figure8 **method, below the first** Do together **tile.**

**2** **Drag an** iceSkater set pose **method tile from the** methods **tab and drop it onto the new** Do together **tile in place of** Do Nothing, **but this time select** iceSkater.pose2 **from the menu.**

**3** **Drag an** iceSkater turn **method tile from the** methods **tab and drop it onto the second** Do together **tile, below the** iceSkater set pose **instruction; point to** right **on the** direction **menu; then select** 1 revolution (all the way around) **from the** amount **menu.**

**4** **Click the** more... **button following the** 1 revolution **parameter, point to** asSeenBy **on the menu that appears and then click** blueCone **to select the blue cone as the target object.**

**5** **Click the** more... **button, select** style **from the menu that appears, and then select** end gently **as the style.**

**6** **Click the** more... **button again, select** duration **from the menu that appears, and then select** 2 seconds **as the duration.**

**7** **Save the world before continuing.**

*The instruction should now read iceSkater turn right 1 revolution asSeenBy = blueCone style = end gently duration = 2 seconds. The method is complete and should match Figure 2-58.*

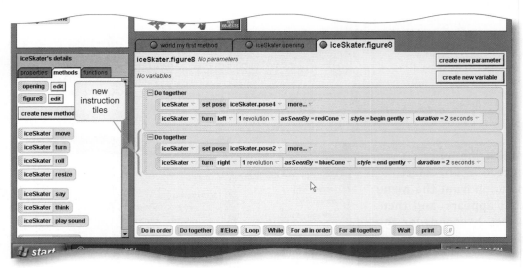

**FIGURE 2-58**

The **figure8** method is now ready for unit testing. The **iceSkater** should perform a figure eight around the two cones and end in the same place where she started, but in a different pose. You'll unit test the method in the following steps.

## To Unit Test the figure8 Method

**1**

• **Drag a copy of the** figure8 **tile from the methods tab in the Details area and drop it in the default event in place of the** world.my first **method tile.**

*The figure8 tile is dropped into place, as shown in Figure 2-59.*

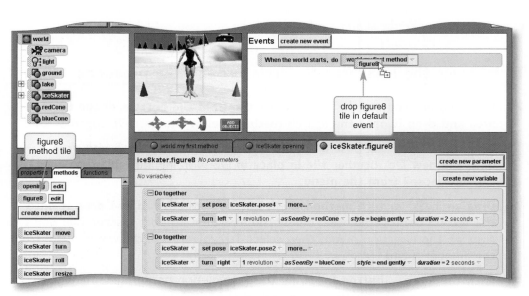

**FIGURE 2-59**

**2**

• **Click the** Play **button to play the world. The** figure8 **method now plays since it is the method in the default event.**

*The ice skater circles around the red cone while changing her pose, and then circles around the blue cone while changing her pose again. She is slightly off of the screen for part of the time that she circles the cones. The skater ends where she started, but in pose 2, as shown in Figure 2-60.*

**FIGURE 2-60**

**3**

• **If the** figure8 **method does not perform as expected, then find and fix any errors before continuing. Remember to save the world again if you make any changes.**

• **Click the** world **tile in the Object tree, then drag the** world.my first method **tile from the methods tab and drop it in the default event in place of** iceSkater.figure8.

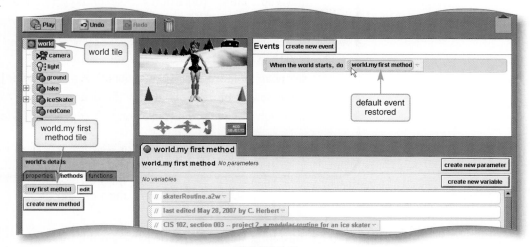

**FIGURE 2-61**

*The default event is restored to its default condition, as shown in Figure 2-61.*

• **Save the world again before continuing.**

The figure8 method is ready for use. Next, you will create the jumpSpin method, and then use these two methods to build the iceSkater's routine method.

## Implementing the Ice Skater World — Coding the jumpSpin Method

To jump, the skater will move up 1 meter and then down 1 meter. In this case, the skater must spin while jumping. The skater should spin around in 2 complete revolutions, so she should spin 1 revolution while jumping up and 1 revolution while coming down. It would also look better if she changed poses while jumping. The jump-and-spin algorithm needs two Do together sequences in order.

This algorithm assumes the instructions within each Do together sequence take the same amount of time to complete, so the duration of each of the three instructions in the first Do together structure should be the same, as should the duration of the three instructions in the second Do together structure. The jump and spin will look smoother if the style for each instruction is set to abruptly. Each of the instructions in the Do together structures should have a duration of .5 seconds and an abrupt style. The skater also needs to skate forward a bit before jumping and again after jumping, so the complete jumpSpin algorithm should match Figure 2-62.

## Skater World — jumpSpin Details

iceSkater move forward 2 meters [style = abruptly]

Do together
    set pose to iceSkater.pose [duration = .5 seconds] [style = abruptly]
    move up 1 meter [duration = .5 seconds] [style = abruptly]
    spin right 1 revolution [duration = .5 seconds] [style = abruptly]

Do together
    set pose to iceSkater.pose2 [duration = .5 seconds] [style = abruptly]
    move down 1 meter [duration = .5 seconds] [style = abruptly]
    spin right 1 revolution [duration = .5 seconds] [style = abruptly]

iceSkater move forward 2 meters [style = abruptly]

**FIGURE 2-62**

The following steps create the jumpSpin method.

## To Begin Creating the jumpSpin Method

**1**

• **If the** iceSkater's **methods are not visible in the Details area, then click the** iceSkater **tile in the Object tree and then click the** methods **tab in the Details area.**

• **Click the** create new method **button, type the name** jumpSpin **in the New Method dialog box that appears, and then press the ENTER key.**

**FIGURE 2-63**

*A new blank method tab with the title, iceSkater.jumpSpin, appears in the Editor area (Figure 2-63).*

**2**

• **Drag an** iceSkater **move tile from the** methods **tab and drop it into the new method in place of** Do Nothing. **Point to** forward **on the** direction **menu and then click** other…. **Type** 2 **in the Custom Number dialog box and click** Okay.

*An iceSkater move forward 2 meters tile appears in the method in the Editor area (Figure 2-64).*

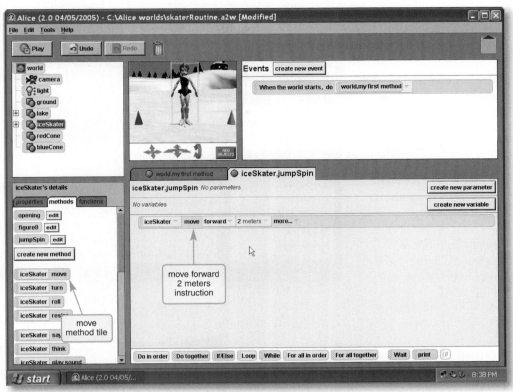

**FIGURE 2-64**

**3**

• **Copy the instruction by right-clicking it and selecting** make copy **from the menu that appears.**

*A second copy of the iceSkater move forward 2 meters tile appears below the first (Figure 2-65).*

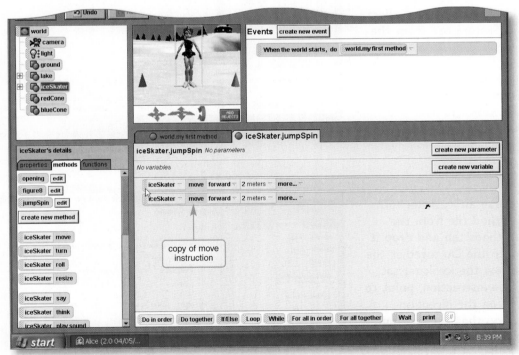

**FIGURE 2-65**

The following steps create the first of the two Do together sequences that are needed in the method.

# To Create the First Do together Sequence in the jumpSpin Method

**1**

• **Drag a copy of the** Do together **tile from the bottom of the Editor area and drop it onto the** jumpSpin **method between the two** iceSkater move forward 2 meters **tiles, as shown in Figure 2-66.**

*An empty Do together instruction tile appears in the method in the Editor area.*

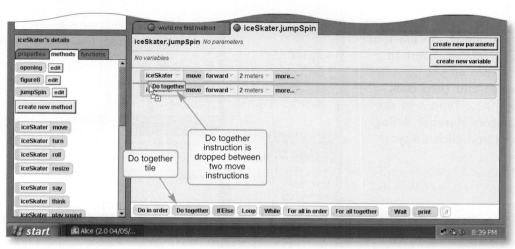

**FIGURE 2-66**

**2**

• **Drag an** iceSkater set pose **method tile from the** methods **tab and drop it onto the** Do together **tile in place of** Do Nothing, **then select** iceSkater.pose **from the menu that appears.**

*The Do together tile now contains an instruction to set the iceSkater's pose to iceSkater.pose (Figure 2-67).*

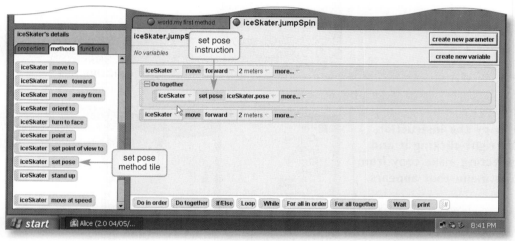

**FIGURE 2-67**

**3**

• **Drag an** iceSkater turn **method tile from the** methods **tab and drop it onto the** Do together **tile below the** iceSkater set pose **instruction, point to** left **on the** direction **menu that appears, and then click** 1 revolution (all the way around) **on the** amount **menu.**

*An iceSkater turn left 1 revolution instruction tile appears in the Do together tile (Figure 2-68).*

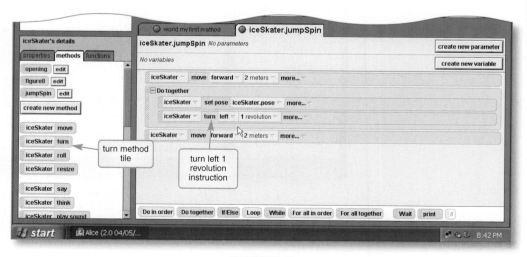

**FIGURE 2-68**

**4**

• **Drag an** iceSkater **move method tile from the** methods **tab and drop it onto the** Do together **tile below the** iceSkater turn left 1 revolution **instruction. Point to** up **on the** direction **menu that appears, and then click** 1 meter **on the** amount **menu.**

*An iceSkater move up 1 meter instruction tile appears in the method (Figure 2-69).*

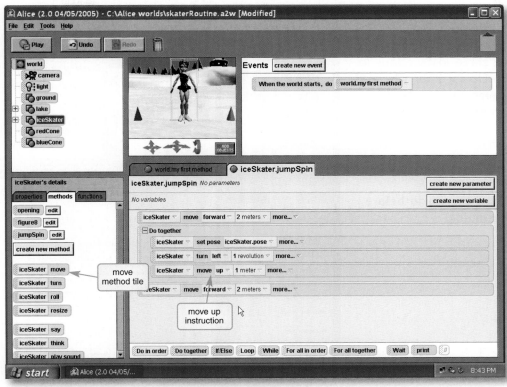

**FIGURE 2-69**

**5**

• **Click the** more... **button on each of the three instructions in the** Do together **tile, and change their durations to** .5 seconds.

*Each of the three instructions now has its duration parameter set to .5 seconds (Figure 2-70).*

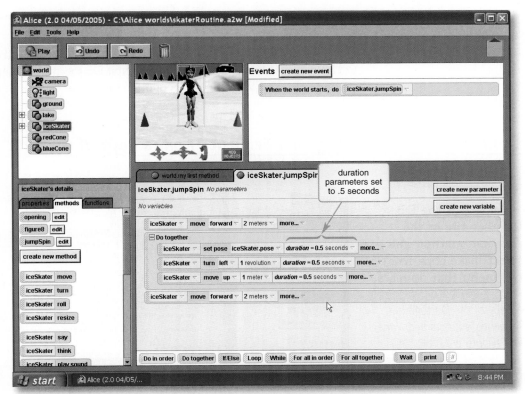

**FIGURE 2-70**

**6**

- **Click the** more... **parameter on each of the three instructions in the** Do together **tile, and change their styles to** abruptly.

*Each of the three instructions now has its style parameter set to abruptly (Figure 2-71).*

- **Save the world before continuing.**

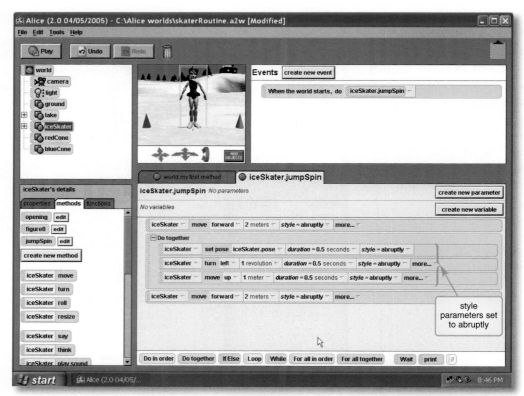

**FIGURE 2-71**

The second **Do together** sequence in the jumpSpin method is very similar to the first, so it can easily be created by copying the first **Do together** sequence and changing two of its parameters. You'll create the second **Do together** sequence in the following steps.

## To Create a Second Do together Sequence from a Copy of the First

**1**

- **Right-click the** Do together **tile in the** jumpSpin **method and select** make copy **from the menu that appears.**

*A copy of the Do together sequence appears below the first (Figure 2-72).*

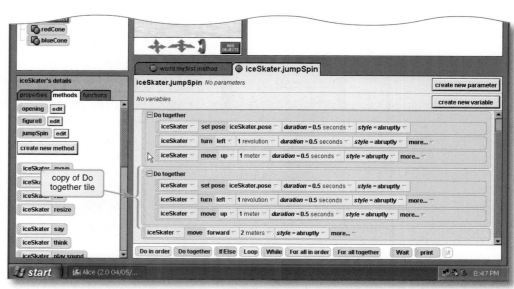

**FIGURE 2-72**

**2**

• **In the second** Do together **tile, click the** iceSkater.pose **parameter in the** iceSkater set pose iceSkater.pose **instruction tile, then select** iceSkater.pose2 **from the menu that appears.**

*The instruction now reads iceSkater set pose iceSkater.pose2 (Figure 2-73).*

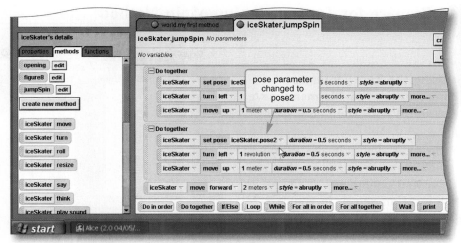

**FIGURE 2-73**

**3**

• **Click the** up **parameter in the** iceSkater move up 1 meter **instruction tile, and select** down **from the menu that appears.**

*The instruction now reads iceSkater move down 1 meter, as shown in Figure 2-74.*

• **Save the world before continuing.**

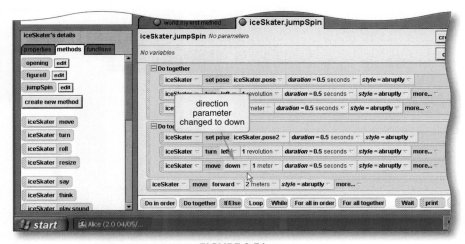

**FIGURE 2-74**

You are now ready to unit test the completed jumpSpin method. It should perform as specified previously in Figure 2-62: The skater should move forward, jump up and spin while changing poses, come back down and spin while changing poses, and then move forward a little more.

You were able to test the iceSkater.opening method and the iceSkater.figure8 methods simply by playing them using the default event. In both of those cases, the iceSkater started in her initial position between the two cones. If you did the same thing with the iceSkater.jumpSpin method, then she would move toward the camera and you would not get a good view of her jumps and spins to see if they look correct. So, you will position the ice skater behind the cones, facing to the left before starting. You will also put the skater into pose4, since this will be her pose in the finished program when the jumpSpin method starts. Rather than making these changes in the skaterRoutine world, you will make a copy of the world for testing so that the original will be preserved. In the following steps, you create a new world for testing and place the iceSkater in the correct starting position.

## To Prepare for Testing the jumpSpin Method

**1**

• **Using the** Save World As **command on the File menu, save the world with the name jumpSpinTest.a2w.**

• **Click the skater in the World window and drag her so that she is located behind the red cone, in the location shown in Figure 2-75.**

*The skater is in the right location, but needs to be positioned correctly.*

**FIGURE 2-75**

**2**

• **Right-click the** iceSkater **tile in the Object tree. When the menu appears, point to** methods, **point to** turn, **point to** right, **and then click** ¼ revolution.

*The skater is in the correct location and facing the correct direction, as shown in Figure 2-76.*

**FIGURE 2-76**

**3**

• **Again, right-click the** iceSkater **tile in the Object tree and point to** methods. **This time, run the** iceSkater set pose **method and choose** iceSkater.pose4 **as the new pose.**

*The skater is now in the correct position and pose for testing, as shown in Figure 2-77.*

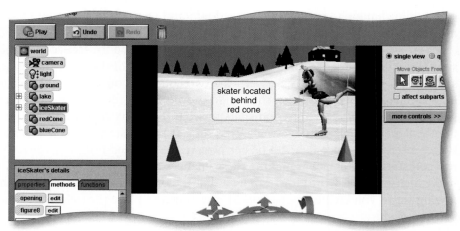

**FIGURE 2-77**

## To Test the jumpSpin Method

**1** **Drag a copy of the** jumpSpin **tile from the** methods **tab in the Details area and drop it in the default event in place of the** world.my first method **tile.**

**2** **Click the** Play **button to play the world.**

*The jumpSpin method plays since it is the method in the default event. The ice skater should perform as specified in Figure 2-62 on page AL 96, and as shown in the sequence of images in Figure 2-78. If the jumpSpin method does not perform as expected, then find and fix any errors before continuing. Remember to make corresponding changes in the jumpSpin method in the original skaterRoutine.a2w world and to save that world again if you do make any changes.*

**FIGURE 2-78**

## Implementing the Ice Skater World — Coding the routine Method

Now that the figure8 and jumpSpin methods are complete, they can be used to create the routine method. The specifications for the method, shown in Figure 2-79, call for the skater to perform the figure eight, skate around into position behind the red cone, jump and spin while moving across the screen from right to left, turn around, then jump and spin again while moving back across the screen from left to right. You'll create this method in the following steps.

> ## Skater World — Routine
>
> perform a figure 8
>
> Do together
> > move 3/4 of the way around the red cone
> > change position to pose4
>
> perform a jump and spin while moving from right to left
>
> turn around 180 degrees
>
> perform a jump and spin while moving from left to right

**FIGURE 2-79**

## To Create the routine Method

### 1

• **Using the File menu, open the original skaterRoutine.a2w world.**

• **Click the** iceSkater **tile in the Object tree and then click the** methods **tab in the Details area.**

• **Click the** create new method **button, type the name** routine **in the New Method dialog box, and then press the** ENTER **key.**

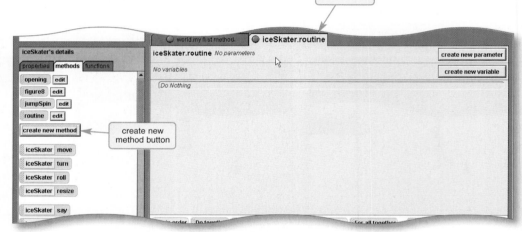

**FIGURE 2-80**

*A new blank method tab with the title iceSkater.routine appears in the Editor area (Figure 2-80).*

### 2

• **Drag a** figure8 **tile from the** methods **tab and drop it onto the new method in place of** Do Nothing.

*An iceSkater.figure8 tile appears in the iceSkater.routine method in the Editor area (Figure 2-81).*

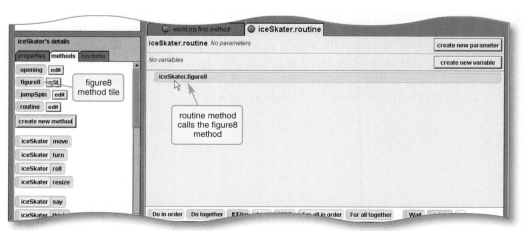

**FIGURE 2-81**

**3**

• **Drag a** Do together **tile from the bottom of the Editor area and drop it onto the** routine **method below the** iceSkater. figure8 **tile.**

*An empty Do together instruction tile appears in the method below the figure8 instruction, as shown in Figure 2-82.*

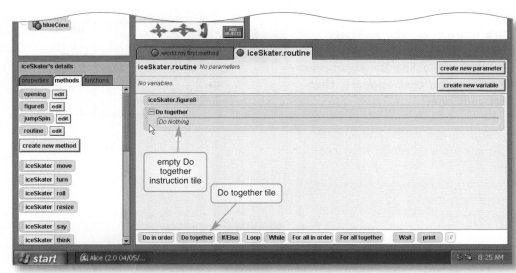

**FIGURE 2-82**

**4**

• **Drag an** iceSkater set pose **method tile from the** methods **tab and drop it onto the** Do together **tile in place of** Do Nothing, **then select** iceSkater.pose4 **from the menu that appears.**

*The Do together tile now contains an instruction to set the iceSkater's pose to iceSkater.pose4 (Figure 2-83).*

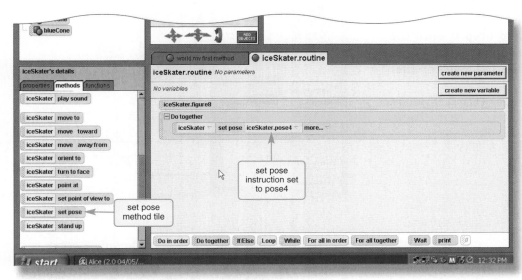

**FIGURE 2-83**

**5**

• **Drag an** iceSkater turn **method tile from the** methods **tab and drop it onto the** Do together **tile above the** iceSkater set pose **instruction. Point to** left **on the** direction **menu, select** other **from the** amount **menu, and then type** .75 **in the Custom Number dialog box. Click the** Okay **button.**

*An iceSkater turn left .75 revolutions instruction tile appears in the Do together tile, as shown in Figure 2-84.*

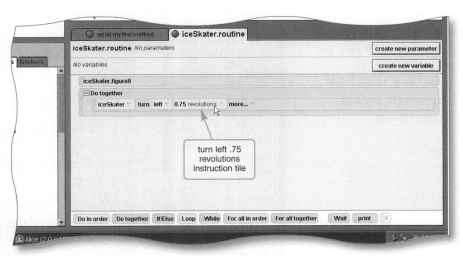

**FIGURE 2-84**

**6**

• **Click** more… **on the** iceSkater turn left .75 revolutions **instruction tile, select the** asSeenBy **parameter from the menu that appears, then select** redCone.

*The instruction now reads iceSkater turn left .75 revolutions asSeenBy = redCone (Figure 2-85).*

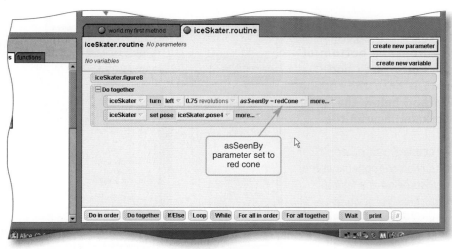

**FIGURE 2-85**

**7**

• **Drag a** jumpSpin **tile from the** methods **tab and drop it onto the** routine **method below the** Do together **tile.**

*An iceSkater.jumpSpin tile appears in the method Editor area (Figure 2-86).*

**FIGURE 2-86**

**8**

• **Drag an** iceSkater turn **method tile from the** methods **tab and drop it onto the** routine **method below the** iceSkater. jumpSpin **tile. Point to** left **on the** direction **menu, and then click** ½ revolution **on the** amount **menu.**

*An iceSkater turn left .5 revolutions instruction tile appears in the method, as shown in Figure 2-87.*

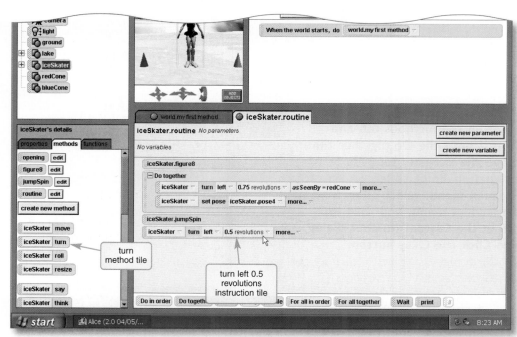

**FIGURE 2-87**

**9**

• **Drag another** jumpSpin **tile from the** methods **tab and drop it onto the** routine **method below the** iceSkater turn left .5 revolutions **tile.**

*Another iceSkater.jumpSpin tile appears as the last instruction in the routine method. The method is now complete, as shown in Figure 2-88.*

**10**

• **Save the world before continuing.**

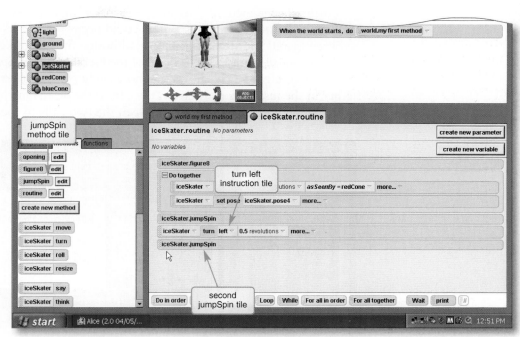

**FIGURE 2-88**

The routine method is now complete and ready for unit testing. Since this method contains calls to the figure8 and jumpSpin methods, the test will also serve as an integration test for those methods, showing how well they work when put in place within the routine method.

The iceSkater should:

- perform a figure eight around the two cones
- move into position behind the cones
- jump and spin while moving across the screen from right to left
- turn around
- jump and spin again while moving back across the screen from left to right

The skater is already in the correct starting position to test the routine method, but the camera should be moved back so that the skater's movements around the cones will be visible.

## To Test the routine Method and the Methods that it Calls

**1** **Right-click the** camera **tile in the Object tree, point to** methods **on the menu that appears, and select a method to** move **the camera** backwards 5 meters.

**2** **Drag a copy of the** routine **tile from the methods tab in the Details area and drop it in the default event in place of the** world.my first method **tile.**

**3** **Click the** Play **button to play the world. The** routine **method will now play.**

*The ice skater should perform a figure eight around the two cones, move into position behind the cones, jump and spin while moving across the screen from right to left, turn around, and then jump and spin again while moving back across the screen from left to right.*

If the routine method does not perform as expected, you should find and fix any errors before continuing. Errors could occur in the two methods that it calls, iceSkater.figure8 and iceSkater.jumpSpin, although the most likely place for errors is in the iceSkater.routine method itself, because the figure8 and jumpSpin methods have already been tested. Figure 2-89 shows the most likely places for errors in the routine method: either in the instructions between the call to the figure8 method and the first call to the jumpSpin method, or in the turn between the two calls to the jumpSpin method.

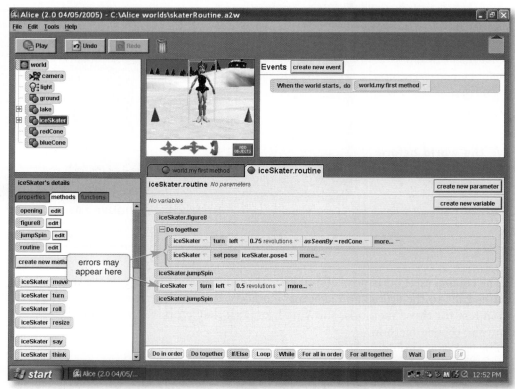

**FIGURE 2-89**

## Implementing the Ice Skater World — Coding the closing Method

The closing method will take place when the skater has finished her routine. The ice skater will turn to face the camera and raise her arm, then the camera will circle around the skater. Figure 2-90 shows the specifications for the closing method.

The iceSkater's right arm is attached to her right shoulder, which is attached to her chest, which is part of her upper body, so it has the name iceSkater.upperBody.chest.rightShoulder.arm. This part of the iceSkater will be used in the closing method. Revealing the tile for this object's subparts in the Object tree will make it easier to use it when the time comes, so you will reveal it in the following steps.

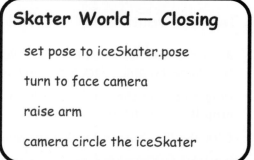

**Skater World — Closing**

set pose to iceSkater.pose

turn to face camera

raise arm

camera circle the iceSkater

**FIGURE 2-90**

## To Reveal the iceSkater's Right Arm Tile in the Object Tree

**1**

• **In the Object tree, click the plus signs next to the** iceSkater **tile, the** upperbody **tile, the** chest **tile, and the** rightShoulder **tile.**

*The iceSkater's rightShoulder and arm tiles are visible in the Object tree, as shown in Figure 2-91.*

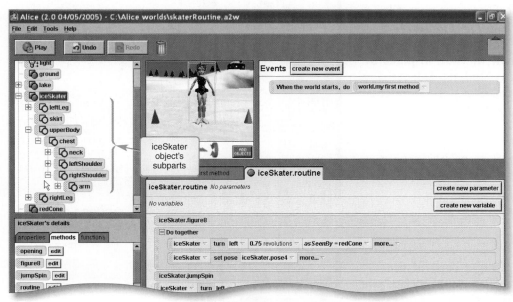

FIGURE 2-91

The closing method will need to make the iceSkater turn to face the camera and then raise her arm before the camera circles the skater. She should change her pose to iceSkater.pose before turning to face the camera. You create the closing method in the following steps.

## To Create the closing Method

**1**

• **Click the** create new method **button on the** iceSkater's **methods tab, type the name** closing **in the New Method dialog box that appears, and then press the ENTER key.**

*A new blank method tab with the title iceSkater.closing appears in the Editor area (Figure 2-92).*

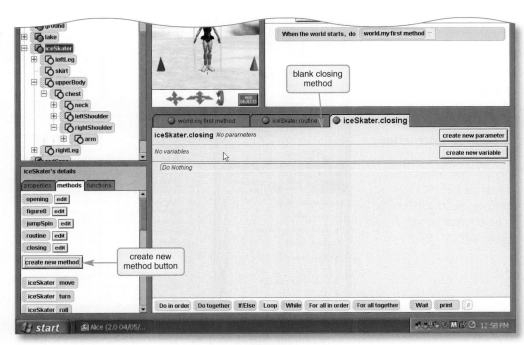

FIGURE 2-92

**2**

• **Drag a copy of the** iceSkater set pose **tile from the** methods **tab and drop it onto the new method in place of** Do Nothing. **Select** iceSkater.pose **from the menu that appears.**

*An iceSkater set pose iceSkater.pose tile appears in the method (Figure 2-93).*

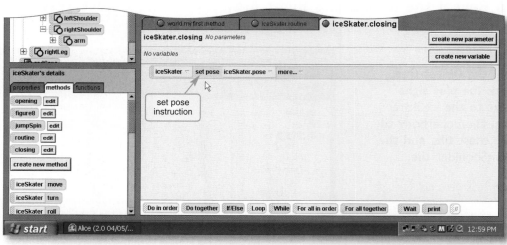

**FIGURE 2-93**

**3**

• **Drag a copy of the** iceSkater turn to face **tile from the** methods **tab and drop it onto the** closing **method below the** iceSkater set pose iceSkater.pose **instruction. Select** camera **from the menu that appears.**

*An iceSkater turn to face camera tile appears in the method, as shown in Figure 2-94).*

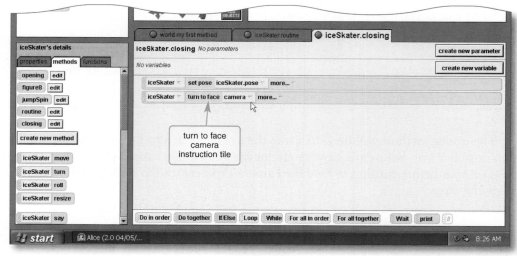

**FIGURE 2-94**

**4**

• **Drag a copy of the** arm **tile from the Object tree and drop it onto the** closing **method below the existing instructions.**

*A menu of the primitive methods for the iceSkater. upperBody.chest.rightShoulder. arm object appears, as shown in Figure 2-95.*

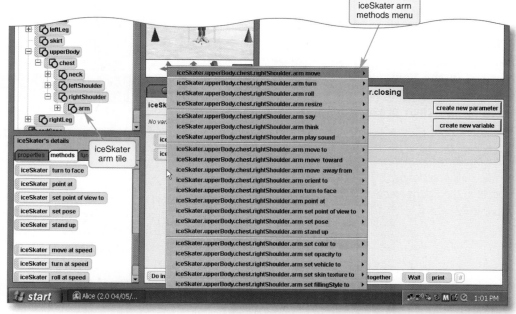

**FIGURE 2-95**

**5**

• **Point to** iceSkater.upperBody. chest.rightShoulder.arm turn **on the menu, point to** backward **on the** direction **menu, and then click** ½ revolution **on the** amount **menu.**

*An iceSkater.upperBody. chest.rightShoulder.arm turn backward .5 revolutions instruction tile appears in the method (Figure 2-96).*

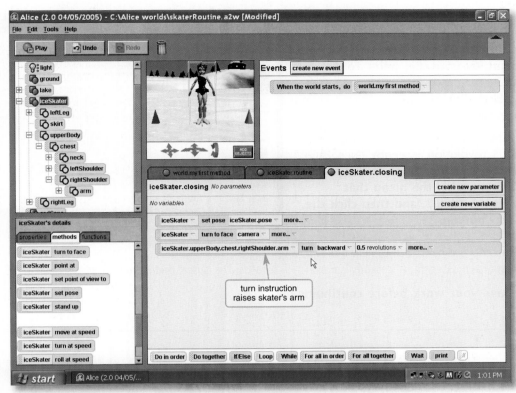

**FIGURE 2-96**

**6**

• **Click the** camera **tile in the Object tree, then drag a** camera turn **tile from the** methods **tab and drop it onto the** closing **method below the existing tiles in the method. Point to** left **on the** direction **menu, and then click** 1 revolution (all the way around) **on the** amount **menu.**

*A camera turn left 1 revolution instruction tile appears in the method (Figure 2-97).*

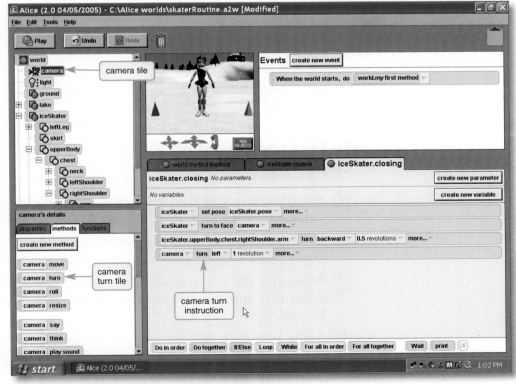

**FIGURE 2-97**

**7**

• **Click** more... **on the** camera turn left 1 revolution **instruction tile, point to** asSeenBy, **point to** iceSkater, **and then click** the entire iceSkater **on the menu that appears.**

• **Click** more... **on the** camera turn left 1 revolution asSeenBy = iceSkater **instruction tile, point to** duration, **click** other **on the menu that appears, type** 7, **and then click the** Okay **button.**

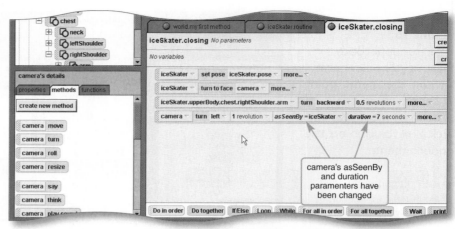

**FIGURE 2-98**

*The instruction now reads camera turn left 1 revolution asSeenBy = iceSkater duration = 7 seconds. The closing method now matches Figure 2-98.*

• **Save your work before continuing,**

---

The closing method is now complete and ready for unit testing. You may recall that earlier in this project you needed to reposition the skater behind the red cone before unit testing the jumpSpin method. You need to do something similar before testing the closing method, since the closing method is called with the skater behind the red cone, not in her current position. You will also need to move the camera back before starting the unit test. Figure 2-99 shows the location and position that the iceSkater should be in when the closing method begins.

In the following steps, you create a new world for testing and position the skater in the correct starting position.

**FIGURE 2-99**

## To Prepare for Testing the Closing Method

**1** **Using the** Save World As **command on the File menu, save the world with the name, ClosingTest.**

**2** **Click the skater in the World window and drag her back behind the red cone, in the location shown in Figure 2-99.**

**3** **Right-click the** iceSkater **tile in the Object tree, point to** methods **on the menu that appears, and run a method to make the** iceSkater **turn right** ¼ **revolution.**

**4** **Again, right-click the** iceSkater **tile in the Object tree and point to** methods. **This time, run the** iceSkater **set pose method and choose** iceSkater.pose4 **as the new pose.**

**5** **Right-click the** camera **tile in the Object tree, point to** methods **on the menu that appears, and run a method to** move **the camera** backwards 5 meters.

*The skater is now in the position and location shown in Figure 2-99, with the camera moved back to widen the scene.*

Now you are ready to test the closing method. According to the specifications, the skater should change her pose and then raise her right arm. Then the camera should circle around the entire scene. The following steps test the closing method.

## To Test the closing Method

**1** **Drag a copy of the** closing **tile from the** methods **tab in the Details area and drop it in the default event in place of the** world.my first method **tile.**

**2** **Click the** Play **button to play the world.**

**3** **If the** closing **method does not perform as described above and as shown in Figure 2-100, then retrace the steps above to find and fix any errors before continuing. Remember to make and save changes in the actual** closing **method in the original skaterRoutine.a2w world that match any changes that were necessary in the closingTest world.**

**FIGURE 2-100**

# Implementing the Ice Skater World — Coding world.my first method

You are now ready to finish the main method, world.my first method. The instructions below the comment tiles in world.my first method are left over from the old world, and will not be needed in the new world.my first method, so they can be deleted.

## To Delete the Unnecessary Instructions from world.my first method

**1**

• **Make sure that the original skaterRoutine. a2w world is open and that** world.my first method **is visible in the Editor area, as shown in Figure 2-101.**

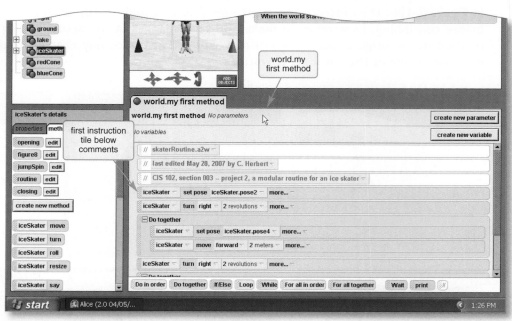

**FIGURE 2-101**

**2**

• **Right-click the first instruction tile below the comments in** world.my first method, **then click** delete **on the menu that appears.**

*The instruction tile is deleted, as shown in Figure 2-102.*

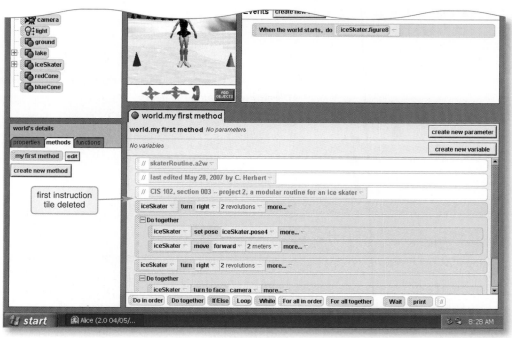

**FIGURE 2-102**

**3**

• **In a similar manner, repeat Step 2 for each of the other instruction tiles below the comments in** world.my first method.

*Only the comments are left in the method (Figure 2-103).*

**4**

• **Save the world again before continuing.**

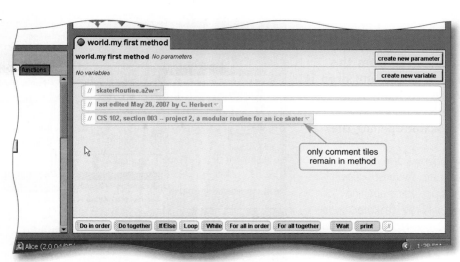

FIGURE 2-103

The unecessary instructions are gone, and you now only need to add calls to the three sub-methods — opening, routine, and closing — to finish world.my first method, as described in the following steps.

## To Add the Necessary Instructions to world.my first method

**1**

• **Click the** iceSkater **tile in the Object tree.**

• **Drag a copy of the** opening **tile from the** methods **tab and drop it onto** world.my first method **below the comment tiles.**

*world.my first method now contains an iceSkater.opening tile, as shown in Figure 2-104.*

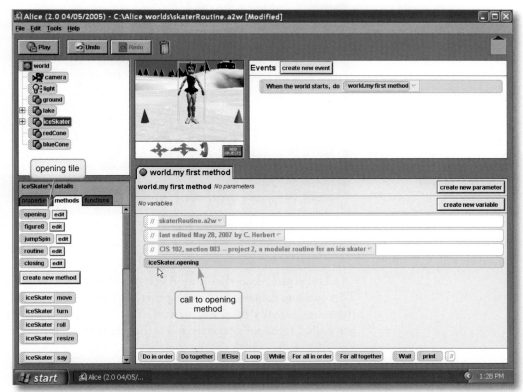

FIGURE 2-104

**2**

• **Drag a copy of the** routine **tile from the** methods **tab and drop it onto** world.my first method **below the** iceSkater.opening **tile.**

*world.my first method now contains two instruction tiles: iceSkater.opening, followed by iceSkater.routine (Figure 2-105).*

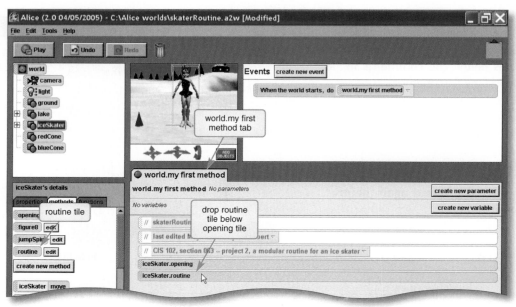

**FIGURE 2-105**

**3**

• **Drag a copy of the** closing **tile from the** methods **tab and drop it onto** world.my first method **below the** iceSkater.routine **tile .**

*world.my first method now contains three instruction tiles – iceSkater.opening, iceSkater.routine, and iceSkater.closing – as shown in Figure 2-106.*

**4**

• **Save the world.**

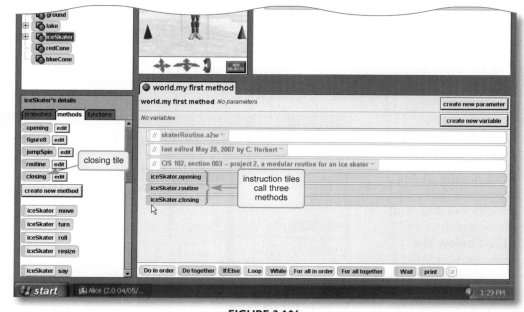

**FIGURE 2-106**

The entire skaterRoutine Alice world is now complete and ready for final testing. The opening, routine, and closing methods should be called one after the other. Each of these has already been unit tested. Your final test is an integration test to see if they are called in order properly from the main method.

## To Test the Completed skaterRoutine World

**1** **Make sure that the finished skaterRoutine world is open in the Alice Interface.**

**2** **Click the** Play **button to play the world. The** iceSkater.opening **method,** iceSkater.routine **method, and** iceSkater.closing **method should be called in order.**

**3** **If the three methods are not called in order as expected, find and fix any errors before continuing. Remember to save the skaterRoutine.a2w world with any changes that you make.**

**4** **Remember to close Alice when you are finished testing the new world.**

## Project Summary

In this project you created a modular routine for the ice skater from Project 1. Before starting to code the project, you reviewed the specifications for the software, engaging in the software development cycle, which you learned has four phases: design, implement, test, and debug. The design phase includes the development of specifications for new software. Implementing software includes establishing the initial state of a software package and coding the software, which includes translating the specifications into a computer programming language, and entering the instructions in that language into a particular computer system. Testing includes unit testing, in which individual software modules are tested to see if they perform correctly according to the specifications, and integration testing, in which modules are tested to see if they work well together. If any errors appear during testing, their causes need to be found and corrected in the debugging phase of the cycle.

You learned that complex software can be developed as a series of small modules that each perform an individual task, and that modular development of computer software makes a large project more manageable, speeds up a project, leads to a higher quality product, makes it easier to correct errors in computer programs, and increases the reusability of your software.

You also learned what software documentation is and how to begin documenting Alice.

## What You Should Know

Having completed this project, you should be able to:

1. List and Describe the Phases in a Software Development Cycle (AL 64)

2. Describe the Concept of Modular Development and List the Advantages (AL 67)

3. Describe Three Different Kinds of Software Documentation (AL 66)

4. Start a New World from an Existing World (AL 69)

5. Position Objects in a New Alice World (AL 71)

6. Position a Camera in an Alice World (AL 79)

7. Add Identifying Comments to an Alice Method (AL 80)

8. Copy an Instruction from One Alice Method to Another (AL 84)

9. Instruct One Object to Circle Around Another Object (AL 93)

10. Prepare a Method for Unit Testing (AL 102)

11. Unit Test a Method (AL 94)

12. Instruct One Method to Call Another (AL 104)

13. Perform an Integration Test on One Method that Calls Another (AL 107)

14. Reveal Tiles for the Subparts of an Object in the Object Tree (AL 109)

15. Delete Unnecessary Instructions from an Existing Method (AL 114)

# Apply Your Knowledge

## 1 Alice in an Alice World

In several places in the Lewis Carroll novels *Alice's Adventures in Wonderland* and *Through the Looking Glass and What Alice Found There*, Alice grows larger, and then smaller again. Your task is to modify an existing Alice world to create a similar scene.

**Instructions:** Open the file, Apply 2 Alice.a2w, from the Data Files for Students. See the inside back cover of this book for instructions for downloading the Data Files for Students or see your instructor for information about accessing the files required in this book. The world contains a scene with Alice, a Cheshire cat, and several other objects, as shown in Figure 2-107.

**FIGURE 2-107**

Play the world to see what happens. The Cheshire cat tells Alice to touch the purple flower but she does nothing. Then he tells Alice to touch the tree, but she still does nothing. The Cheshire cat then fades away, with only his smile showing, and Alice says "What a silly cat."

Your task is to modify the world so that Alice does touch the flower when the cat tells her to do so, which causes her to grow larger. She then touches the tree when the cat says to do so, and she grows smaller.

1. You will need to design and build two new methods: Alice.touchFlower and Alice.touchTree.
   In Alice.touchFlower, Alice should turn to face the flower, reach out to touch the flower, and then grow to four times her size, as follows:

   Alice turn to face greenFlower

# Apply Your Knowledge

Do together

    Alice turn forward 0.05 revolutions

    Alice.leftArm roll right 0.1 revolutions

    Alice.leftArm.forearm turn backward 0.1 revolutions

    Alice.leftArm turn left 0.1 revolutions

Do together

    Alice resize 4

    Alice turn backward 0.05 revolutions

    Alice.leftArm roll left 0.1 revolutions

    Alice.leftArm.forearm turn forward 0.1 revolutions

    Alice.leftArm turn right 0.1 revolutions

2. In Alice.touchTree, Alice should turn to face the tree, reach out to touch the tree, and then shrink to 0.25 times her size, as follows:

Alice turn to face Tree

Do together

    Alice.rightArm roll left 0.1 revolutions

    Alice.rightArm turn backward 0.1 revolutions

    Alice.rightArm turn backward 0.05 revolutions

Do together

    Alice resize 0.25

    Alice.rightArm roll right 0.1 revolutions

    Alice.rightArm turn forward 0.1 revolutions

    Alice.rightArm turn forward 0.05 revolutions

3. You will also need to modify world.myfirst method, as follows:

cheshireCat say Touch the purple flower. duration = 2 seconds

Alice.touchFlower

Alice say Oh my! duration = 2 seconds

cheshireCat say Touch the tree. duration = 2 seconds

Alice.touchTree

Alice say Oh dear! duration = 2 seconds

cheshireCat.fade

Alice turn to face camera

Alice say What a silly cat. duration = 3 seconds

4. Once the methods are built you should test the world to see if they work properly. When you are finished, save your world with the name, Apply 2 Alice grow.a2w.

# 1 Three Penguin Dance

**Instructions:** In this exercise you will create an Alice world in which three penguins – Peter, Paul, and Pamela – perform a short dance. You will start with a blank snow template, create and save the scene for the world, and then create the methods needed for the world. There are six methods – one routine for each penguin, an opening method, a closing method, and world.my first method. There are two parts to this exercise. In the first part, you will set the scene for the world. In the second part, you will create, test, and debug the six methods.

## Instructions for Part 1 — Setting the Scene

1. Open the Alice software and begin a new world with the snow template.
   a. Click the ADD OBJECTS button to enter Scene Editor mode.
   b. Click the tile for the Animals folder.
2. Find and click the Class Penguin tile to open the Penguin information dialog box, and then click the Add instance to world button.
   a. Right-click the penguin tile in the Object tree and run a method to make the penguin turn to face camera.
   b. Right-click the penguin tile in the Object tree and rename the penguin Peter.
3. Click the Class Penguin tile a second time and again click the Add instance to world button.
   a. Right-click the penguin tile in the Object tree and run a method to make the penguin turn to face camera.
   b. Right-click the penguin tile in the Object tree and run a method to make the penguin move left 1 meter.
   c. Right-click the penguin tile in the Object tree and rename the second penguin Paul.
4. Click the Class Penguin tile a third time and again click the Add instance to world button.
   a. Right-click the penguin tile in the Object tree and run a method to make the penguin turn to face camera.
   b. Right-click the penguin tile in the Object tree and run a method to make the penguin move right 1 meter.
   c. Right-click the penguin tile in the Object tree and rename the third penguin Pamela. You should now have three penguins in the world, as shown in Figure 2-108.

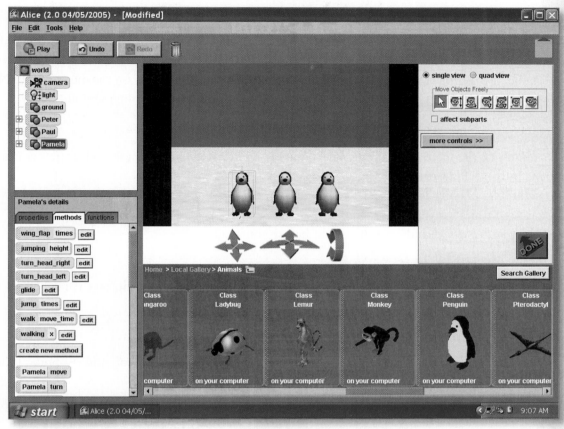

**FIGURE 2-108**

5. Click the **DONE** button to exit Scene Editor mode, then save your world with the name, Lab 2-1 penguinDance.a2w, before continuing.

## Instructions for Part 2 — Creating Methods for the World

### The Peter.routine Method

1. Click Peter's tile in the Object tree and then click the **create new method** button on the **methods** tab. Name the method routine, and then click **OK**. Add the following two instructions to the method:
   a. turn left 1 revolution asSeenBy Paul duration = 3 seconds
   b. turn right 1 revolution asSeenBy Pamela duration = 3 seconds
2. Prepare to unit test the method by dragging the routine tile from the **methods** tab and dropping it in place of **world.my first method** in the default event.
3. Test the method by playing the world. The middle penguin should circle the penguin on the viewer's right and then the penguin on the viewer's left.
4. Fix any errors in the world and save the world before continuing.

*(continued)*

## Creating Methods for the World *(continued)*

### The Paul.routine Method

1. Click Paul's tile in the Object tree and then click the **create new method button** on the **methods** tab. Name the method `routine`, and then click **OK**. Add the following two instructions to the method:
   c. jump times = 3
   d. turn left 3 revolutions duration = 3 seconds
2. Prepare to unit test the method by dragging the **routine** tile from the **methods** tab and dropping it in place of **Peter.routine** in the default event.
3. Test the method by playing the world. The penguin on the viewer's right should jump up and down 3 times, then spin around to its left 3 times.
4. Fix any errors in the world and save the world before continuing.

### The Pamela.routine Method

1. Click Pamela's tile in the Object tree and then click the **create new method** button on the **methods** tab. Name the method `routine`, and then click **OK**. Add two instructions to the method:
   e. turn right 3 revolutions duration = 3 seconds
   f. jump times = 3
2. Prepare to unit test the method by dragging the **routine** tile from the **methods** tab and dropping it in place of **Paul.routine** in the default event
3. Test the method by playing the world. The penguin on the viewer's left should spin around to its right 3 times, then jump up and down 3 times.
4. Fix any errors in the world and save the world before continuing.

### The world.Opening method

1. Click the **world** tile in the Object tree and then click the **create new method** button on the methods tab. Name the method `opening`, and then click **OK**. Add the following four instructions to the method:
   a. Peter say Hello.
   b. Paul say Hello.
   c. Pamela say Hello.
   d. Peter say Welcome to the Penguin Dance.
2. Prepare to unit test the method by dragging the **opening** tile from the methods tab and dropping it in place of **Pamela.routine** in the default event.
3. Test the method by playing the world.
4. Fix any errors in the world and save the world before continuing.

### The world.Closing method

1. Click the **create new method** button on the methods tab. Name the method `closing`, and then click **OK**. Add the following instructions to the method:
   a. In a **Do together** tile,
      Peter turn right ¼ revolution
      Paul turn right ¼ revolution
      Pamela turn right ¼ revolution

b. Pamela glide

c. Peter glide

d. Paul glide

2. Prepare to unit test the method by dragging the closing tile from the methods tab and dropping it in place of world.opening in the default event.

3. Test the method by playing the world. The three penguins should turn to their right together, then one at a time in order they should glide off of the screen on their bellies.

4. Fix any errors in the world and save the world before continuing.

**The world.my first method method**

1. Click the edit button next to my first method on the methods tab. Add the following instructions to the method from the methods tab for each respective object:

a. world.opening

b. In a Do together tile:

Peter.routine

Paul.routine

Pamela.routine

c. world.closing

2. Prepare to test the method by dragging the world.my first method tile from the methods tab and dropping it in place of world.closing in the default event. This will prepare you for a unit test of world.my first method and an integration test of the other methods. It will also return the default event to its original condition.

3. Test the method by playing the world. The opening method should perform as it did during unit testing, then the three penguins should perform their routines together, then the closing method should perform as it did during unit testing.

4. Fix any errors and then save the world.

# 2 A Short Airport Animation

A modern computer game or simulation often contains a series of short animation sequences that together tell a story, in the same way that a Hollywood film is a collection of short separate scenes. In this exercise you will create a short animated scene showing some activity at a busy airport. Your task is to create several methods to animate a world with an airport scene, in which a jet will land and taxi from the runway to the terminal, a biplane will taxi to the runway and take off, and then a helicopter will take off and fly away.

You will start with an airport scene with the aircraft in place and an invisible cone to mark a spot on the runway where airplanes land and take off. Your task is to create five short methods – jet.land, jet.taxi, biplane.taxi, biplane.takeoff, and helicopter.takeoff – and then modify world.my first method to call these five methods in sequence to animate the airport scene.

**Instructions:** Open the file, Lab 2-2 airport.a2w, from the Data Files for Students. See the inside back cover of this book for instructions for downloading the Data Files for Students or see your instructor for information about accessing the files required in this book. The world contains the airport scene shown in Figure 2-109. Notice that the object tree contains an airport, a jet, a biplane, a helicopter, and an invisible cone. The cone marks a spot near the start of the runway. The helicopter and biplane can be seen at the airport, but the jet is still in the air, off camera.

*(continued)*

## A Short Airplane Animation *(continued)*

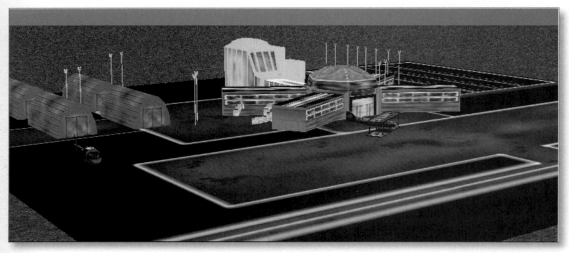

**FIGURE 2-109**

**To create the** jet.land **method:**

1. Click the jet tile in the Object tree and then click the **create new method** button on the **methods** tab. Name the new method **land**, then click the **OK** button.
2. Drag a copy of the **Do together** tile from the bottom of the Editor area and drop it in the new method in place of **Do Nothing**.
3. Drag a jet move instruction tile from the **methods** tab and drop it in the new method in the **Do together** tile in place of **Do Nothing**. Select **forward** as the direction and **30 meters** as the amount.
4. Click **more...** on the jet move instruction that you just created and change the duration to **2 seconds**.
5. Right click the jet move instruction that you just created and select **make copy** from the menu that appears.
6. Change the direction to **down** and the amount to **10 meters** in the new copy of the jet.move instruction.
7. Drag a jet move instruction tile from the **methods** tab and drop it in the new method below the **Do together** tile. Select **forward** as the direction and **40 meters** as the amount.
8. Click **more...** on the last jet move instruction and change the style to **abruptly**.
9. Click **more...** on the last jet move instruction and change the duration to **2 seconds**.

**To create the** jet.taxi **method:**

1. Click the **create new method** button on the **methods** tab. Name the new method **taxi**, then click the **OK** button.
2. Drag a copy of the jet turn instruction tile from the **methods** tab and drop it in the new method in the **Do together** tile in place of **Do Nothing**. Select **left** as the direction and **other** for the amount. Enter the number **3/8** using the Custom Number dialog box, then click **Okay**.
3. Drag a jet move instruction tile from the **methods** tab and drop it in the new method below the jet turn instruction tile. Select **forward** as the direction and **30 meters** as the amount.
4. Click **more...** on the jet move instruction and change its duration to **2 seconds**.

**To create the** biplane.taxi **method:**

1. Click the **biplane** tile in the Object tree and then the **create new method** button on the **methods** tab. Name the new method **taxi**, then click the **OK** button.

2. Drag a copy of the **Do together** tile from the bottom of the Editor area and drop it in the new method in place of **Do Nothing**.
3. Drag a **biplane move** instruction tile from the **methods** tab and drop it in the **Do together** tile in place of **Do Nothing**. Select **forward** as the direction and **5 meters** as the amount.
4. Drag a **biplane turn to face** instruction tile from the **methods** tab and drop it in the **Do together** tile below the **biplane move** instruction. Click **cone** on the **target** menu that appears.
5. Drag a **biplane move to** instruction tile from the **methods** tab and drop it in the new method below the **Do together** tile. Click **cone** on the **target** menu that appears.
6. Click **more...** on the last **biplane move to cone** instruction tile and change the duration to **2 seconds**.
7. Drag a copy of the **biplane orient to** instruction tile from the **methods** tab and drop it in the new method below all of the other instructions. Select **cone** from the menu that appears. This instruction lines up the plane with the invisible cone facing down the runway.

**To create the biplane.takeoff method:**

1. Click the **create new method** button on the **methods** tab. Name the new method **takeoff**, then click the **OK** button.
2. Drag a **biplane move** instruction tile from the **methods** tab and drop it in the new method in place of **Do Nothing**. Select **forward** as the direction and **5 meters** as the amount.
3. Click **more...** on the **biplane move** instruction tile and change the **style** to **begin gently**.
4. Drag a copy of the **Do together** tile from the bottom of the Editor area and drop it in the new method below the **biplane move** instruction.
5. Drag a **biplane move** instruction tile from the **methods** tab and drop it in the new method in the **Do together** tile in place of **Do Nothing**. Select **forward** as the direction and **30 meters** as the amount.
6. Click **more...** on the **biplane move** instruction that you just created and change the **style** to **abruptly**.
7. Click **more...** on the **biplane move** instruction that you just created and change the **duration** to **2 seconds**.
8. Right click the **biplane move** instruction that you just created and select **make copy** from the menu that appears.
9. Change the direction to **up** and the amount to **10 meters** in the new copy of the **biplane move** instruction.

**To create the helicopter.takeoff method:**

1. Click the **helicopter** tile in the Object tree and then the **create new method** button on the **methods** tab. Name the new method **takeoff**, then click the **OK** button.
2. Drag a **helicopter move** instruction tile from the **methods** tab and drop it in the new method in place of **Do Nothing**. Select **up** as the direction and **10 meters** as the amount.
3. Drag a **helicopter turn** instruction tile from the **methods** tab and drop it in the new method below the first instruction. Select **left** as the direction and ¼ **revolution** as the amount.
4. Drag a copy of the **Do together** tile from the bottom of the Editor area and drop it in the new method below the two existing instructions.
5. Drag a **helicopter turn** instruction from the **methods** tab and drop it in the **Do together** tile in place of **Do Nothing**. Select **left** and ½ **revolution** from the menus that appear.
6. Click **more...** on the **helicopter turn** instruction tile, and change the duration to **4 seconds**.
7. Drag a **helicopter move** instruction from the **methods** tab and drop it in the **Do together** tile below the **helicopter turn** instruction. Select **forward** and **100 meters** from the menus that appear.
8. Click **more...** on the **helicopter move** instruction tile, and change the duration to **4 seconds**.

*(continued)*

## In the Lab

### A Short Airplane Animation *(continued)*

To put the necessary method calls in world.my first method:

1. Click the world tile in the Object tree and then click the edit button next to my first method on the methods tab.
2. Drag a Do together tile from the bottom of the Editor area and drop it in world.my first method in place of Do Nothing.
3. Click the helicopter tile in the Object tree and then drag a copy of the heli blade method tile and drop in the Do together tile in place of Do Nothing. This will cause the helicopter's blades to keep spinning while the other methods are being executed.
4. Drag a Do in order tile from the bottom of the Editor area and drop it in the Do together tile below the helicopter.heli blade tile.
5. Drag a copy of the takeoff instruction from the methods tab and drop it onto the Do in order tile in place of Do Nothing.
6. Click the jet tile in the Object tree and then drag a copy of the land method tile from the methods tab and drop it in the Do in order tile above the helicopter.takeoff tile.
7. Drag a copy of the taxi method tile from the methods tab and drop it in the Do in order tile between the jet.land tile and the helicopter.takeoff tile.
8. Click the biplane tile in the Object tree and then drag a copy of the taxi method tile from the methods tab and drop it in the Do in order tile between the jet.taxi tile and the helicopter.takeoff tile.
9. Drag a copy of the takeoff method tile from the methods tab and drop it in the Do in order tile between the biplane.taxi tile and the helicopter.takeoff tile.

Your new airport world is now complete. Save the world with the name, Lab 2-2 airport animation.a2w. You can now play the world to see the animation.

## 3 Ballerina Movements

**Problem:** In this exercise you will develop an Alice world in which a ballerina, similar to the one in Figure 2-110, demonstrates her movements. To do so, you need methods for the ballerina that will enable her to move her arms up, move her arms down, bow, jump, and spin. Your task is to create an Alice world with methods for each of these five actions, along with a sample routine in which the ballerina demonstrates each of the five movements.

# In the Lab

**FIGURE 2-110**

Figure 2-111 shows the specifications for each of the movements.

*(continued)*

## Ballerina Movements *(continued)*

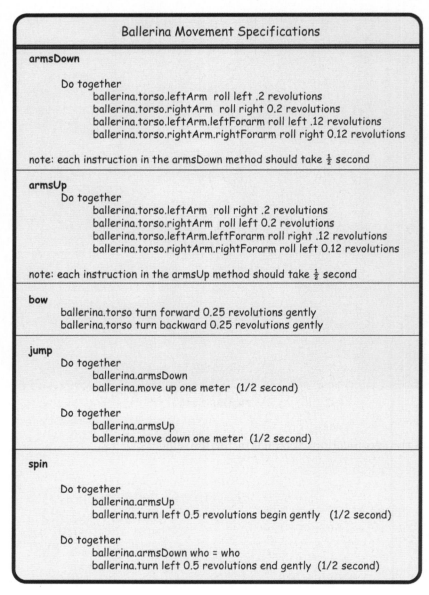

```
                    Ballerina Movement Specifications

armsDown

        Do together
                ballerina.torso.leftArm  roll left .2 revolutions
                ballerina.torso.rightArm  roll right 0.2 revolutions
                ballerina.torso.leftArm.leftForarm roll left .12 revolutions
                ballerina.torso.rightArm.rightForarm roll right 0.12 revolutions

    note: each instruction in the armsDown method should take ½ second

armsUp
        Do together
                ballerina.torso.leftArm  roll right .2 revolutions
                ballerina.torso.rightArm  roll left 0.2 revolutions
                ballerina.torso.leftArm.leftForarm roll right .12 revolutions
                ballerina.torso.rightArm.rightForarm roll left 0.12 revolutions

    note: each instruction in the armsUp method should take ½ second

bow
        ballerina.torso turn forward 0.25 revolutions gently
        ballerina.torso turn backward 0.25 revolutions gently

jump
        Do together
                ballerina.armsDown
                ballerina.move up one meter  (1/2 second)

        Do together
                ballerina.armsUp
                ballerina.move down one meter  (1/2 second)

spin

        Do together
                ballerina.armsUp
                ballerina.turn left 0.5 revolutions begin gently   (1/2 second)

        Do together
                ballerina.armsDown who = who
                ballerina.turn left 0.5 revolutions end gently  (1/2 second)
```

**FIGURE 2-111**

## Instructions:

1. Start Alice with a grass template, and then enter Scene Editor mode. Navigate to the **People** folder in the **Local Gallery**. Add either a **blueBallerina** or a **pinkBallerina** to the world and rename it simply, ballerina.
2. Add identifying comments to world.my first method.
3. Create five methods for the ballerina, one for each of the movements in the specification in Figure 2-111.
4. Add code to world.my first method to have the ballerina say the name of a movement, and then call the method to perform the movement for each of the five movements.
5. Once you have a properly working world, save your world with the name Lab 2-1 ballerinaMovements.a2w.

# Cases and Places

**1** The Television program *Sesame Street* often uses the theme of commercial endorsements to teach young children about the alphabet, such as segments on the program that are supposedly "… brought to you by the letter W…" Your task is to create an Alice world that picks up on this theme to teach children about a letter of the alphabet in an Alice world with animation and sound.

The Alice world, Case 2-1 letter P.a2w, has the letter P added to a world as an object, as shown in Figure 2-112. Your task is to find objects in the Alice object galleries that begin with the letter P and use them to create a world with the theme "This Alice world is brought to you by the letter P."

**FIGURE 2-112**

*(continued)*

# Cases and Places

**1** *(continued)*

**Instructions:** Open the file, Case 2-1 letter P.a2w, from the Data Files for Students. See the inside back cover of this book for instructions for downloading the Data Files for Students or see your instructor for information about accessing the files required in this book. The world contains a scene with the letter P.

1. Look through the Alice object galleries and find at least five objects that begin with the letter P.
2. Add the objects you found to the world, and design and create one method for each object that animates the object in some way or has the object say something.
3. Add instructions to world.my first method after the existing instructions so that the letter P will say things like "Petunia", after which the petunia method is called so that it performs its action, such as waving back and forth or spinning around. Note that this is only an example, there is no petunia in the object gallery. The letter P should say the name of the object (or something close to its name), then the object's action method should be called.
4. When you are finished, save the world with the name, Case 2-1 P.a2w.

**2** This exercise will test your storytelling ability as well as your Alice programming skills. The Alice world Case 2-2 aquarium.a2w contains an aquarium with three fish: a blueFish, a pinkFish, and a greenFish (Figure 2-113). Your task is to write a short story that can be enacted by the three fish. You may work alone or with another student. Your story should have a clear beginning, middle, and end. In the beginning, the viewer should become familiar with the world of the aquarium and the behavior and attitudes of the characters in your story: the three fish. In the middle some incident or action should occur. In the end, the fish should react to the incident or action that occurs. Remember not to make things too complicated or lengthy. This should be a very short fish story.

**FIGURE 2-113**

# Cases and Places

You will need to create methods to provide the behaviors for the fish needed for your story, such as moving forward while swimming, turning left or right, floating up and down, and swimming around in a circle. Exactly what they are able to do is up to you. Each of the three fish already has a swim method, which moves the fish's tail back and forth. world.my first method in the current world demonstrates the use of this method. You should create modules that call the necessary behaviors for each part of your story, then call these modules from world.my first method. You can delete the demonstration code currently in world.my first method after you see how it works.

You can begin by starting Alice and opening the file, Case 2-2 aquarium.a2w, from the Data Files for Students. See the inside back cover of this book for instructions for downloading the Data Files for Students or see your instructor for information about accessing the files required in this book. Remember to use good modular design in creating your fish story world. An outline and an organizational chart of the modules in your world may be useful. Your finished world should be saved with the name Case 2-2 fish story.a2w.

**3** The American Film Institute's list of *The 100 Greatest Movie Quotes Of All Time* is on the Web at www.afi.com/tvevents/100years/quotes.aspx#list. Working alone, with another student, or with several students, pick one of the quotes and develop an Alice world that enacts a short scene using the quote. Complete the following tasks:

1. Find a quote from the American Film Institute's list that would fit in a scene using objects from the Alice galleries. You will need to look through the folders in the Alice galleries and find several objects that can be used to create the scene for your new world. If you have high-speed Internet access, you may want to look in the Web Gallery, which is more extensive than the Local Gallery. You may also want to create new characters for your story using the heBuilder and sheBuilder tools in the local object gallery's people folder.

2. Develop an outline for a short animation using the quote and the objects from the gallery. Be careful not to get too carried away describing a long and complex scene that will be too difficult and time consuming to implement.

3. Create an organizational chart that shows the modules in the story, and develop a list of the Alice methods that you would need to write to implement your story as an Alice world. Identify any reusable methods.

4. Implement your story as an Alice world with separate methods showing good modular design. Save the finished world with the name Case 2-3 AFIScene.a2w.

# Learning Exercises

**1** **Writing Directions**  Common, everyday tasks can sometimes be hard to describe in an algorithm, because people often carry out such tasks without thinking about the individual steps. For each of the following tasks, break the task down into several more detailed modules, describe the steps in each module, and draw an organizational chart showing how the modules fit together. Identify any of the modules that are reusable for other activities:

    A. Making a pot of coffee and serving it to several people.
    B. Traveling from the White House in Washington, D.C. to the Golden Gate Bridge in San Francisco, CA.
    C. Assembling a bicycle from a box of its parts.
    D. Searching for a name in a telephone directory.
    E. Sorting a list of names alphabetically by last name.
    F. Solving your favorite math problem.

**2** **Analyzing the Modular Design of an Existing World**  Early in Project 1 you used the lakeSkater.a2w example world that is provided with Alice. The world can be found on the Examples tab after starting Alice. It exhibits good modular design for some of its methods, but not for others.
Complete the following tasks:

1. Click the IceSkater tile in the Object tree, click the methods tab in the Details area, and then examine the IceSkater's methods. Use the edit button next to a method's name to view the code in the Editor area. Some of the methods are long and complex, using features that you have not yet learned about in Alice, but you should be able to read though most of the code.
2. List several examples of one user-created method calling another one among the IceSkater's methods. Describe how these instances are examples of modular design and the concept of reusable code.
3. Click the world tile in the Object tree and then click the edit button to examine the code in the world.my first animation method.
4. Create an organizational chart showing an improved design for world.my first animation that exhibits better modularity.

**3** **Describing Alice Programming Tasks**  Briefly describe how to complete each of the following tasks in Alice:

    A. add identifying comments to a method
    B. copy an instruction from one method to another
    C. instruct one object to circle around another object
    D. instruct one method to call another method
    E. unit test a method
    F. perform an integration test on one method that calls another method

# Programming with Logical Structures

## CASE PERSPECTIVE

Dr. Dodgson is pleased with what you've done so far in your Alice world. However, she points out that all of the methods contain only linear sequences of instructions—that is, the instructions follow one after another as if in a straight line, with no branching or looping. Dr. Dodgson would like to show her students some examples of branching and looping, along with the Boolean logic used for the conditions used in such statements. She asks you for at least one example each of a binary bypass, a binary choice, a count-controlled loop, and a sentinel loop.

In this project you will respond to Dr. Dodgson's request by adding the branching and looping routines she suggested. To provide all the examples that Dr. Dodgson has requested, you will add four new features to your world:

- A selection sequence to have the skater say "Happy New Year!" if it is the first day of the year.

- A selection sequence to have the skater say either "Good morning." or "Good afternoon.", depending on the time of day .

- A count-controlled loop to make the skater complete her figure eight three times as part of her routine.

- A sentinel loop to make the skater skate over to a flagpole when her routine is done.

First, you will take a look at the logical structure of algorithms, including branching and looping, and a form of conditional logic known as Boolean logic, which is most important in modern computer programming.

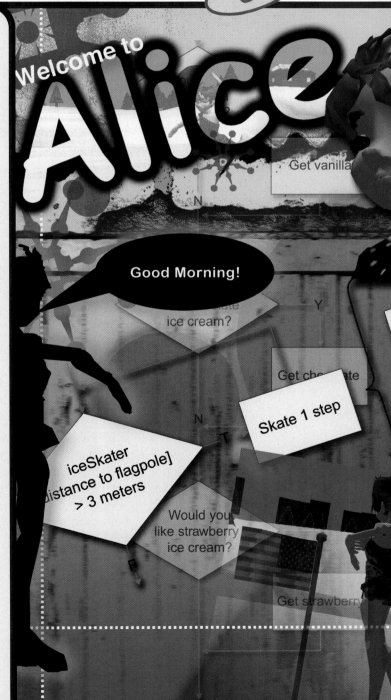

## Alice 2.0

# Programming with Logical Structures

PROJECT

3

### Objectives

**You will have mastered the material in this project when you can:**

- List and describe the three major elements of logical structure found in algorithms
- List several criteria that should be met by each linear sequence in an algorithm
- Describe the difference between binary bypass and binary choice branching routines
- Describe the difference between a pretest loop and a posttest loop
- List and describe the four major parts of a count-controlled loop
- List and describe the six logical comparison operations used in computer programming

- List and describe the three major operations in Boolean logic
- Create methods in Alice that implement each of the following:
  - a binary bypass
  - a binary choice
  - a count-controlled loop
  - a sentinel loop that is not count controlled
- Create a compound Boolean expression in an Alice looping or branching instruction

## Project Three — Programming with Logical Structures

You will start Project 3 by modifying the skaterRoutine.a2w world from Project 2, using logical structures to control the behavior of the skater. You will focus on learning how to implement these logical structures in the Alice interface using Alice's built-in functions and methods. Along the way, you'll also add a flagpole to the Alice world, as shown in Figure 3-1. To start Project 3, you will open the world, change the documentation in world.my first method, and then save the world with the new name, skaterLogic.a2w.

**FIGURE 3-1**

## To Create a New World from an Existing World

**1**

• **Start Alice as described in Project 1, then click the** Open a world **tab.**

*The Open a world tab appears (Figure 3-2).*

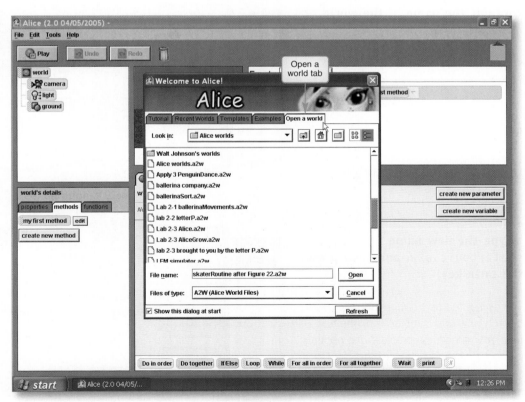

**FIGURE 3-2**

**2**

• **Navigate to the folder that contains the Alice file skaterRoutine.a2w and open the file by selecting it and clicking the Open button.**

*world.my first method from the skaterRoutine world appears in the standard Alice interface, with the identifying comments visible at the top of the method (Figure 3-3).*

• **Save the world with the name** skaterLogic.a2w **before continuing. Remember or write down the name of the world and where you saved it.**

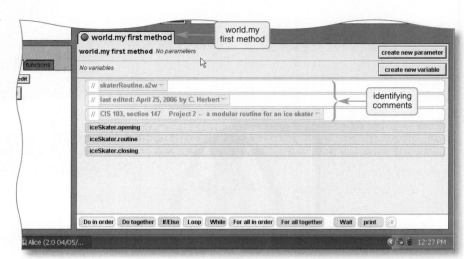

**FIGURE 3-3**

## To Update the Identifying Comments in the New World

**1**

• **Click the comment tile that contains the name of the world,** skaterRoutine.a2w.

*The text in the tile is highlighted and is now accessible for editing (Figure 3-4).*

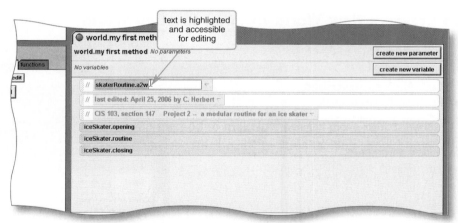

**FIGURE 3-4**

**2**

• **Type the new name** skaterLogic.a2w, **and then press the ENTER key.**

*The highlighted text disappears when you begin typing, and is replaced by the new text. Your change is complete and appears in the instruction when you press the ENTER key (Figure 3-5).*

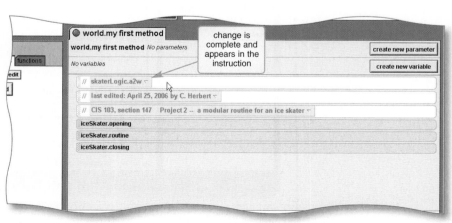

**FIGURE 3-5**

**3**

• **Change the date in the** last edited **comment tile to be today's date, in the same way that you modified the first comment tile.**

*The second comment shows the current date (Figure 3-6).*

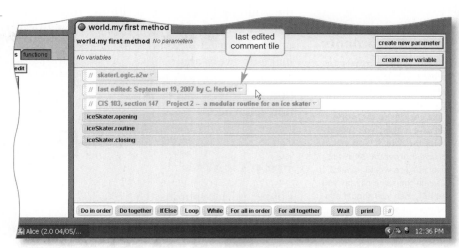

**FIGURE 3-6**

**4**

• **Update the description in the third comment tile to include the text** CIS 103, section 147 Project 3 — branching and looping in an iceSkater routine.

*The three comment tiles are complete and are similar to those in Figure 3-7.*

• **Save the world before continuing.**

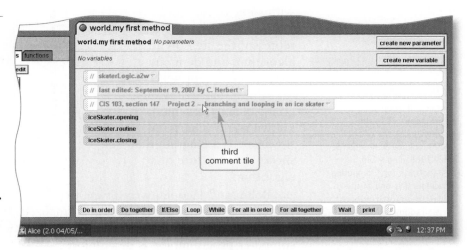

**FIGURE 3-7**

*Other Ways*

1. If the skaterRoutine.a2w world appears on the **Recent Worlds** tab, then you can open the world by clicking the **Recent Worlds** tab and then double-clicking the icon for that world.

# The Logical Structure of Algorithms

Every computer program is an algorithm — a step-by-step process. In modern object-oriented programming, each method is an algorithm, and a collection of methods together make up the components of a more complex algorithm. So, when you design and build methods for objects, you are designing and building algorithms.

Algorithms are sequential in nature. Sometimes several instructions are executed at the same time, such as in a **Do together** tile, but generally we can think of an algorithm as a set of steps being executed one after another. The steps in an algorithm form a kind of sequential logic. Modern approaches to developing software recognize that this is only part of the story, but programmers still need to be able to design, manipulate, and implement sequential algorithms. They need to understand sequential logic.

Certain patterns exist in the design of sequential logic. These patterns can be understood as elements of logical structure. In the 1960s, two Italian mathematicians, Corrado Böhm and Giuseppe Jacopini, showed that all algorithms are composed of just three elements of logical structure: branching routines, loops, and linear sequences, which have no branches or loops. They showed that these elements are

Alice 2.0

the building blocks of algorithms. Today, branching routines are referred to as selection sequences and loops are called repetition sequences. So, the three major elements of logical structure that make up every algorithm are linear sequences, selection sequences, and repetition sequences.

## Flowcharts

Böhm and Jacopini used a system they called flow diagrams to describe their work. Figure 3-8 shows part of their manuscript with some of their diagrams, in which rectangles represent the steps in an algorithm, and diamond-shaped boxes represent branching. Their flow diagrams quickly became known as flowcharts. A flowchart is a diagram that shows the structure of an algorithm.

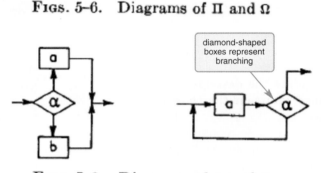

**FIGS. 5-6.** Diagrams of Π and Ω

**FIGS. 7-8.** Diagrams of Δ and Φ

**FIGURE 3-8**

Bohm and Jacopini weren't the first people to use flowcharts, but they formalized them in their work on algorithms. Today, computer programming is much more sophisticated than in the 1960s, and many different types of diagrams are used to design and document software, but flowcharts are still commonly used to help people understand the logical structure of algorithms. Flowcharts are also used to diagram many other algorithms, such as business processes, rules for decision making, and biological processes.

A simple version of flowcharting will be used in the rest of this project to help describe the elements of logical structure found in algorithms. Three symbols will be used: rectangles and diamonds, as Böhm and Jacopini used, along with oval-shaped boxes to mark the beginning and end of an algorithm, as shown in Figure 3-9.

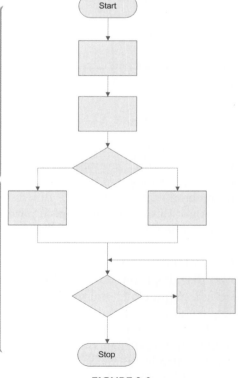

**FIGURE 3-9**

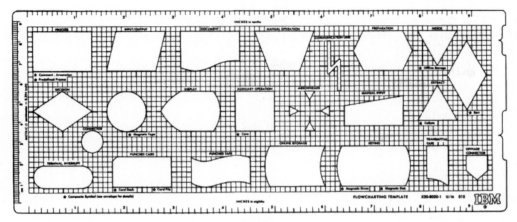

**FIGURE 3-10**

# More About

## Creating Flowcharts

In the late 1960s, IBM (International Business Machines Corporation) introduced a green plastic flowcharting template, shown in Figure 3-10, that was used to draw flowcharts by hand. It was accompanied by a 40–page instruction manual on how to use the various shapes. At the time, IBM was by far the world's largest producer of both computer hardware and software and this template heavily influenced the way flowcharting symbols have appeared since. Today the world's largest software company, Microsoft, has more than 25,000 flowcharts on its Microsoft.com and MSDN.com Web sites. For more information about creating flowcharts with Microsoft PowerPoint or Microsoft Visio visit http://office.microsoft.com/en-us/assistance/HA010785431033.aspx.

## Linear Sequences

The Alice methods you have created so far are all examples of linear sequences of instructions. There have been some occasions when two or more instructions were executed at the same time using Alice's Do together tile, but generally, the instructions in the methods you have written are steps in an algorithm that are executed one after another, as if in a straight line.

Linear sequences seem very simple, but computer programmers need to make sure that they meet the following criteria:

- They should have a clear starting and ending point.
- Entry and exit conditions need to be clearly stated. What conditions need to exist before the sequence starts? What can we expect the situation to be when the sequence is finished?
- The sequence of instructions needs to be complete. Programmers need to be sure not to leave out any necessary steps. (This is more difficult than it sounds.)
- The sequence of instructions needs to be in the proper order.
- Each instruction in the sequence needs to be correct. If one step in an algorithm is incorrect, then the whole algorithm is incorrect.

In short, linear sequences must have clearly stated entry and exit conditions, and they need to be complete, correct, and in the proper order. You have already created linear sequences in your program, so you will not carry out any additional tasks involving linear sequences at this time.

## Selection Sequences — Branching

A selection sequence, or branching routine, occurs whenever the flow of instructions in a computer program splits into separate paths. There must be a condition to determine which path the computer will follow each time the selection sequence is being executed. Binary branching occurs when the flow of logic in the program splits into two possible paths with a simple true-or-false condition. Multiple branching occurs when the path of logic in an algorithm divides into more than two paths, based on a single condition with many possible values. Figure 3-11 shows examples of both binary branching and multiple branching.

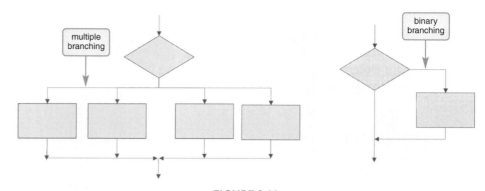

**FIGURE 3-11**

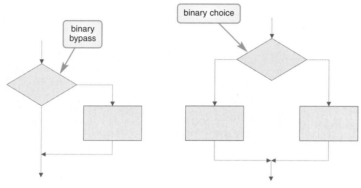

**FIGURE 3-12**

There are two different kinds of binary branching sequences: a binary bypass and a binary choice. In a binary bypass, an instruction is either executed or bypassed. In a binary choice, one of two instructions, but not both, is executed. The two structures are shown in Figure 3-12.

The difference between a bypass and a choice is subtle but significant. In a binary bypass, it is possible that nothing will happen and the algorithm will move on to the next step, whereas in a binary choice, one of the two instructions will definitely be executed.

Having the iceSkater say "Happy New Year!" on the first day of the year is an example of a bypass, which you can see in Figure 3-12. If it is the first day of the year, then the skater will say "Happy New Year!". If it is not, then the iceSkater will simply ignore the say instruction and move on to whatever comes next. Either she will say "Happy New Year!", or the instruction will be bypassed.

Having the iceSkater say "Good morning" if it is before noon and "Good afternoon" if it is after noon is an example of a binary choice, shown in Figure 3-12. The iceSkater will always say either "Good morning" or "Good afternoon", but not both. One of the two say instructions, but not both, will be executed whenever the method runs.

Binary bypasses and binary choices are both implemented in Alice using an If/Else instruction tile, shown in Figure 3-15 on page AL 141. The If/Else tile has a place to put a true-or-false condition following the word If, and places to put an instruction set below the word If and again below the word Else. An instruction set could be a single instruction or several instructions. If the condition is true, then the instruction set below the word If will be executed; if not, then the instruction set below the word Else will be executed.

To implement a binary bypass in Alice, simply leave the phrase Do Nothing in place below the word Else. If the condition is true, then the instruction set below the word If will be executed, but if the condition is false, then nothing will happen and the computer will move on to the next instruction.

To implement a binary choice, place the instruction to be executed when the condition is true below the word If, and the instruction to be executed if the condition is false below the word Else.

You will use two of Alice's built-in functions to create the true-or-false condition in the new If/Else instruction. The day of year function is used to return the day of the year from the computer's system clock. Each day of the year is numbered starting with 1 on January 1st. The a == b math function will be used to see if the day of the year is equal to 1. This is an example of a Boolean comparison function, which will be discussed in more detail later in this Project. If day of year does equal 1, then the function will be true and the say instruction will be executed. If day of year does not equal 1, then the condition will be false and the say instruction will not be executed. You add a binary bypass to the opening method in the next set of steps.

## To Add a Binary Bypass to the opening Method

**1**

• **If the** iceSkater's **methods are not visible in the Details area, click the** iceSkater **tile in the Object tree and then click the** methods **tab in the Details area.**

*The iceSkater's methods appear in the Details area (Figure 3-13).*

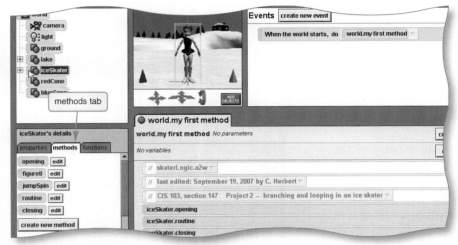

**FIGURE 3-13**

**2**

• **Click the** edit **button next to the** opening **tile on the** methods **tab.**

*The opening method is visible in the Editor area (Figure 3-14).*

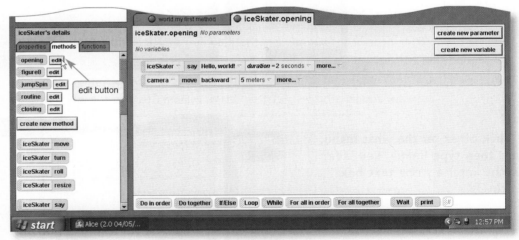

**FIGURE 3-14**

**3**

• **Drag a copy of the** If/Else **tile from the set of logic and control tiles at the bottom of the Editor area and drop it in the method below the two existing instructions.**

*A condition menu appears (Figure 3-15).*

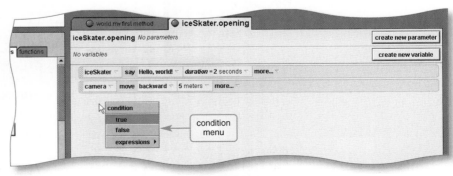

**FIGURE 3-15**

**4**

• **Click** true **on the** condition **menu.**

*A blank If/Else instruction, with true following the word If, appears in the method. (Figure 3-16).*

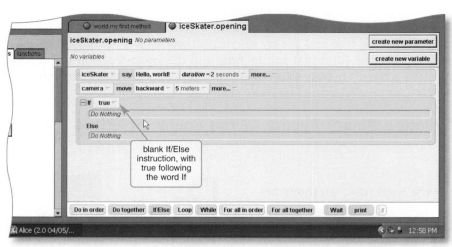

**FIGURE 3-16**

**5**

• **Drag a copy of the** iceSkater say **tile from the** methods **tab and drop it in the** If/Else **tile in place of** Do Nothing **just below the word If.**

*A menu appears, asking what you want the skater to say (Figure 3-17).*

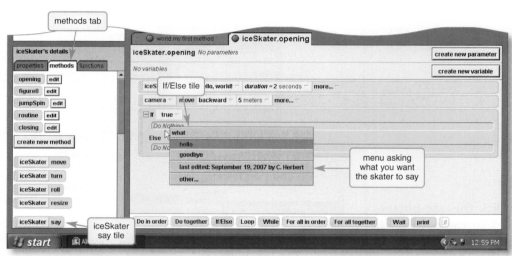

**FIGURE 3-17**

**6**

• **Click** other **on the** what **menu, and then type** Happy New Year! **in the** Enter a string **text box. Click** OK.

*The method now contains an instruction that reads If true iceSkater say Happy New Year! Else Do Nothing (Figure 3-18).*

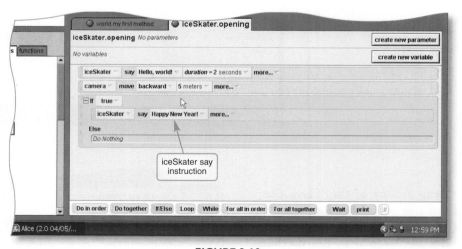

**FIGURE 3-18**

**7**

• **Click the** world **tile in the Object tree and then click the** functions **tab in the Details area.**

*Alice's world-level functions appear in the Details area (Figure 3-19).*

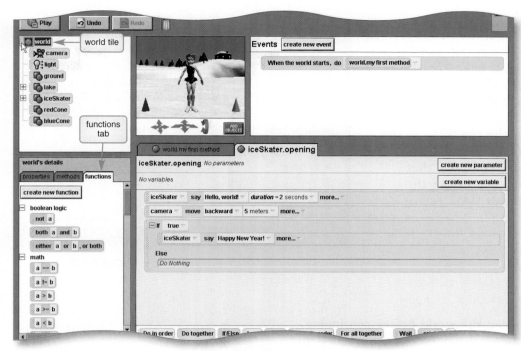

**FIGURE 3-19**

**8**

• **Drag a copy of the** math **function** a == b **and drop it in the** If/Else **instruction tile in place of the word** true.

*A menu appears, allowing you to choose a value for a (Figure 3-20).*

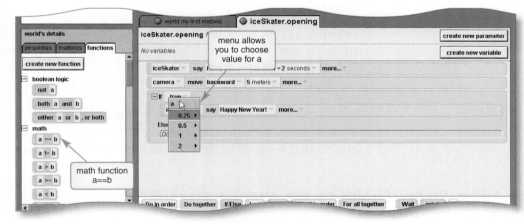

**FIGURE 3-20**

**9**

• **Point to 1 on the** a **menu and then click 1 on the** b **menu.**

*The condition in the If/Else instruction now reads 1 == 1 (Figure 3-21).*

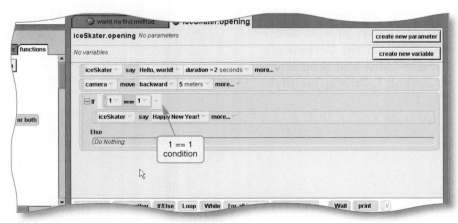

**FIGURE 3-21**

**10**

• **Scroll down the** functions **tab until you see the** time **function** day of year. **Drag a copy of the** day of year **function tile and drop it in the condition in the** If/Else **instruction in place of the** 1 **that appears before the equals sign.**

*The condition in the If/Else instruction now reads day of year == 1. The entire If/Else instruction is now complete and should match Figure 3-22.*

• **Save the world before continuing.**

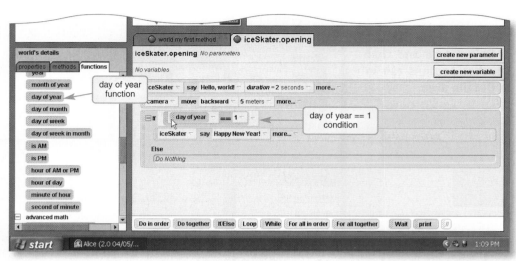

**FIGURE 3-22**

Next you will add a binary choice routine to the opening method to have the iceSkater say "Good morning." if the current time is in the morning and "Good afternoon." if the current time is in the afternoon. You will simply have the ice skater say "Good morning." if the time is AM, and "Good afternoon." if it is not AM.

Alice has a world-level, built-in function is AM, which returns a value of true if the time on the system clock is before 12:00 PM and false if it is not. You will use this function in the condition in the new If/Else instruction. Since it returns a value of true or false instead of returning a number like the day of year function, the is AM function can be used by itself as the condition in the If/Else instruction.

## To Add a Binary Choice to the opening Method

**1**

• **Drag a second copy of the** If/Else **tile from the set of logic and control tiles at the bottom of the Editor area and drop it in the method following the first** If/Else **tile.**

*A condition menu appears (Figure 3-23).*

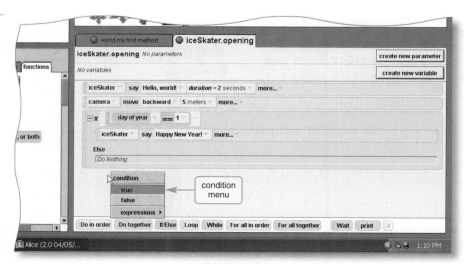

**FIGURE 3-23**

**2**

• **Click** true **on the** condition **menu.**

*A blank If true tile appears in the method below the If day of year == 1 tile (Figure 3-24).*

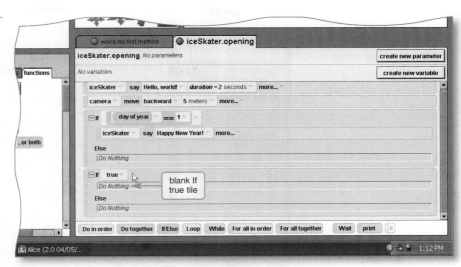

**FIGURE 3-24**

**3**

• **Find the** is AM **function tile on the** world**'s** functions **tab in the Details area, then drag a copy of it and drop it in the new** If/Else **tile in place of** true.

*The condition in the If/Else instruction now reads is AM (Figure 3-25).*

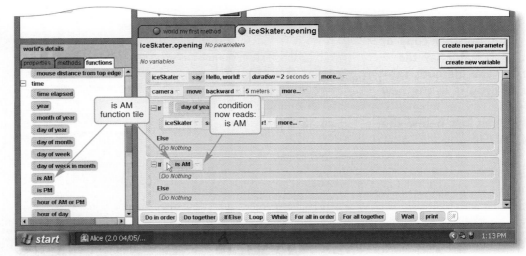

**FIGURE 3-25**

**4**

• **Click the** iceSkater **tile in the Object tree, click the** methods **tab in the Details area, and then drag a copy of the** iceSkater say **tile from the** methods **tab and drop it in the new** If/Else **tile in place of** Do Nothing, **just below the word** If.

*The what menu appears, asking you what you want the skater to say (Figure 3-26).*

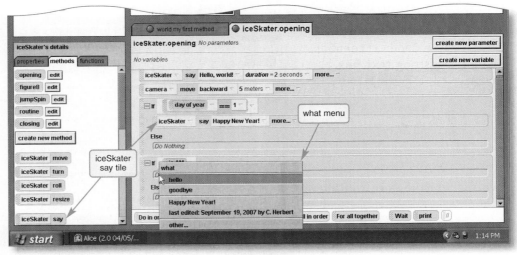

**FIGURE 3-26**

**5**

• **Click** other... **on the** what **menu, and then** **type** Good morning. **in the** Enter a string **text box. Click** OK.

*The method now contains an instruction that reads If is AM iceSkater say Good morning. Else Do Nothing (Figure 3-27).*

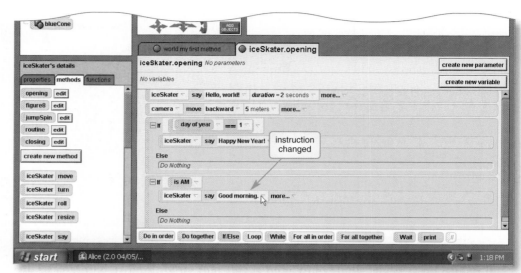

**FIGURE 3-27**

**6**

• **Drag another copy of the** iceSkater say **tile from the** methods **tab and drop it in the new** If/Else **tile in place of** Do Nothing **just below the word** Else.

*The what menu appears, asking you what you want the skater to say (Figure 3-28).*

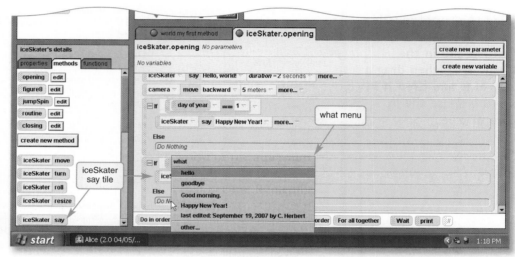

**FIGURE 3-28**

**7**

• **Select** other **from the menu, and then enter** Good afternoon. **in the** Enter a string **text box. Click** OK.

*The method should now contain an instruction that reads If is AM iceSkater say Good morning. Else iceSkater say Good afternoon. (Figure 3-29).*

• **Save the world before continuing.**

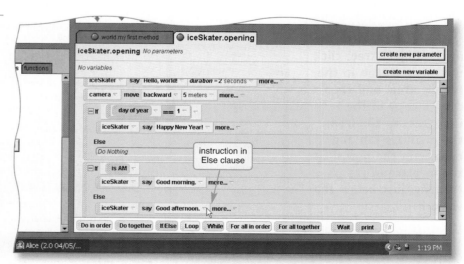

**FIGURE 3-29**

## Multiple Branching

Consider the question "What flavor ice cream would you like?" It is not a true-or-false question, but one with many different possible answers. A flowchart showing this might look something like a pitchfork, as shown in Figure 3-30.

This is multiple branching, not binary branching, yet the same results can be achieved by asking a series of binary questions, such as "Would you like vanilla ice cream?", "Would you like chocolate ice cream?", "Would you like strawberry ice cream?", and so on.

Multiple branching routines are not really necessary in algorithms, since multiple branching can always be rewritten as a series of binary branching routines, or as a series of nested If/Else instructions. Figure 3-31 shows the same process as Figure 3-30 written as a series of binary branching routines. Figure 3-32 shows the same process again, but written as a series of nested If/Else instructions. The difference between the two is subtle, but important. It is possible to follow a path through a series of If/Else instructions and answer yes to more than one instruction, as in Figure 3-31. A series of nested If/Else instructions can be layered so that only one true answer is possible, as in Figure 3-32, which has the same effect as multiple branching. Figure 3-33 shows how this would be implemented in Alice.

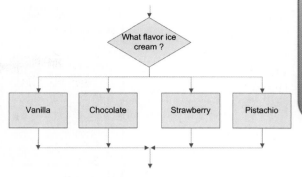

**FIGURE 3-30**

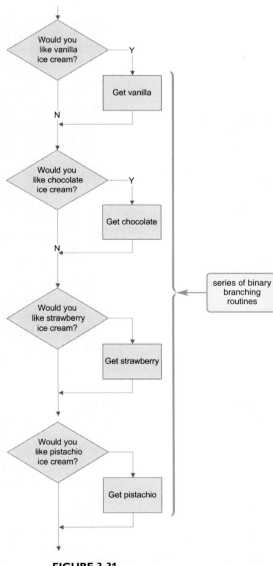

**FIGURE 3-31**

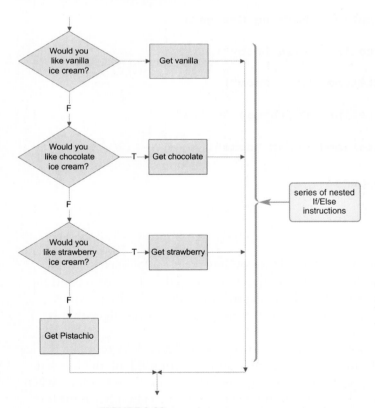

**FIGURE 3-32**

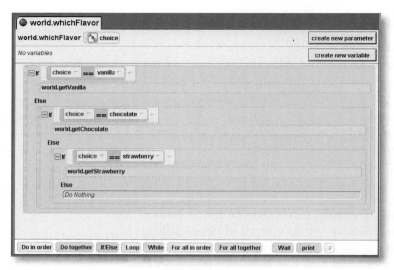

**FIGURE 3-33**

Many computer programming languages have multiple branching instructions for the convenience of programmers using the language, such as the Select Case instruction from Visual Basic, shown in Figure 3-34. Alice does not have an instruction for multiple branching.

```
Select Case FloorNumber
    Case 1, 2
        Elevator.WriteLine("Parking Garage")
    Case 3
        Elevator.WriteLine("Main Lobby")
    Case 4
        Elevator.WriteLine("Ball Room")
    Case 40
        Elevator.WriteLine("Penthouse Suites")
    Case Else
        Elevator.WriteLine("Guest Rooms")
End Select
```

multiple
branching
instructions

**FIGURE 3-34**

# Repetition Sequences — Looping

The algorithms in the branching routines that you have seen so far each split into different paths that all moved forward; nothing was repeated. A loop or repetition sequence is formed whenever a branch in an algorithm leads back to a previous instruction, instead of forward to a new instruction, and part of the algorithm is repeated.

Consider the algorithm described by the flowchart in Figure 3-35 to make the ice skater skate to a flagpole. Inside the loop there is an instruction telling the ice skater to skate forward one step. A separate linear sequence shows that a step occurs when the ice skater pushes with her left foot and then glides two meters on her right foot. The ice skater will continue to push and glide, gently moving across the ice until she is within three meters of the flagpole.

Figure 3-36 shows the Alice instruction tile for this loop. The word While is used for looping instead of the word If that was used for branching. As in many programming languages, this tells the computer to loop back to the conditional expression when the block of code following the While instruction is finished. Each time the condition following the word While is true, the computer will execute the block of code, and then come back to the condition again. When the condition is not true, the block of code will be ignored, much like a binary bypass, and the computer will move on to whatever comes next in the algorithm.

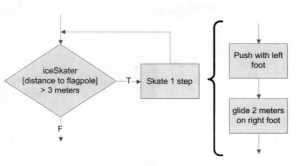

FIGURE 3-35

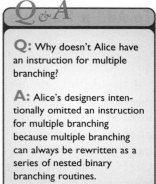

**Q:** Why doesn't Alice have an instruction for multiple branching?

**A:** Alice's designers intentionally omitted an instruction for multiple branching because multiple branching can always be rewritten as a series of nested binary branching routines.

FIGURE 3-36

This loop has a condition that controls whether or not the repetition sequence will be executed. In this loop, the distance to the flagpole is used to keep track of how many times to go through the loop. If the distance to the flagpole is greater than 3, then the instructions in the loop will be executed. When the computer finishes with the instructions in the loop, it will again test to see if the condition is true to determine whether to execute the loop again, or to move on to whatever comes next in the algorithm.

In the next several sets of steps, you will add a flagpole with an American flag to your ice skater world, create a simple method to make the skater glide across the ice, and then use that method inside a loop to make the skater move to the flagpole as part of the closing method. The ice skater will move to a position near the flagpole, but not too close to it.

The flagpole needs to be positioned and doubled in size to be appropriate for this world. You will do this as part of the process of adding the flagpole to the world.

**Q:** What is the primary difference between an IF instruction and a WHILE instruction?

**A:** The IF instruction and the WHILE instruction both contain tests to determine if an instruction set should be executed. In both cases, when the condition is true the instruction set will be executed. The computer then will go on to whatever comes next in an IF instruction, but will loop back to repeat the test again in a WHILE instruction. The instruction set will be ignored when the condition is false in both the IF and WHILE instructions, and in both cases the computer will go on to whatever comes next.

## To Add a Flagpole to the skaterLogic World

**1**

• **If the** skaterLogic **Alice world is not open, locate the world and open it, then click the large green** ADD OBJECTS **button in the lower-right corner of the World window.**

*Alice enters Scene Editor mode, as shown in Figure 3-37.*

**FIGURE 3-37**

**2**

• **Scroll through the** Local Gallery **near the bottom of the interface until you can see the** Objects **folder, shown in Figure 3-38, and then click the tile to open the** Objects **folder.**

*Tiles for the items in the Objects folder are visible in place of the Local Gallery (Figure 3-39).*

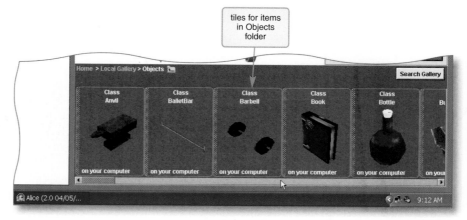

**FIGURE 3-38**

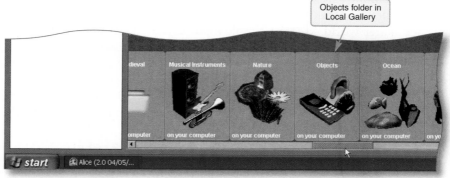

**FIGURE 3-39**

**3**

• **Find and click the** Class Flagpole **tile, shown in Figure 3-40.**

*The Flagpole information dialog box appears (Figure 3-41).*

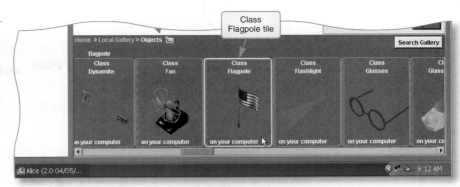

**FIGURE 3-40**

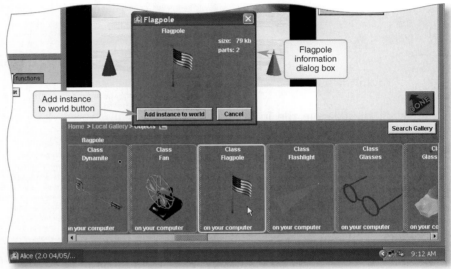

**FIGURE 3-41**

**4**

• **Click the** Add instance to world **button to add an instance of the** Flagpole **class to your world.**

*A flagpole is now visible in the World window, and a flagpole tile has been added to the Object tree (Figure 3-42). If you cannot see the flagpole in your World window, then use the blue camera control arrow keys to find it and then move it so that it is near the iceSkater. Start by pulling the camera back a bit to see more of the world.*

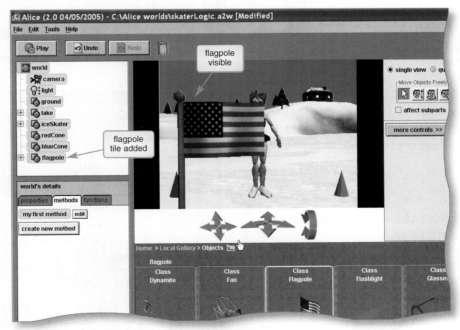

**FIGURE 3-42**

**5**

• **Click the** flagpole **in the World window and drag it back, well behind the skater, as shown in Figure 3-43.**

*The flagpole is in position, behind the iceSkater.*

**FIGURE 3-43**

**6**

• **Right-click the** flagpole **tile in the Object tree and point to** methods **on the menu that appears.**

*A menu of the flagpole's methods appears (Figure 3-44).*

**FIGURE 3-44**

**7**

• **Point to** flagpole resize **on the** methods **menu, then click** 2 (twice as big) **on the** amount **menu.**

*The menus disappear and the flagpole and its flag double in size (Figure 3-45).*

• **Save the world before continuing.**

**FIGURE 3-45**

Next you will create a simple method to make the skater gently glide a single step. She will move one meter while pushing with her left foot, and then glide two meters on her right foot with her left foot raised behind her. To do this, you will need to put the ice skater in a new position, and capture that position as a new pose. The new pose, shown in Figure 3-46, will be called leftFootUp.

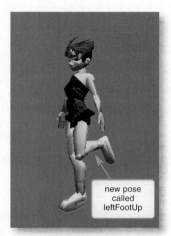

new pose
called
leftFootUp

**FIGURE 3-46**

## To Capture the iceSkater in a New Pose

**1**

• **Click the plus sign next to the** iceSkater **tile in the Object tree to see its subparts, then click the plus sign next to the** leftLeg **tile to see the** leftLeg's **subparts.**

*Tiles for the the iceSkater's subparts and the leftLeg's subparts appear in the Object tree (Figure 3-47).*

iceSkater's
subparts and
leftLeg's subparts

**FIGURE 3-47**

**2**

• **Right-click the** lowerLeg **tile found in the Object tree under the** leftLeg **tile, then point to** methods **on the menu that appears.**

*A menu of the iceSkater.leftLeg.lowerLeg's methods appears (Figure 3-48).*

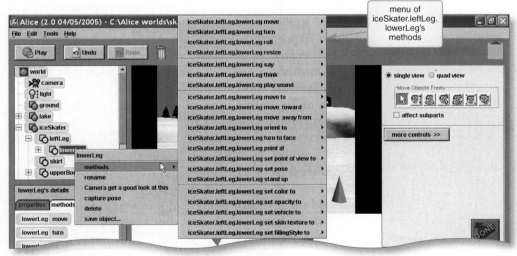

menu of
iceSkater.leftLeg.
lowerLeg's
methods

**FIGURE 3-48**

**3**

• **Point to** iceSkater.leftLeg. lowerLeg turn **on the** methods **menu, point to** forward **on the** direction **menu, and then click** ¼ revolution **on the** amount **menu.**

*The iceSkater's lower-left leg moves into the desired position, with her left knee bent and left foot raised behind her, as shown in Figure 3-49.*

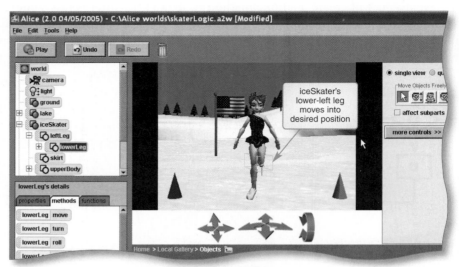

**FIGURE 3-49**

**4**

• **Click the** iceSkater **tile in the Object tree and then click the** properties **tab in the Details area.**

*The iceSkater's properties are visible in the Details area (Figure 3-50).*

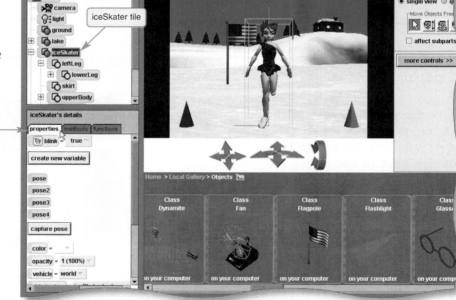

**FIGURE 3-50**

**5**

• **Click the** capture pose **button.**

*A new pose tile appears, with the name pose5 opened for editing (Figure 3-51).*

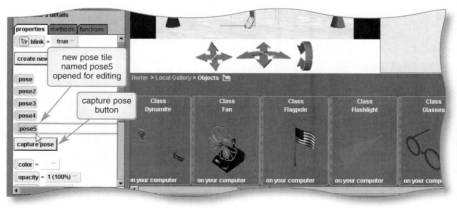

**FIGURE 3-51**

**6**

• **Change the name from** pose5 **to** leftFootUp**, then press the ENTER key.**

*The pose tile now appears on the properties tab, with the name leftFootUp (Figure 3-52).*

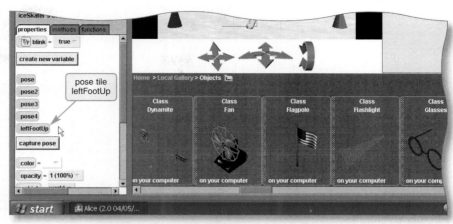

**FIGURE 3-52**

**7**

• **Right-click the** iceSkater **tile in the Object tree, point to** methods **on the menu that appears, and then point to** iceSkater set pose **on the** methods **menu.**

*A menu of the iceSkater's poses appears next to the methods menu (Figure 3-53).*

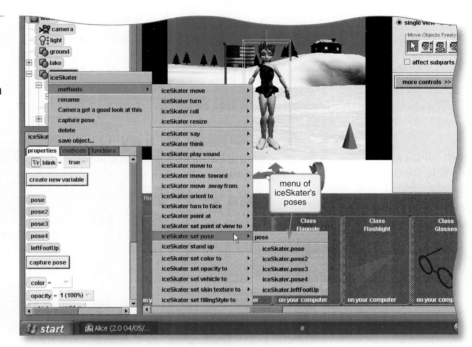

**FIGURE 3-53**

**8**

• **Click** iceSkater.pose **on the** pose **menu.**

*The iceSkater returns to her original pose, with both feet on the ground (Figure 3-54).*

• **Save the world before continuing.**

**FIGURE 3-54**

The new pose that you have captured can now be used to create the new glideStep method for the iceSkater. Figure 3-55 shows what the new method will look like. The iceSkater will start in her original pose, move forward 1 meter while changing to the new leftFootUp pose, then glide forward 2 meters while slowly putting her foot back down.

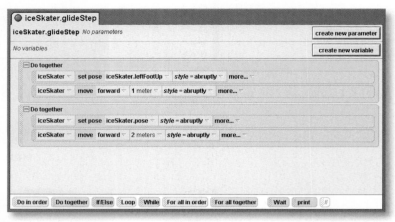

**FIGURE 3-55**

## To Create the New glideStep Method

**1**

• **Click the** iceSkater **tile in the Object tree if it is not already selected, then click the** methods **tab in the Details area.**

*The iceSkater's methods appear in the Details area (Figure 3-56).*

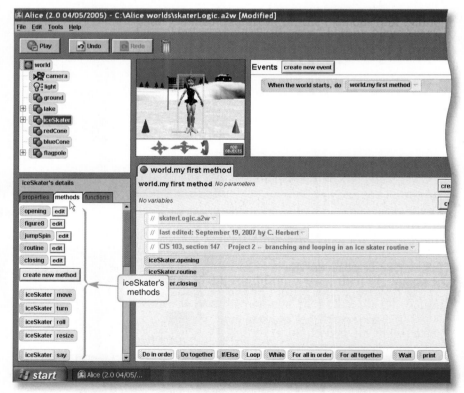

**FIGURE 3-56**

**2**

• **Click the** create new method **button, type** glideStep **in the New Method dialog box that appears, and then click the** OK **button.**

*A new blank method tab for the iceSkater.glideStep method appears in the Editor area (Figure 3-57). If you were still in Scene Editor mode, notice that you have been returned to the standard Alice interface.*

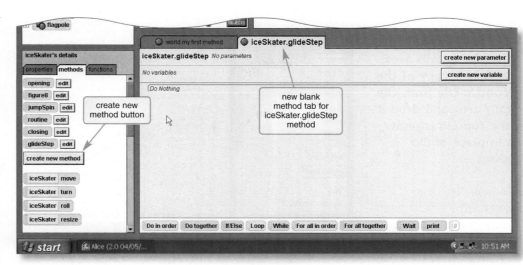

**FIGURE 3-57**

**3**

• **Drag a blank** Do together **tile from the bottom of the Editor area and drop it in the new method in place of Do Nothing.**

*A blank Do together tile appears in the method (Figure 3-58).*

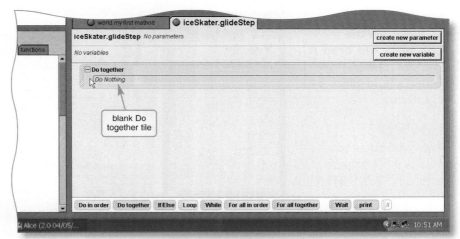

**FIGURE 3-58**

**4**

• **Right-click the** Do together **tile and click** make copy **on the menu that appears.**

*There are now two blank Do together tiles, one above the other, in the new method (Figure 3-59).*

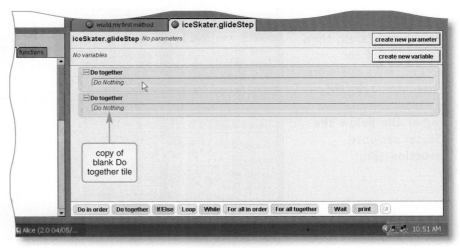

**FIGURE 3-59**

**5**

• **Click the** properties **tab in the Details area, then drag a copy of the** leftFootUp **tile from the Details area and drop it in the top** Do together **tile in place of** Do Nothing.

*An iceSkater set pose iceSkater.leftFootUp instruction appears in the top Do together tile (Figure 3-60).*

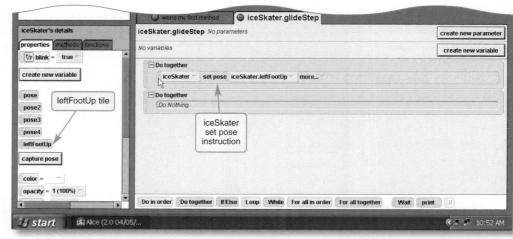

**FIGURE 3-60**

**6**

• **Drag a copy of the** pose **tile from the Details area and drop it in the bottom** Do together **tile in place of** Do Nothing.

*An iceSkater set pose iceSkater.pose instruction appears in the bottom Do together tile (Figure 3-61).*

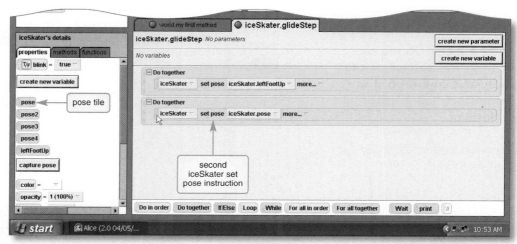

**FIGURE 3-61**

**7**

• **Click the** methods **tab in the Details area, then drag a copy of the** iceSkater move **tile from the** methods **tab and drop it in the top** Do together **tile below the** iceSkater set pose **instruction tile.**

*A direction menu appears (Figure 3-62).*

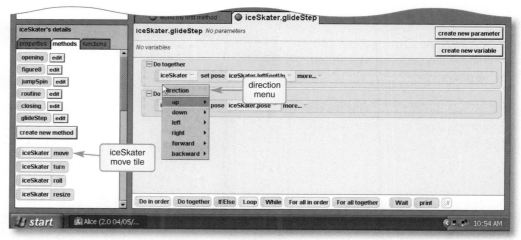

**FIGURE 3-62**

**8**

• **Point to** forward **on the** direction **menu, then click** 1 meter **on the** amount **menu.**

*An iceSkater move forward 1 meter instruction appears in the top Do together tile below the iceSkater set pose iceSkater.leftFootUp tile (Figure 3-63).*

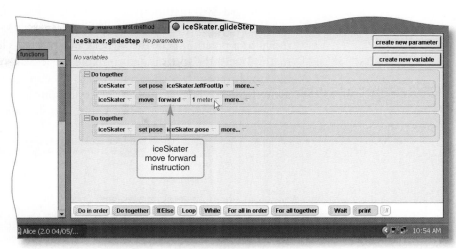

**FIGURE 3-63**

**9**

• **Drag another copy of the** iceSkater move **tile from the** methods **tab and this time drop it in the bottom** Do together **tile below the** iceSkater set pose iceSkater.pose **instruction tile. Point to** forward **on the** direction **menu, click** other... **on the** amount **menu, type** 2 **in the Custom Number dialog box, and then click** OK.

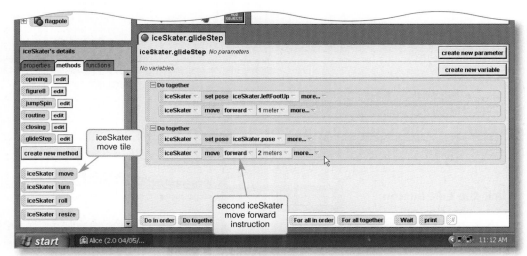

**FIGURE 3-64**

*An iceSkater move forward 2 meters instruction tile appears in the bottom Do together tile, below the iceSkater set pose iceSkater.pose tile (Figure 3-64).*

**10**

• **One at a time, click** more **on each of the four instruction tiles inside the two** Do together **tiles, and add** Style = abruptly **to each of the instructions.**

*The two instructions in the top Do together tile and the two instructions in the bottom Do together tile each have the style parameter set to abruptly (Figure 3-65).*

• **Save the world before continuing.**

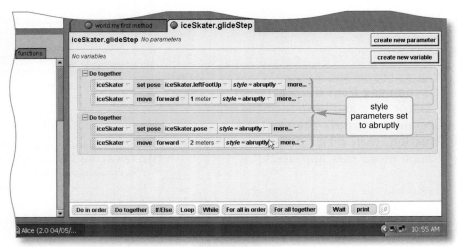

**FIGURE 3-65**

The glideStep method is now complete and can be used inside a while loop in the closing methods to make the iceSkater skate gently over to the flagpole. The skater will move to a position near the flagpole, but not too close to it. Figure 3-66 shows the closing method with the loop added to make the iceSkater skate to the flagpole. First she turns to face the flagpole, then she continues to execute glide steps while she is more than 3 meters away from the flagpole. When the condition iceSkater distance to flagpole > 3 meters is no longer true, the loop will stop. You'll add this while loop next.

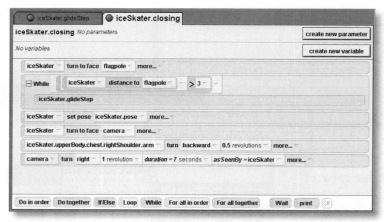

**FIGURE 3-66**

## To Add a While Loop to the closing Method

**1**

• **Click the** edit **button next to the** closing **method tile in the Details area.**

*The iceSkater.closing method opens in the Editor area (Figure 3-67).*

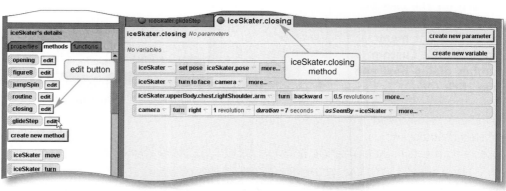

**FIGURE 3-67**

**2**

• **Drag a copy of the** While **instruction tile from the bottom of the Editor area and drop it in the** closing **method above the first instruction, then click** true **on the** condition **menu that appears.**

*A blank While true instruction tile appears as the first instruction in the closing method (Figure 3-68).*

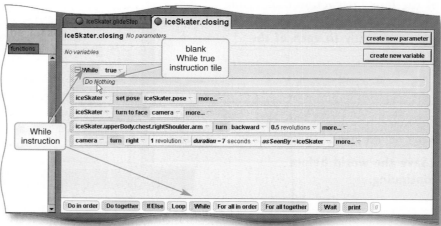

**FIGURE 3-68**

**3**

• **Click the** world **tile in the Object tree and then click the** functions **tab in the Details area.**

*The world-level functions are now visible in the Details area (Figure 3-69).*

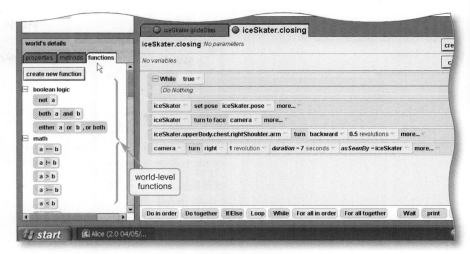

**FIGURE 3-69**

**4**

• **Drag a copy of the math function** a > b **and drop it in the** While **instruction tile in place of the word** true **that follows the word** While.

*A menu appears, allowing you to choose a value for a (Figure 3-70).*

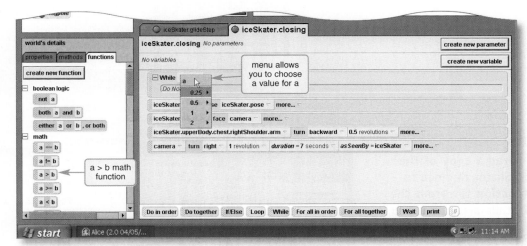

**FIGURE 3-70**

**5**

• **Point to 1 on the** a **menu and then click 3 on the** b **menu. If 3 is not available on the** b **menu, click** other..., **type 3 in the** Custom Number **dialog box, and then click** OK.

*The condition in the While instruction now reads 1 > 3 (Figure 3-71).*

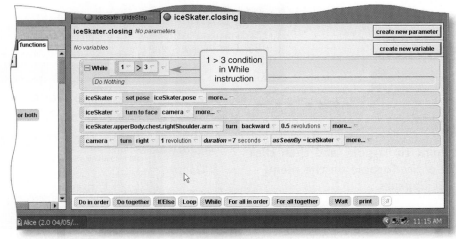

**FIGURE 3-71**

**6**

• **Click the** iceSkater **tile in the Object tree.**

*The iceSkater's functions are now visible in the Details area (Figure 3-72).*

**FIGURE 3-72**

**7**

• **Drag a copy of the** iceSkater distance to **function tile from the Details area and drop it into the** While **instruction in place of the value** 1 **in the condition** 1 > 3.

*An object menu appears (Figure 3-73).*

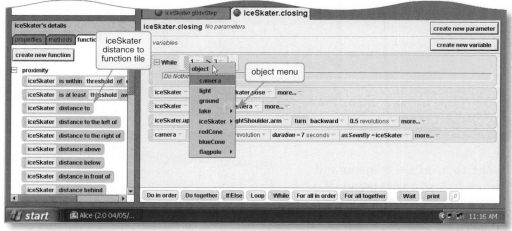

**FIGURE 3-73**

**8**

• **Point to** flagpole, **and then click the entire** flagpole **on the menu that appears.**

*The condition in the While instruction now reads iceSkater distance to flagpole >3 (Figure 3-74).*

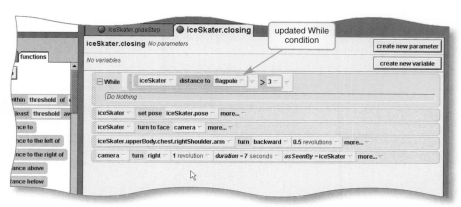

**FIGURE 3-74**

**9**

- **Click the** methods **tab in the Details area, then drag a copy of the** glideStep **method and drop it into the** While **instruction in place of** Do Nothing.

*The loop now contains the glideStep method tile (Figure 3-75).*

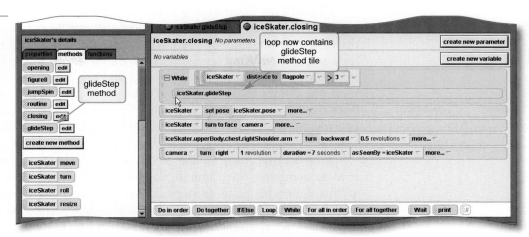

**FIGURE 3-75**

**10**

- **One instruction is needed before the loop. Drag a copy of the** iceSkater turn to face **method from the Details area and drop it in the** iceSkater.closing **method as the first instruction (above the** While **loop). Point to** flagpole **on the** target **menu, and then click** the entire flagpole **on the menu that appears.**

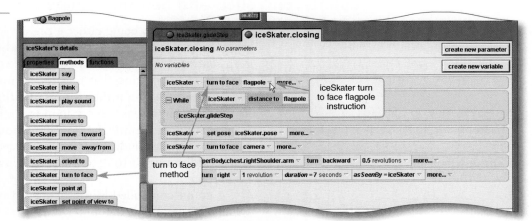

**FIGURE 3-76**

*The method now contains an iceSkater turn to face flagpole instruction (Figure 3-76).*

- **Save the world before continuing.**

---

The While loop that you have just added to the **skaterLogic** world is an example of a pretest sentinel loop. Every loop is either a pretest loop or a posttest loop, and every loop is either a count-controlled loop or a sentinel loop that is not count controlled. In this section you will read about these characteristics of loops, then add a count-controlled loop to the **skaterLogic** world.

## Pretest and Posttest loops

The set of instructions to be repeated in a loop is called the body of the loop. It could be just one instruction or many instructions. Every loop, except for an infinite loop that never ends, has a condition to test whether or not the body of the loop should be executed. This test can occur before or after the body of the loop. The loop is a pretest loop if the test comes before the body of the loop, and a posttest loop if the test comes after the body of the loop, as shown in Figure 3-77.

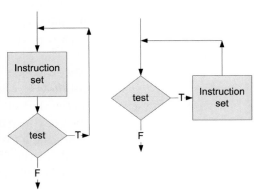

**FIGURE 3-77**

The difference between a pretest loop and a posttest loop is subtle but significant. The body of a pretest loop will not be executed if the test is negative the first time it is encountered. The body of a posttest loop is always executed at least once, even if the test is negative the first time through the repetition sequence, since the test doesn't occur until after the body of the loop. In the case of a pretest-loop, the computer asks "Should I do this?" and, if the answer is yes, the computer does the instruction and then asks "Should I do this again?". In the case of a posttest loop, the computer does something without asking first, and then asks "Should I do that again?".

A **while** instruction, similar to the one in the loop you implemented above, is used in most computer programming languages for pretest loops. Some languages also have an instruction for posttest loops; however, many computer scientists suggest that all loops should be set up as pretest loops and that posttest loops should not be used. Alice does not contain an instruction for a posttest loop.

## Count-Controlled and Sentinel Loops

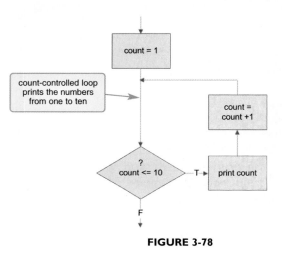

**FIGURE 3-78**

In addition to being either a pretest loop or a posttest loop, every loop in a computer program is either a count-controlled loop or a sentinel loop that is not count controlled. A sentinel is a marker or a condition that tells the computer when to stop executing a loop. Every loop that is not an infinite loop must have such a sentinel—so in a sense, every loop is a sentinel loop. In the **While** loop that you added to the **closing** method, shown previously in Figure 3-70, the condition **iceSkater distance to flagpole > 3** is the sentinel condition used to determine whether or not the loop should be executed.

A count-controlled loop is a special type of sentinel loop in which the sentinel is a counter that is not allowed to go beyond a certain value. A counter is a variable that is updated each time the program runs through the loop. Figure 3-78 shows a count-controlled loop that prints the numbers from 1 to 10.

A counter must have an initial value, a final value, and an increment. A count-controlled loop has four parts, as follows:

- **Initialization** — an instruction that sets the first value of the control variable
- **Test** — the instruction that looks at the control variable to see if the loop should be executed
- **Processing** — the instruction or set of instructions to be repeated inside the loop
- **Update** — an instruction that changes the value of the control variable each time through the loop.

In the loop shown in Figure 3-78, the initial value is 1, the final value is 10, and the increment is 1. The loop starts with the counter equal to 1, adds 1 to the counter each time though the loop, and ends after the counter reaches 10.

The while instruction can be used in Alice to create a count-controlled loop, but Alice also has a special instruction, the **Loop** instruction, used specifically for creating count-controlled loops. The **Loop** instruction can be viewed in a simple version or in a complicated version. Figure 3-79 shows a loop in Alice using the simple version of the **Loop** instruction. The simple version shows only one parameter, the number of times the loop is to be repeated. The counter, initial value, and final value are all hidden from the user and handled internally by the instruction. This is an example of encapsulation, which was discussed briefly in Project 1.

The **Loop** instruction's control variable, named **index**, along with its initial value, final value, and increment can be seen in Figure 3-80, which shows the complicated version of the same loop instruction shown in Figure 3-79. You can see that the index starts at zero, increases by 1 each time through the loop, and stops before reaching the final value of 3. So, if you instructed the loop to do something 3 times, it would do it once with the loop index set to 0, once with the loop index set to 1, and once with the loop index set to 2, but it would stop before reaching 3. Elementary school children learn that the counting numbers start with 1, but it is very common for computers to start counting at 0.

In the next set of steps, you will use the simple version of the **Loop** instruction to add a count-controlled loop to the skater's **routine** method to make her repeat the figure eight three times. Figure 3-81 shows what the finished **skaterLogic** routine should look like.

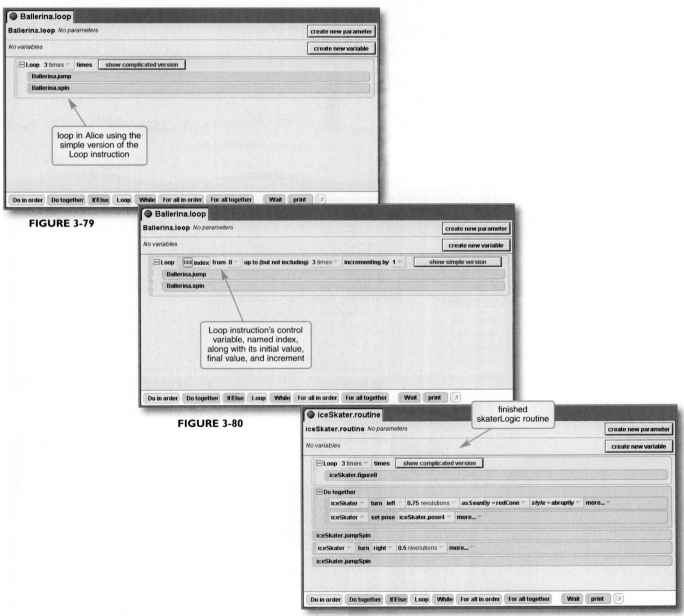

**FIGURE 3-79**

**FIGURE 3-80**

**FIGURE 3-81**

# To Add a Count-Controlled Loop to the Routine Method

**1**

• **If necessary, click the** iceSkater **tile in the Object tree and then click the** methods **tab in the Details area.**

*The iceSkater's methods are visible in the Details area (Figure 3-82).*

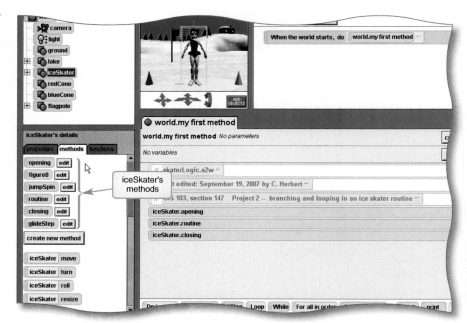

**FIGURE 3-82**

**2**

• **Click the** edit **button next to the** routine **tile in the Details area.**

*The iceSkater.routine method opens in the Editor area (Figure 3-83).*

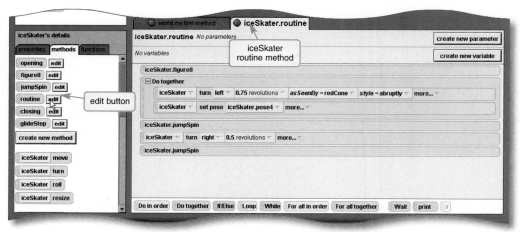

**FIGURE 3-83**

**3**

• **Drag a copy of the** Loop **instruction tile from the bottom of the Editor area and drop it in the** iceSkater.routine **method above the** iceSkater.figure8 **tile.**

*An end menu appears, asking you for the final value of the loop index, which is the number of times the loop is to be repeated (Figure 3-84).*

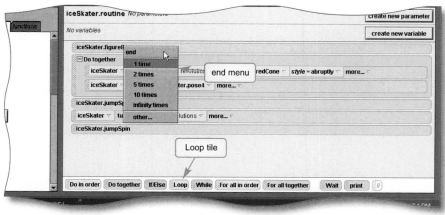

**FIGURE 3-84**

**4**

• **Click** other... **on the end menu, type** 3 **in the Custom Number dialog box, and then click the OK button.**

*A blank Loop tile appears in the method, with the value 3 as the number of times the loop is to be repeated (Figure 3-85).*

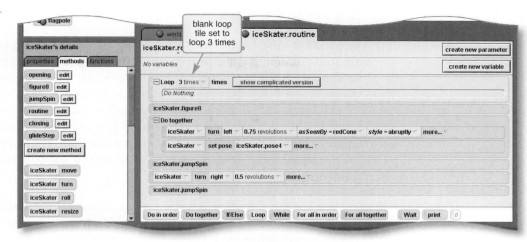

**FIGURE 3-85**

**5**

• **Drag the** iceSkater.figure8 **instruction tile from below the** Loop **instruction tile and drop it into the** Loop **instruction in place of** Do Nothing.

*The Loop tile now contains the iceSkater.figure8 instruction (Figure 3-86).*

• **Save the world again before continuing.**

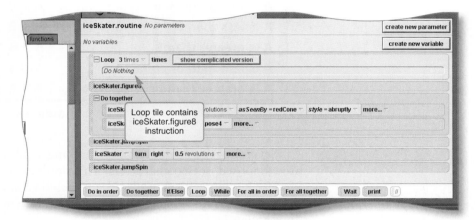

**FIGURE 3-86**

The modified routine method is now complete and ready for testing. The skater should complete her figure eight three times before starting the part of her routine in which she jumps and spins. To test the method, simply run the world and observe whether or not this happens. If it does, then you can move on. If not, find and fix your errors before continuing.

## Boolean Logic

The true-or-false conditions that exist in selection sequences and repetition sequences are most often a comparison of two values, such as the expression iceSkater distance to flagpole > 3. If the distance from the iceSkater to the flagpole is greater than 3, the condition will be true; otherwise, the condition will be false.

The symbol ">" in the above example stands for "is greater than." There are six such logical comparison operators used in mathematics and computer programming: equals, is not equal to, is less than, is greater than, is less than or equal to, and is greater than or equal to. Figure 3-87 shows the symbols most commonly used for these operators.

| Condition | In Mathematics | In Computer Programming |
|---|---|---|
| A equals B | A = B | A = B or A == B |
| A does not equal B | A ≠ B | A <> B or A != B |
| A is less than B | A < B | A < B |
| A is greater than B | A > B | A > B |
| A is less than or equal to B | A ≤ B | A <= B |
| A is greater than or equal to B | A ≥ B | A >= B |

**FIGURE 3-87**

*More About*

**Boolean Logic**

Boolean logic is the basis for all modern digital electronic technology. To read an article about how computers implement Boolean logic, visit http://computer.howstuffworks.com/boolean.htm. In 1858, Boole's original book was republished as *An Investigation of the Laws of Thought*. Copies of the 1973 reprint of this edition can still be found in many bookstores and online. The complete text of an 1848 paper by Boole titled "The Calculus of Logic" is available on the Web at www.maths.tcd.ie/pub/HistMath/People/Boole/CalcLogic. The site is maintained by the University of Dublin's Trinity College School of Mathematics. They also maintain links to information about George Boole at www.maths.tcd.ie/pub/HistMath/People/Boole.

Several of the computer programming symbols, such as " < > " for "not equals," are composed of two characters. This doubling of characters is required because modern computer keyboards do not include a single symbol for these comparison operators, in contrast to standard algebra, in which the symbol ≠ is often used for "not equals".

In 1854, a mathematician named George Boole outlined a system of logic and a corresponding algebraic language in which the only values used are true and false. Today that type of logic is called Boolean logic, and his language is called Boolean algebra. The true-or-false conditions that exist in branching and looping routines are a form of Boolean logic. Boolean logic has three basic operations: AND, OR, and NOT, as described in Figure 3-88.

| AND | OR | NOT |
|---|---|---|
| true ***and*** true = true | true ***or*** true = true | ***not*** true = false |
| true ***and*** false = false | true ***or*** false = true | ***not*** false = true |
| false ***and*** true = false | false ***or*** true = true | |
| false ***and*** false = false | false ***or*** false = false | |

**FIGURE 3-88**

The AND and OR operations are binary operations, meaning that they need two operands. When two values are combined in the **AND** operation, the result is true only if both values are true. Otherwise, the result is false. In the **OR** operation, the result is true if either of the two values is true.

The **NOT** operation is a unary operation, which means that it works on only one operand. It simply reverses the true or false value of its operand. In other words, NOT true yields false and NOT false yields true.

The Boolean operations AND, OR, and NOT can be combined with the six logical comparison operators to create compound logical expressions. Consider the following instruction: If month = December AND day of the month = 22 then iceSkater say "Today is the shortest day of the year." You will add this instruction to the opening method in the following set of steps. Rather than starting from scratch, you will copy one of the existing If/Else instructions and modify it to build the new instruction.

## To Add a Compound Boolean Expression to the opening Method

**1**

• **If necessary, click the** iceSkater **tile in the Object tree, click the** methods **tab in the Details area, and then click the** edit **button next to the** opening **tile on the** methods **tab.**

*The iceSkater's opening method is visible in the Editor area (Figure 3-89).*

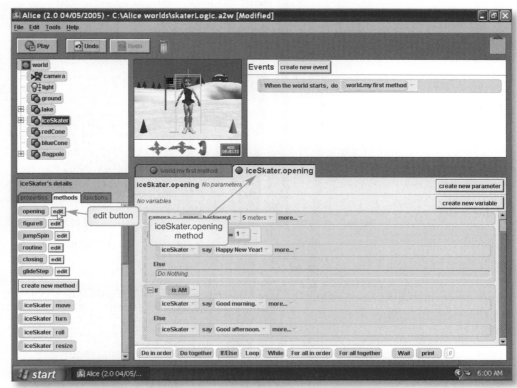

**FIGURE 3-89**

**2**

• **Right-click the** If/Else **tile with the condition** If day of the year == 1 **and select** make copy **from the menu that appears. Be sure to click the background of the tile itself and not one of the parameter boxes inside the tile.**

*A second copy of the If/Else tile appears below the first (Figure 3-90).*

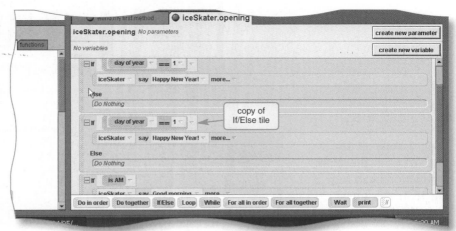

**FIGURE 3-90**

**3**

• **Select the** world **tile in the Object tree and then click the** functions **tab in the Details area.**

*The Boolean logic and mathematical comparison tiles appear as shown in Figure 3-91.*

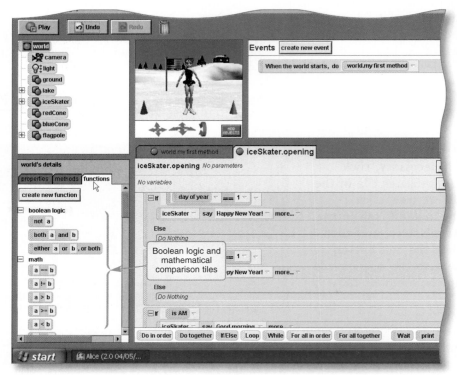

**FIGURE 3-91**

**4**

• **Scroll down in the** functions **tab until the time functions are visible.**

*The time functions are now visible on the functions tab (Figure 3-92).*

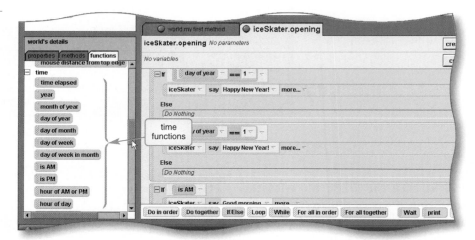

**FIGURE 3-92**

**5**

• **Drag a copy of the** month of year **tile from the** functions **tab and drop it in the new** If/Else **tile in place of** day of year.

*The condition now reads month of year == 1 (Figure 3-93).*

**FIGURE 3-93**

**6**

• **Click the value** 1 **in the** month of year == 1 **condition, click** other... **on the menu that appears, type** 12 **in the Custom Number dialog box, and then click the** Okay **button.**

*The method should now contain an instruction that reads If month of year == 12 (Figure 3-94).*

**FIGURE 3-94**

**7**

• **Drag a copy of the Boolean function** both a and b**, and drop it in the new** If/Else **instruction tile in place of the condition** month of year == 12.

*A menu appears, allowing you to choose a value for b (Figure 3-95).*

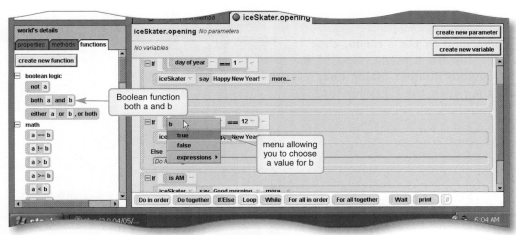

**FIGURE 3-95**

**8**

• **Click** true **on the** b **menu.**

*The condition in the If/Else instruction now reads both month of year == 12 and true (Figure 3-96).*

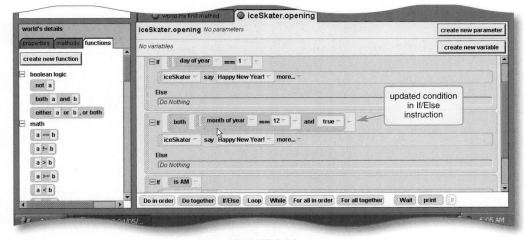

**FIGURE 3-96**

**9**

• **Drag a copy of the** a == b **function tile and drop it carefully in place of** true **in the** both month of year == 12 and true **condition.**

*A menu appears asking you for the value of a (Figure 3-97)*

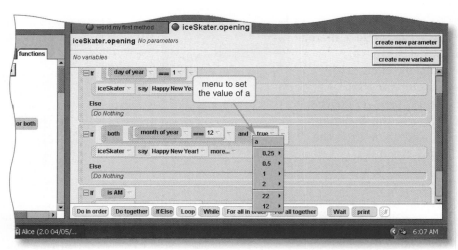

**FIGURE 3-97**

**10**

• **Point to** 1 **on the** a **menu, click** other... **on the** b **menu, type** 22 **in the Custom Number dialog box, and then click the** Okay **button.**

*The condition in the If/Else instruction now reads both month of year == 12 and 1 = 22. (Figure 3-98)*

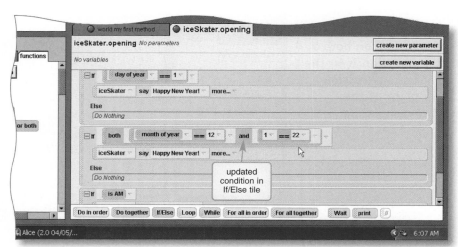

**FIGURE 3-98**

**11**

• **Drag a copy of the** day of month **function from the Details area and drop it in the condition** both month of year == 12 and 1 = 22 **in place of the value 1.**

*The condition in the If/Else instruction now reads both month of year == 12 and day of month = 22 (Figure 3-99).*

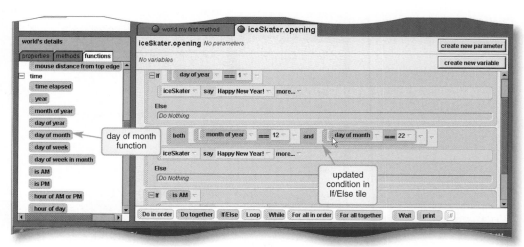

**FIGURE 3-99**

**12**

• **Click the arrow at the end of the** Happy New Year! **parameter in the** If both month of year == 12 and day of month = 22 iceSkater say Happy New Year! **instruction tile, click** other... **on the menu that appears, and then type** Today is the shortest day of the year. **in the** Enter a string **text box. Click the** OK **button.**

*The If/Else instruction is now complete and should read If both month of year == 12 and day of month = 22 iceSkater say Today is the shortest day of the year. (Figure 3-100).*

• **Save the world and exit Alice.**

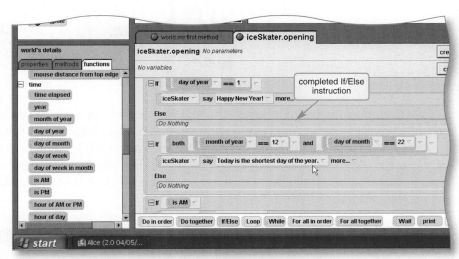

**FIGURE 3-100**

## Project Summary

In this project, you added branching and looping to the ice skater's routine. You learned that these are examples of the elements of logical structure, which are the building blocks of algorithms. You learned that there are three different elements of logical structure: linear sequences, selection sequences, and repetition sequences.

You learned that a linear sequence must be complete, correct, and in the correct order; that a binary selection sequence may be either a binary bypass or a binary choice; and that a repetition sequence is either a pretest loop or a posttest loop. You also learned that some loops are count controlled while others are not, and that a count-controlled loop must have a counter with an initial value, a final value, and an increment.

You saw that simple flowcharts composed of just three symbols can be used to show the structure of algorithms.

You learned that the conditions inside branching and looping instructions are most often comparisons of values using the six logical comparison operations: equals, not equals, less than, less than or greater than, greater than, and greater than or equal to. You also learned that they may be combined with the Boolean operators AND, OR, and NOT to form compound logical expressions.

Finally, you learned how to include branching and looping in Alice methods by using the If/Else instruction tile, the While instruction tile, the comparison functions, and the Boolean logic functions built into Alice.

## What You Should Know

Having completed this project, you should be able to:

1. Create a New World from an Existing World (AL 135)
2. Update the Identifying Comments in a World (AL 136)
3. Add a Binary Bypass to a Method (AL 141)
4. Add a Binary Choice to a Method (AL 144)
5. Add an Object to an Alice World (AL 150)
6. Capture an Object in a New Pose (AL 153)
7. Create a New Method (AL 156)
8. Add a While Loop to a Method (AL 160)
9. Add a Count-Controlled Loop to a Method (AL 166)
10. Add a Compound Boolean Expression to a Method (AL 169)

# Apply Your Knowledge

## 1 Jumping in Wonderland

Alice has a world-level function to ask the user a yes-or-no question. In this exercise you will add two questions to world.my first method in an Alice world with Alice, the White Rabbit, and the Chesire Cat from *Alice's Adventures in Wonderland*. First, the method will ask if the user wants Alice to jump. If the answer is yes, then Alice will jump. If the answer is no, the method will ask if the user wants the White Rabbit to jump. If the second answer is yes, the White Rabbit will jump; if the answer is no, then the Cheshire Cat will jump. Figure 3-101 shows the Alice code for this routine.

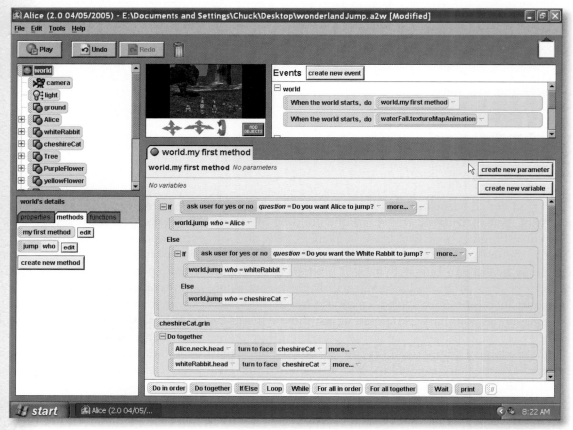

**FIGURE 3-101**

### Instructions:

1. Start Alice. Open the file, Apply 3 wonderlandJump.a2w, from the Data Files for Students. See the inside back cover of this book for instructions for downloading the Data Files for Students, or see your instructor for information about accessing the files required in this book.
2. Play the world to see what happens.
3. Add an If/Else instruction to world.my first method below the three world.jump instructions but before cheshireCat.grin. To do this, drag a copy of the If/Else tile from the bottom of the Editor area and drop it into the method just below the three jump instructions.
4. Select true on the menu that appears.

# Apply Your Knowledge

5. Select the world tile in the Object tree, and then click the functions tab in the Details area. Scroll through the list of functions and find the ask user for yes or no function. Drag and drop a copy of this function into the If/Else tile in place of true following the word If.

6. On the menu that appears, click other... to open the Enter a String dialog box. The character string you enter will be the question the user will see. Type Do you want Alice to jump? as the string, and then click the OK button. The question will now appear as the condition for the If/Else instruction.

7. Drag the world.jump who = Alice tile and drop it into the If/Else instruction in place of Do Nothing, immediately below If and above the word Else.

8. If the user answers "no" to the first question, he or she should see a second question. Drag another If/Else tile from the bottom of the Editor area and drop it in place of Do Nothing following the word Else in the first If/Else tile. Click true when the menu appears. You now have nested If/Else instructions, one inside the other.

9. You need to put another question in place of true in the second (nested) If/Else instruction. Again, drag a copy of the ask user for yes or no function and drop it into the second If/Else tile in place of true following the word If.

10. Click other... on the menu that appears, type Do you want the White Rabbit to jump?, and then click the OK button. Your second question will now appear in the If/Else tile in place of true as the condition for the If/Else instruction.

11. If the user answers "yes," the whiteRabbit should jump. Drag the world.jump who = whiteRabbit tile and drop it in the instruction in place of Do Nothing, below the If clause and above the word Else.

12. Drag the world.jump who = cheshireCat tile, and drop it in the instruction in place of Do Nothing below the word Else.

13. The method is complete and should match Figure 3-101 above. Save the world with the name, Apply 3 wonderland jump.a2w, and then test it to see if it works as expected.

# In the Lab

## 1 Japanese Dance Routine

An Ougi Mai is an ancient Japanese dance performed with fans made from bamboo and silk in gratitude for the land and to honor one's ancestors. Each dancer's Ougi Mai is unique, but all of the dancers follow certain rules, moving in circles and trying to keep their bodies very still except for a few fan movements. In this exercise you will create an Ougi Mai routine for the Japanese fan dancer that appeared in the In the Lab 1-1 exercise. Each morning and evening she performs the same Ougi Mai.

You will start with an existing Alice world that includes a dancer and the environment in which she will dance. The dancer's properties tab has four poses that she may assume. The world already has an entrance method and a method to make the dancer bow. Your task is to modify the world so that she will perform her routine. You will add a branching routine and a count-controlled loop to the world.

**Instructions:** Start Alice and open the file, Lab 3-1 fan dancer.a2w. The dancer is not visible on the screen because she did not make her entrance yet. Play the world to see her entrance, then click the Stop button after she makes her bow.

First, modify world.my first method so that the dancer will greet us before starting her dance.

*(continued)*

## Japanese Dance Routine *(continued)*

1. world.my first method should be visible in the Editor area. Drag a copy of the If/Else tile from the bottom of the Editor area and drop it in world.my first method below the two existing instructions. Select true from the menu that appears.
2. Select the world tile in the Object tree, click the functions tab in the Details area, and then scroll down to find the is AM function. Drag a copy of it from the functions tab and drop it in the new If/Else tile in place of true.
3. Click the fanDancer tile in the Object tree, click the methods tab in the Details area, and then drag a copy of the fanDancer say tile from the methods tab and drop it in the new If/Else tile in place of Do Nothing, just below the word If.
4. Select other... on the menu that appears, then type I will now perform my morning Ougi Mai. in the Enter a string text box and click OK.
5. Drag another copy of the fanDancer say tile from the methods tab and drop it in the new If/Else tile in place of Do Nothing just below the word Else.
6. Select other... from the menu, then enter I will now perform my evening Ougi Mai. in the Enter a string text box and click OK.
7. On each of the fanDancer say tiles, click more... and change the duration to 2 seconds.

Your initial changes to world.my first method are complete. Next, create the dancer's routine method.

1. Click the create new method button on the methods tab, then type the name routine in the New method dialog box and click the OK button.
2. Drag a copy of the Loop instruction tile from the bottom of the Editor area and drop it in the fanDancer.routine method in place of Do Nothing.
3. Click other... on the menu that appears, then use the Custom Number dialog box to enter 3 as the ending value for the loop.
4. Drag a copy of the Do together tile from the bottom of the Editor area and drop it into the loop tile in place of Do Nothing.
5. Drag a fanDancer turn method tile from the methods tab and drop it into the Do together tile, in place of Do Nothing. Select left and then 1 revolution from the menus that appear.
6. Click the more... parameter box on the new fanDancer turn instruction tile and set the duration to 4 seconds.
7. Click the more... parameter box again and change asSeenBy to lantern2, the entire lantern2.
8. Click the properties tab, then drag a copy of the left arm up tile and drop it in the Do together tile below the fanDancer turn instruction.
9. Right-click the Do together tile and select make copy from the menu that appears. Make sure to select the Do together tile by clicking on its purple background area.
10. Click the appropriate parameter boxes and make the following changes in the bottom copy of the Do together tile:
    - Change the direction in the fanDancer turn tile from left to right.
    - Change the as seen by target in the fanDancer turn tile from lantern2 to lantern1, the entire lantern1.
    - Change the pose in the fanDancer set pose tile from fanDancer.left arm up to fanDancer.right arm up.

The routine method is now complete. Complete the project by further modifying world.my first method to call routine and make the dancer bow when her routine is finished.

# In the Lab

1. Click the tab on the world.my first method tile in the Editor area to reveal the method.
2. Click the methods tab in the Details area, then drag a copy of the routine tile from the methods tab and drop it in world.my first method below the existing instructions.
3. Drag a copy of the bow tile from the methods tab and drop it in world.my first method below the routine tile.
4. Click the properties tab, then drag a copy of the arms down tile and drop it in the method below the routine instruction but above the bow instruction that you just added to the method.

The world is now complete. Save the world with the filename, Lab 3-1 fan dancer routine.a2w, then play the world to see the dancer perform her Ougi Mai.

## 2 Jumping Ballerinas

**Problem:** Your task is to modify the five ballerina worlds supplied with the data files for this book to include a loop to make the ballerinas each jump a certain number of times. You will use the Loop instruction to make the ballerinas jump up and down three times. One ballerina, Bronwyn, will jump up and down with the height of the jump equal to the index for the loop. The other four will jump up and down 1 meter each time through the loop. Figure 3-102 shows what the finished method will look like.

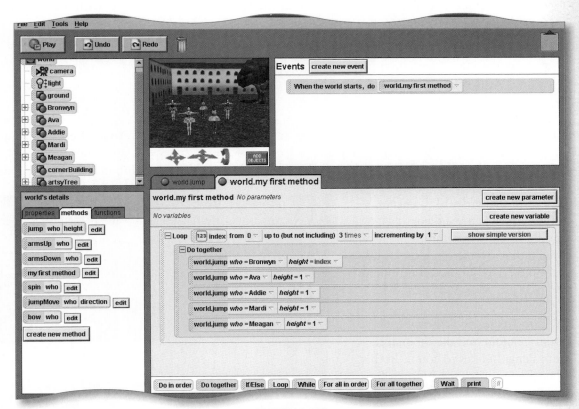

**FIGURE 3-102**

*(continued)*

## In the Lab

### Jumping Ballerinas *(continued)*

1. Start Alice. Open the file, Lab 3-2 five ballerinas.a2w, from the Data Files for Students. See the inside back cover of this book for instructions for downloading the Data Files for Students, or see your instructor for information about accessing the files required in this book.
2. Play the world to see how it works.
3. Open the method world.myfirst method for editing.
4. Drag a copy of the Loop instruction tile from the bottom of the Editor area and drop it in the method below the Do together instructions.
5. Select other... from the menu that appears and then use the Custom Number dialog box to enter the value 3 as the number of times to repeat the loop.
6. Drag the Do together instruction tile from above the loop and drop it into the loop in place of Do Nothing.
7. Click the show complicated version button on the Loop instruction tile to reveal the details of the Loop instruction.
8. Drag the index parameter tile in the loop instruction and drop it in the world.jump who = Bronwyn height = 1 instruction in place of the height parameter.
9. Your changes are complete and the method should match Figure 3-102. Test your method before continuing, to see if it functions as expected. Remember that the value of the index starts with 0 and stops before reaching 3.
10. Save your file with the name, Lab 3-2 five ballerinas jumping.a2w.

## 3 Fibonacci Penguin

What is the next number in this sequence: 1, 1, 2, 3, 5, 8, 13...? The answer is 21. You get each new number in the sequence by adding the previous two numbers: 1 + 1 = 2, 1 + 2 = 3, 2 + 3 = 5, and so on to 8 + 13 = 21. The next number after 21 will be 13 + 21, which is 34. This is the world-famous Fibonacci sequence, described by the Italian mathematician Leonardo Fibonacci of Pisa in the early 13th century. Numbers in the sequence are called Fibonacci numbers. They are important in many fields, including architecture, art, biology, and economics. The Fibonacci numbers less than 100 are 1, 2, 3, 5, 8, 13, 21, 34, 55, and 89.

Your task is to create a world with two penguins: Count Penguin and the Fibonacci Penguin. Count Penguin likes to count. In this Alice world he will count from 1 up to 100. The Fibonacci Penguin is fascinated by Fibonacci numbers. He will jump up and down and say "Fibonacci! Fibonacci! That's a Fibonacci number!" every time Count Penguin gets to a Fibonacci number. Figure 3-103 shows the Fibonacci Penguin reacting to Count Penguin.

**FIGURE 3-103**

In the Lab

You will create a world with a loop to count from 1 up to 100, and a series of If/Else instructions, similar to the following, to check for Fibonacci numbers:

```
If index = 21
    FibonacciPenguin.react
Else
    Do nothing
```

The program is actually a very simple one, with no mathematical calculations involved, simply a loop to go from 1 to 100, with a series of If/Else instructions inside the loop. There are 10 Fibonacci counting numbers less than 100, so your program will have 10 If/Else instructions to check for each of these 10 Fibonacci numbers.

You will start a world with the two penguins, create a react method for the Fibonacci Penguin, then put a loop in world.my first method to make Count Penguin count up to 100. The loop will also have 10 If/Else instructions to test each number to see if it is in the Fibonacci sequence. Your finished world will be a short one, and this exercise should progress fairly quickly.

First, create the scene for your new world.

1. Start Alice and open a new world with the snow template.
2. Enter Scene Editor mode and add a penguin to your world.
3. Right-click the penguin tile in the Object tree and rename it CountPenguin.
4. Move CountPenguin slightly to his left so that he is about halfway between the center and left edge of the World window.
5. Right-click CountPenguin and then run a method to make it turn to face the camera.
6. Add a second penguin to your world and rename it FibonacciPenguin.
7. Move the FibonacciPenguin slightly to its right so that he is about halfway between the center and right edges of the world window.
8. Right-click the FibonacciPenguin and then run a method to make it turn to face the camera.
9. Click the DONE button to exit Scene Editor mode and then save your world with the filename, Lab 3-3 Fibonacci penguin, before continuing.

Next, create a method to make the FibonacciPenguin react when he hears CountPenguin say a number that is a Fibonacci number. You will use this method in If/Else instructions that you will place in world.my first method.

1. Click the FibonacciPenguin tile in the Object tree and then click the create new method button on the methods tab. Type react as the name for the new method.
2. Drag a copy of the Loop tile from the bottom of the Editor area and drop it in the new method in place of Do Nothing. Select 2 times from the menu that appears.
3. Drag a copy of the Do together tile from the bottom of the Editor area and drop it in the new Loop tile in place of Do Nothing.
4. Drag a copy of the FibonacciPenguin say instruction tile from the methods tab and drop it in the Do together tile in place of Do Nothing. Select other... from the menu that appears, then enter the string Fibonacci! and click OK.
5. Drag a copy of the jump times tile from the methods tab and drop it in the Do together tile below the FibonacciPenguin.say instruction. Select 1 from the menu that appears.
6. Drag a copy of the wing_flap times tile from the methods tab and drop it in the Do together tile below the FibonacciPenguin.jump instruction. Select 1 from the menu that appears.

(continued)

## Fibonacci Penguin *(continued)*

7. Drag a copy of the FibonacciPenguin turn instruction tile from the methods tab and drop it in the Do together tile below the FibonacciPenguin.wing_flap instruction. Select left and 1 revolution from the menu that appears.

8. Drag a copy of the FibonacciPenguin say instruction tile from the methods tab and drop it in the new method below the Do together tile. Select other..., enter the string That's a Fibonacci number!, and then click the OK button.

The react method is complete. Next, add a count-controlled loop to world.my first method.

1. Drag a copy of the Loop tile from the bottom of the Editor area and drop it in world.my first method in place of Do Nothing. Select other, then enter 100 in the Custom Number dialog box and click the Okay button.

2. Click the show complicated version button on the loop tile to see the complicated version of the Loop instruction.

3. Click the gray 0 parameter box that follows the word from in the Loop instruction and change the starting value to 1.

4. Click the CountPenguin tile in the Object tree, then drag a copy of the CountPenguin say instruction tile from the methods tab and drop it in the Loop instruction in place of Do Nothing. Click hello on the menu that appears.

In the current structure of the loop, CountPenguin says hello each time through the loop. Instead, he should count by saying the value of the loop index each time through the loop. However, the loop index is a number but the say command uses strings. You will need to use a world-level function to convert the value of the index to a string, so that CountPenguin can count.

1. Click the world tile in the Object tree and then click the functions tab in the Details area. Scroll through the functions to find the what as a string function. This function converts other types of values, such as numbers, to strings.

2. Drag a copy of the what as a string function tile and drop it in the CountPenguin say instruction in place of the word hello. Select expressions, then index from the menu that appears.

The CountPenguin say instruction now tells CountPenguin to say the value of index as a string each time through the loop. index goes from 1 up to (but not including) 100, which means CountPenguin will count from 1 to 99. Unfortunately, he will say the numbers with a decimal point and a zero, such as 1.0, 2.0, 3.0, and so on. That is not an easy problem to fix in Alice, so you will leave it that way for now. Next, you only need to add the If/Else instructions to the loop, and your Fibonacci Penguin world will be complete.

1. Drag a copy of the If/Else tile from the bottom of the Editor area and drop it in the Loop tile below the CountPenguin say instruction tile. Click true on the menu that appears.

2. Drag a copy of the a == b function tile from the functions tab and drop it in the If/Else instruction tile in place of the word true. A menu will appear. Select expressions and then index for the value of a, and then select 1 for the value of b. The first part of the If/Else tile should now read If index == 1.

3. Click the FibonacciPenguin tile in the Object tree, click the methods tab in the Details area, and then drag a copy of the react method and drop it in the If/Else tile in place of the phrase Do Nothing that is below the word If but above the word Else.

4. Drag a copy of the completed If/Else tile from world.my first method in the Editor area and drop it on the Clipboard. Make sure you drag the entire If/Else instruction and only the If/Else instruction.

5. Drag the contents of the Clipboard and drop it in the Loop tile but below the If/Else tile. You need to be careful, because there is only a small space between the bottom of the If/Else tile and the bottom of the Loop tile.

6. Click the value 1 in the comparison tile that reads index == 1 in the new copy of the If/Else instruction and change it to 2.

## In the Lab

7. You now have If/Else instructions to check for 1 and to check for 2. In a similar manner, again drag the contents of the Clipboard into the space between the Loop and the last If/Else instruction, then change the value in the If/Else tile to 3 so that its comparison reads index == 3. Repeat this process for each of the remaining seven Fibonacci numbers less than 100: 5, 8, 13, 21, 34, 55, and 89.

Your Fibonacci Penguin world is now complete. Save the world with the name, Lab 3-3 Fibonacci penguin.a2w, then play the world to see Count Penguin and the Fibonacci Penguin at work.

(If you would like to know more about Fibonacci numbers, and see some fascinating images related to the Fibonacci sequence, search the Web for the terms Fibonacci numbers, Fibonacci sequence, or simply Fibonacci.)

## Cases and Places

**1** The Alice world, Case 3-1 random100.a2w, supplied with the data files for this text, uses Alice's random number function to pick a random number between 1 and 100. The world contains a numeric variable called pick. The only instruction in the current world sets the value of pick to a random number, which will be different each time the world is played. Your task is to create an Alice "guessing game" world with two characters of your choice, in which the user tries to guess what the number is, with the two characters providing feedback to the user. It might be best to create a flowchart to help design your world.

Your world should function as follows:

a. Ask the user to guess the number. Alice has a world-level function to ask the user for a number.
b. Have one of the characters tell the user if the guess is too low. Have the other character tell the user if the guess is too high.
c. Set up a sentinel loop to repeat the process while the user's guess is not equal to the number the computer picked.
d. Have both characters tell the user when the guess is correct and react, such as with a dance.

When you are finished, save your new world with the name, Case 3-1 guessingGame.a2w.

**2** Cases and Places 2-2, at the end of the last chapter, asked you to write a story for the Aquarium world that contains three fish. For this exercise you should start with the same world, but this time there is a shark in the aquarium. The Alice world, Case 3-2 aquarium with shark.a2w, contains the aquarium with three fish—a blueFish, a pinkFish, and a greenFish—and a shark (Figure 3-104).

(continued)

# Cases and Places

**2** *(continued)*

**FIGURE 3-104**

Your task is to create an animation of life in the fish tank, using at least one branching routine and several loops in your code. The entire animation can be put in an infinite loop that can be allowed to play so the world will appear as if someone is watching an aquarium. Some people have made a lot of money selling similar commercial software, only with much better graphics. You may work alone or with another student. As always, be careful not to make things too complicated or lengthy, and remember to use good modular design.

You may begin by starting Alice and opening the file, Case 3-2 aquarium with shark.a2w, from the Data Files for Students. See the inside back cover of this book for instructions for downloading the Data Files for Students, or see your instructor for information about accessing the files required in this book. You should save your finished world with the name, Case 3-2 aquarium animation.a2w.

**3** The Alice world, Case 3-3 boats.a2w, contains two sailboats, one green and one yellow. (See Figure 3-105.) Each sailboat has a **random move** method that will cause the boat to move a random distance forward each time it is used, anywhere from one to three meters in each movement.

# Cases and Places

**FIGURE 3-105**

Your task is to create a sailboat race. The movement commands for the two boats can be put into a **Do together** tile inside a **while** loop to make them move together until one of them reaches the finish line. Look through the Alice object galleries to find other objects that you can add to the world to make things more interesting. Create methods to make the two boats race and to react one way if the green boat wins and another way if the yellow boat wins.

You may begin by starting Alice and opening the file, Case 3-3 boats.a2w, from the Data Files for Students. See the inside back cover of this book for instructions for downloading the Data Files for Students, or see your instructor for information about accessing the files required in this book. Save your finished world with the name, Case 3-3 boat race.a2w.

# Learning Exercises

**1** **Writing Directions** Create a set of instructions for a simple everyday process that contains a number of steps, such as making a cup of coffee or getting from your school to where you live. Exchange directions with another student, and critique each other's work. In particular, are the linear sequences in the algorithm complete, correct, and in the proper order?

# Learning Exercises

**2** **Creating a Loop to Read Data from a File**   John's Corner Store and Food Emporium has a data file to keep track of items in the store's inventory. There is one record in the data file for each item in the inventory, containing the item's stock number, description, price, and a Boolean field named "taxable" that has the value **true** if the item is subject to sales tax and **false** if it is not. The last record in the file is a special record called an End of File marker (EOF). Using a flowchart, describe an algorithm that will read and print each record no matter how many records are in the file when the algorithm is executed. For each item, the algorithm should test to see if it is the EOF and, why it is not, then print the stock number, description, and price. It should also print the message "taxable" after the price if an item is subject to sales tax. Design problems like this one are very common in business software.

**3** **Writing Boolean Expressions**   Complete each of the following, which involve writing rules as Boolean expressions:

a.  Information about leap years can be found on the U.S. Naval Observatory's Web site at http://aa.usno.navy.mil/faq/docs/leap_years.html. Write as a single Boolean expression the rule for determining if a year is a leap year.

b.  The following rule is often used to help children learn to spell words that contain "ie" or "ei": I before E except after C, or when sounding as A as in "neighbor" or "weigh." Rewrite the rule as a single Boolean expression using an If instruction.

c.  In most states, a vehicle must stop at an intersection with a traffic light when the traffic light is red, except when making a right turn, in which case the driver must pause and can then make a right turn on red if the way is clear, unless otherwise posted. At a particular intersection there is a sign that says, "No right turn on red, 6 am to 6 pm, except Saturdays and Sundays." Write the complete set of rules and conditions for stopping at this intersection as a set of nested If/Else instructions with Boolean expressions.

d.  Rule 6 of the National Horseshoe Pitchers Association (NHPA) governing scoring for the game of horseshoes can be found on the Web at www.horseshoepitching.com/rules/nhparul.shtml. Scoring according to the American Horseshoe Pitchers Association (AHPA) rules can be found on the Web at www.geocities.com/ahpa1949/rules/rules2.htm. Write one set of nested If/Else instructions for the NHPA scoring rules and one set for the AHPA scoring rules.

Alice 2.0

# Event-Driven Programming in Alice

PROJECT

4

## CASE PERSPECTIVE

You've heard from Dr. Carole Dodgson again. This time she would like you to build a skate simulator world with an interactive interface similar to the flight simulator example world supplied with the Alice software. This is the final product that she would like you to develop for her students.

Your task is to examine the flight simulator world to see how it works, explore events in Alice so that you understand them better, and then build the skate simulator for Dr. Dodgson's course by modifying the existing skaterLogic world from Project 3.

Alice 2.0

# Event-Driven Programming in Alice

*Objectives*

**You will have mastered the material in this project when you can:**

- Describe the concept of an event in computer programming
- List and briefly describe the nine event types used in Alice
- Add an invisible object to mark a spot in an Alice world
- Create new Boolean and numeric properties for an object

- Create an event to move an object
- Create events to allow a user to control a moving object
- Create a billboard object and position it in an Alice world
- Create an event to make a billboard disappear

## User Interfaces and Event-Driven Programming

A **graphical user interface (GUI)** is a combination of computer software and hardware that allows users to operate a computer by manipulating icons and menus on a computer screen, most commonly with a mouse that controls a pointer. Modern applications software — such as word processing programs, electronic spreadsheets, Internet browsers, and computer games — depends on the use of a GUI. Before GUIs were developed, the most common interface was a **command-driven** user interface, in which users operated a computer by typing commands. This required users to be familiar with programming languages or with the language of the operating system, rather than simply pointing and clicking with a mouse as one can do with Microsoft Windows.

The use of a GUI on a computer system requires **event-driven programming**. An **event** occurs whenever an event listener detects an event trigger and responds by running a method called an event handler. An **event listener** is a combination of hardware and software that continuously checks the computer system for an event trigger. Modern computer systems contain facilities to let programmers set up event listeners in their software. An **event trigger** can be any activity or condition selected by the programmer, such as someone clicking on a button to print a document, pressing the ENTER key, or clicking a URL on a Web page. It could also be a change that occurs in a computer system itself, such as a bank account balance going below zero. An **event handler** is a method that is activated when the event trigger occurs. Almost any method can serve as an event handler. When the event listener detects the event trigger, the event handler is called into action.

Events are used in Alice to let the user control objects while a world is playing. Some Alice worlds are narrative worlds which simply tell a story like an animated film, while others are interactive worlds, with mouse and keyboard controls that work while the world plays, like a video game. Most Alice worlds are somewhere in between, with some user controls and some narrative sequences.

In this project, you will look at the events in an existing Alice world, then modify the ice skater world from the previous chapters so that it includes an event-driven user interface, as shown in Figure 4-1.

### More About

### Xerox PARC

The modern graphical user interface was developed at the Xerox Palo Alto Research Center (Xerox PARC) in California. We see the innovations of Xerox PARC every time we use a modern computer. Local area networks, the laser printer, the mouse, and even object-oriented programming were developed or refined at Xerox PARC. The Apple Macintosh approach to computing and the Microsoft Windows operating system are each based directly on developments at Xerox PARC. For more information on Xerox PARC, visit www.parc.com.

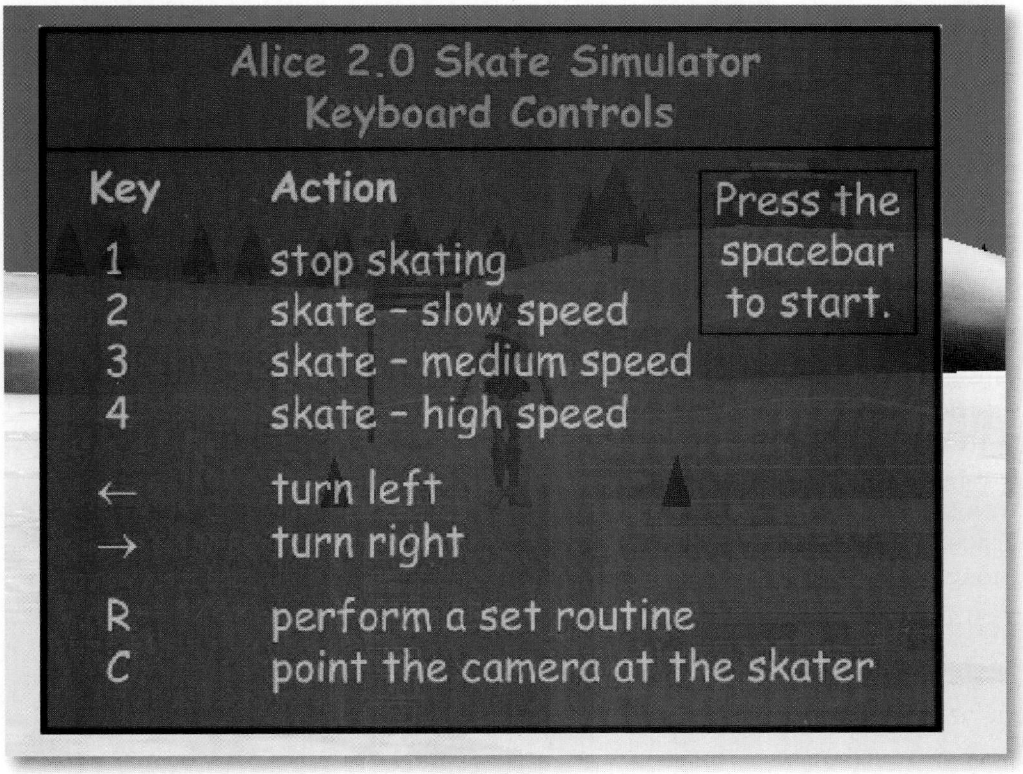

**FIGURE 4-1**

## Examining Events in an Existing Alice World

In this set of steps, you will load the flight simulator example world that comes with the Alice software and examine the events it contains. The world that you will examine is named flightSimulator.a2w.

# To Start the Flight Simulator World

**1**

• **Start Alice as described in previous projects.**

**2**

• **Click the** Examples **tab.**

**3**

• **Click the thumbnail sketch of the flightSimulator world and then click the** Open **button.**

*The flightSimulator world is displayed and the world's events appear in the Events area (Figure 4-2).*

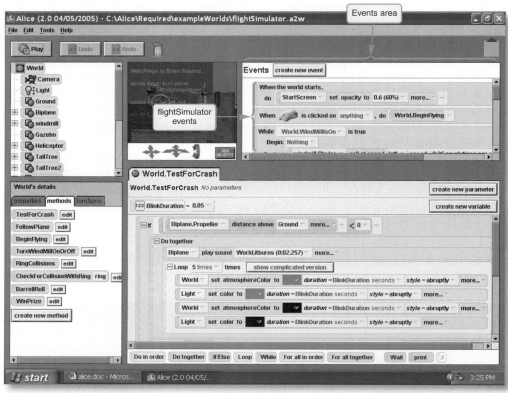

**FIGURE 4-2**

**FIGURE 4-3**

The first event says When the world starts, do StartScreen set opacity to 0.6 (60%). This event tells the computer to set the opacity property of the StartScreen object to six tenths, which equals sixty percent.

The StartScreen object is the image with text that you can see in the World window (Figure 4-3). The opacity property has a value between 0 and 1 (100%), with 0 meaning completely invisible and 1 meaning completely solid. Setting the opacity to 0.6 will make the image solid enough to read the text, but transparent enough to see through. Later in this project, you will learn how to add an image to an Alice world as an object.

The trigger for this event is When the world starts. The event handler is the single instruction do StartScreen set opacity to 0.6 (60%). This event has the same event trigger as the default event for previous worlds that you have seen, but with a different event handler. This event will change the opacity of the image when the world starts, instead of running the method world.my first method, as the default event does. This world does not have a method named world.my first method, nor does it have the default event. Nothing happens when the world starts except the opacity change for the image.

The second event is a mouse-control event. The method World.Begin Flying will run whenever the mouse is clicked on anything in the World window.

The trigger for the third event is contained in the phrase, While World. WindMillIsOn is true. It has places for three different event handlers, one to be run when the trigger begins, one to be run during the time that the triggering condition is true, and one to be run when the triggering condition ends. This is called a **BDE event type**, for Before, During, and End.

In this case, nothing will happen when the triggering condition begins or ends, but while the triggering condition is true, the instruction windmill.Blades roll at speed left speed = 0.25 revolutions per second will be executed. In other words, whenever the Boolean variable World.WindMillIsOn is true, the windmill.Blades object will roll, which means the user will see the windmill blades turning. World.WindMillIsOn is like a switch for the windmill blades; the blades can be turned on by setting its value to true, and turned off by setting its value to false. The event listener is constantly checking for the triggering condition—a true value for the Boolean variable—and will execute the event handler while the event trigger is present.

The remaining methods for this world provide user controls for the flight simulator. You will examine these events in the next set of steps to determine how the user controls in the flight simulator work. In general, you can discover how the user controls work in any interactive world before playing the world by examining the events in that world.

# Exploring How User Controls Work in an Alice World

In this set of steps, you will look at the flight simulator's user controls to determine how they work, then play the world and try those controls.

## To Determine How the World's User Controls Work

**1**

• **Scroll up and down through the flight simulator's events by using the scrollbar on the right side of the Events area.**

*The different events in the world appear in the Events area (Figure 4-4).*

**FIGURE 4-4**

**2**

• **Adjust the scrollbar so that the second event is visible.**

*The second event is visible, as shown in Figure 4-5. Notice that it has a picture of a mouse in the event handler, and uses this picture to say When the mouse is clicked on anything, do World.BeginFlying.*

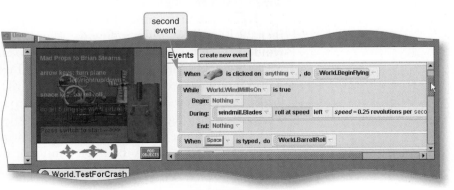

**FIGURE 4-5**

**3**

• **Adjust the scrollbar so that the fourth event is visible.**

*The fourth event, When Space is typed, do World.BarrellRoll, is visible (Figure 4-6). Notice that the event handler is the method World.BarrellRoll, and that it will be executed whenever someone presses the spacebar.*

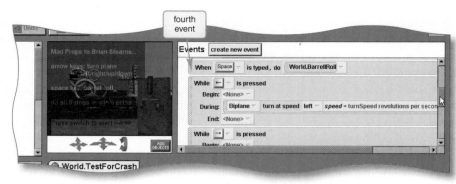

**FIGURE 4-6**

**4**

• **Move the scrollbar to the bottom so that the last event is visible.**

*Notice that the last event is a BDE event that will cause the Biplane to turn forward while the up arrow key is pressed (Figure 4-7).*

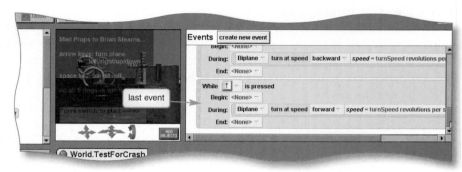

**FIGURE 4-7**

**5**

• **Slowly move the scrollbar up and look at each of the three events above the last event.**

*Notice that these events are similar to the last event, but are used for turning left, right, or down when the corresponding arrow key is pressed (Figure 4-8).*

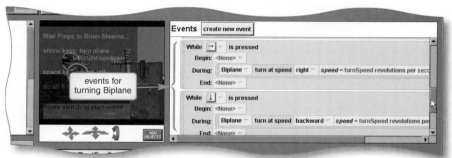

**FIGURE 4-8**

You have just seen that there are six user controls for the flight simulator. The four arrow keys—left, right, up, and down—are used to steer the airplane. The spacebar causes the plane to execute a barrel roll. The sixth control is the mouse, which starts the flight simulator when the mouse is clicked on anything.

To use the flight simulator, you start the world by clicking the Play button, and then click in the World window to begin. (You may click anywhere in the World window, even though the instructions say to click on the switch.) This will run the method World.BeginFlying, which makes the flight simulator work.

You will not examine the details of the flight simulator's methods now, since this project focuses on events in Alice. The creator of this world actually built a game. The person playing the world should try to fly the plane through all five of the rings in the world. Once this is accomplished, a prize will appear on the screen. In the next set of steps, you will run the flight simulator to see how these controls work, then try the game. You should know that the world has sound effects, and that a method in the software causes a reaction if the plane hits the ground. The user can play the world without listening to the sound, but it may be more interesting if the sound can be heard. In this particular case, the sound is rather loud and startling, so be careful not to have the volume too high.

## To Play the Flight Simulator

**1**

• **Click the** Play **button to start the world. Read the instructions for the flight simulator, but do not click the mouse until instructed to do so in Step 3, below.**

*The World window opens with the image containing text visible, but semitransparent (Figure 4-9). Several objects appear in the world behind the image, including the biplane, several rings, and the windmill with its blades turning.*

**FIGURE 4-9**

**2**

• **Press the SPACEBAR a few times to try the barrel roll control.**

*The biplane performs a barrel roll behind the text image. Notice that it rolls in a different direction each time you press the spacebar: first left, then right, then left again, and so on.*

• **Press the arrow keys a few times to turn the biplane.**

*The biplane turns in response to your key presses. It is still behind the text image and not moving except to turn in place (Figure 4-10).*

**FIGURE 4-10**

**3**

• **Click anywhere in the World window to start the flight simulator, and then experiment with the controls to get a feel for flying the plane.**

*The switch moves, and then the switch and text image disappear. The biplane begins moving and responds to your use of the controls (Figure 4-11).*

• **Once you begin to get a feel for the controls, click the** Restart **button in the World Running window to restart the flight simulator, then click the mouse anywhere in the World window to** begin flying again. **See if you can fly the plane through all five rings to win the prize.**

• **Restart the world and try again, if necessary. When you have finished with the flight simulator, press the** Stop **button in the World Running window.**

**FIGURE 4-11**

In the steps above, you saw several different types of events. Altogether, there are nine different types of events in Alice. Before adding events to the ice skater world to make it interactive, you will take a brief look at the nine different event types.

## To View the Event Types Available in Alice

**1**

• **Click the** create new event **button in the Event area.**

*A menu showing the nine Alice event types appears (Figure 4-12).*

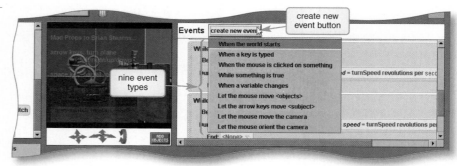

**FIGURE 4-12**

Five of the nine event types in Alice allow you to create events that will cause something to happen when the world starts, when a key is typed, when the mouse is clicked on something, when something (meaning a Boolean condition or Boolean variable) is true, or when the value of a variable changes. Four of the event types are more complex events that have built-in controls to let you move an object with the mouse or the keyboard, or use the mouse to move or orient the camera.

The first five event types each respond to a different event trigger, and you have the flexibility to specify or build your own event handler. The last four event types respond to specific event triggers tied to specific event handlers. They may appear to make programming events a bit easier, but they limit your flexibility.

# Creating a Skate Simulator with Interactive User Controls

Now that you are more familiar with the Alice events, you can begin to build an interactive ice skater world. You will modify the skaterLogic world from Project 3 so that it includes user controls, and rename it as skateSimulator. In the following steps, you prepare the new world by modifying the world's documentation and removing several instructions in world.my first method that won't be needed. You will also move the camera back to give the viewer a wider view of the world.

## To Create the skateSimulator World from the skaterLogic World

**1**

• **Start Alice, if necessary. Click** File **on the menu bar, click** Open World **on the File menu, navigate to the folder that contains the Alice file, skaterLogic.a2w, and open the world.**

• **Save the world with the name, skateSimulator.a2w, before continuing. Remember or write down the name of the world and where you saved it.**

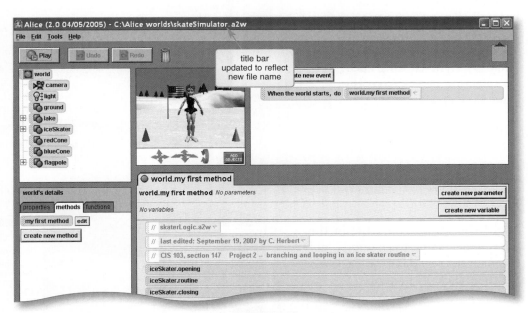

**FIGURE 4-13**

*A new world is saved with the name skateSimulator.a2w. The title bar at the top of the Alice interface is updated to reflect the new name (Figure 4-13).*

**2**

• **Click the comment tile with the name of the world,** skaterLogic.a2w, **change the name to** skateSimulator.a2w, **and then press the** ENTER **key.**

• **Change the date in the** last edited **comment tile to the current date.**

• **Update the description in the third comment tile to include the text** Project 4 - an interactive skater simulation world.

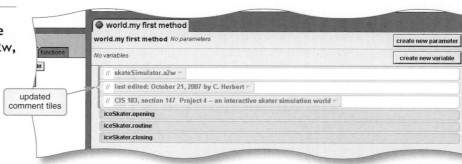

updated comment tiles

**FIGURE 4-14**

The three comment tiles are now similar to those shown in Figure 4-14.

**3**

• **Delete the three instructions that call the** iceSkater.opening, iceSkater.routine, **and** iceSkater.closing **methods one at a time by right-clicking each and selecting** delete **from the menu that appears.**

The three instruction tiles no longer appear below the comments in world.my first method (Figure 4-15).

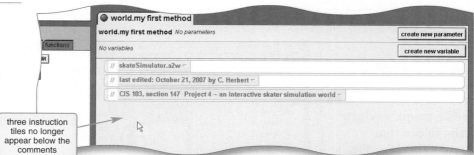

three instruction tiles no longer appear below the comments

**FIGURE 4-15**

**4**

• **Right-click the** camera **tile in the Object tree, point to** methods, **point to** camera move, **point to** backward, **and then click** 10 meters.

The camera moves backward 10 meters, giving a wider view of the skater and her environment (Figure 4-16).

• **Save the world before continuing.**

camera moves backward 10 meters, giving wider view

**FIGURE 4-16**

*Other Ways*

1. Drag instruction tiles to be deleted and drop them on the Trash Can

Although you have deleted the three method calls from world.my first method, the skateSimulator world still contains the methods that you created for the skaterLogic world: figure8, jumpSpin, glideStep, opening, closing, and routine. You will create keyboard controls in the new world to allow the user to freely control the skater and to cause the skater to use the existing methods to perform her set routine. You will also create a keyboard control to allow the user to point the camera at the skater if she moves off camera. Table 4-1 summarizes the keyboard controls you will create.

**Table 4-1   Skate Simulator Keyboard Controls**

| KEY | ACTION |
| --- | --- |
| 1 | The skater will change to *pose* and stop moving. |
| 2 | The skater will change to *pose2* and begin moving *½ meter per second*. |
| 3 | The skater will change to *pose3* and begin moving *1 meter per second*. |
| 4 | The skater will change to *pose4* and begin moving *2 meters per second*. |
| ← | The skater will turn *left* while the key is held down. |
| → | The skater will turn *right* while the key is held down. |
| R | The skater will perform her set routine. |
| C | The camera will turn to face the skater. |

You will also create an event to automatically stop the skater from skating off the frozen lake by turning around if she gets too far away from the cones. This is not listed in the table above because it is an automatic event triggered when a particular condition occurs, and not a user control triggered by pressing a key.

Before creating the events, you will need to add a few new features to the world. You will create two new properties for the iceSkater object and add a variable named Moving to the iceSkater's properties. You will also create an event to keep the skater moving when this property is set to true; then you can change the value of the property to start or stop the skater. You will also add a property to keep track of the skater's speed.

In the following steps, you will start by adding an invisible cone to the world to mark the spot where the skater's set routine begins, halfway between the red and blue cones. Then, when the user presses the R key to start the set routine, the skater can move to the correct spot to begin.

This may seem like a lot to do, but it is really a collection of small steps that will move along rather quickly.

## To Add an Invisible Cone to an Alice World to Mark a Specific Location

**1**

• **Click the** ADD OBJECTS **button to enter Scene Editor mode, then scroll through the** Local Gallery **near the bottom of the interface until you can see the** Shapes **folder. Click the tile to open the** Shapes **folder.**

*The Shapes folder opens (Figure 4-17).*

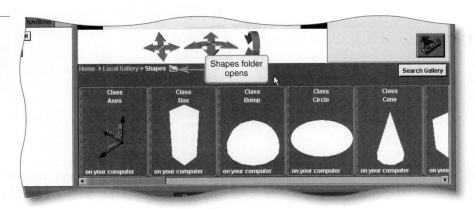

**FIGURE 4-17**

**2**

• **Find and click the**
Cone **tile to open the**
**Cone information dialog**
**box, and then click the**
Add instance to world
**button to add an**
**instance of the cone to**
**your world.**

*A white cone appears in the*
*world and a cone tile appears*
*in the Object tree, as in*
*Figure 4-18, although the cone*
*may appear in a slightly different*
*location.*

**FIGURE 4-18**

**3**

• **Right-click the** cone **tile in the**
**Object tree and then point to**
methods **on the menu that**
**appears.**

*A menu of the cone's built-in methods*
*appears (Figure 4-19).*

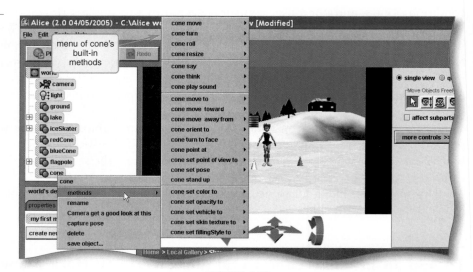

**FIGURE 4-19**

**4**

• **Point to** cone move to**, point to**
iceSkater**, and then click** the entire
ice skater**.**

*The cone moves to the same spot as the*
*iceSkater. It is hard to see because it blends*
*in with the ice and snow and is positioned*
*between the skater's feet (Figure 4-20).*

**FIGURE 4-20**

**5**

• **Right-click the** cone **tile in the Object tree and then point to** methods **on the menu that appears. This time, point to** cone turn to face, **and then click** camera.

• **Click the** cone **tile in the Object tree, and then click the** properties **tab in the Details area.**

*The cone's properties appear in the Details area (Figure 4-21).*

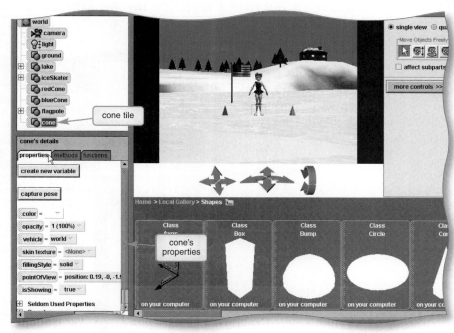

**FIGURE 4-21**

**6**

• **Click the list box next to the** isShowing **property, and select** false**, as shown in Figure 4-22.**

*The cone marking the iceSkater's starting position is now invisible.*

• **Click the** DONE **button to exit Scene editor mode, and save the world before continuing.**

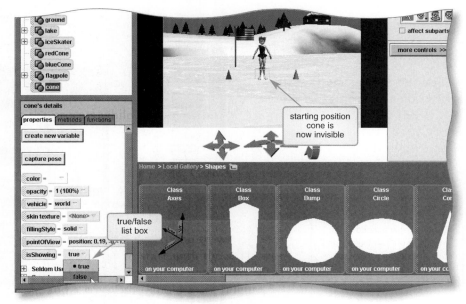

**FIGURE 4-22**

Next, you will create an object variable to hold the new Moving property for the iceSkater object. An object variable is a storage location in the computer's memory that stores a property of an object. It has a name and a data type. The iceSkater's new variable will be a Boolean variable named Moving, which will store a property that is true if the skater should be moving and false if the skater should not be moving. You will then create a new event to make the skater move when the Moving property is true. By default, the event will not make the skater move when the property is false, which means she will stand still.

Alice 2.0

## To Create a Boolean Moving Property for an Object

**1**

• **Click the** iceSkater **tile in the Object tree and, if necessary, click the** properties **tab to display the** iceSkater**'s properties in the Details area.**

*The iceSkater's properties appear in the Details area (Figure 4-23).*

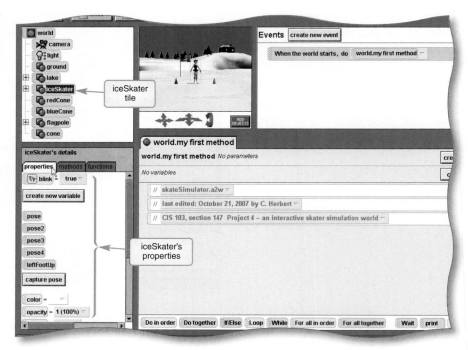

**FIGURE 4-23**

**2**

• **Click the** create new variable **button on the properties tab.**

*The create new variable dialog box appears (Figure 4-24).*

*Q & A*

**Q:** Why is a Boolean Moving property needed when we could simply set an object's speed to zero to stop it from moving?

**A:** It might seem redundant to have a Moving property when you could just set the speed to zero, but this is the correct way to manage an object's properties. Computers sometimes round off numbers, especially if a long chain of calculations occurs inside the computer. If the speed is not exactly zero, then the object might drift a bit instead of remaining still. Moving the object only when the Boolean Moving property is true prevents this from happening.

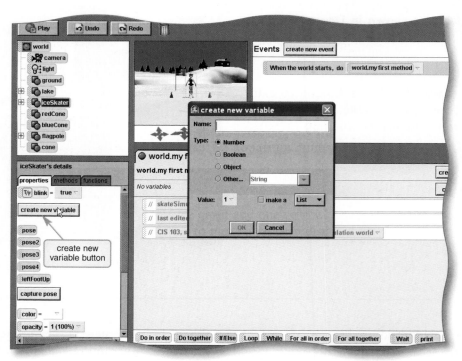

**FIGURE 4-24**

**3**

• **Type the name** Moving **in the text box, select** Boolean **as the type, select** false **as the value, and then click the OK button.**

*A new Boolean variable named Moving appears on the properties tab with the initial value false (Figure 4-25).*

• **Save the world before continuing.**

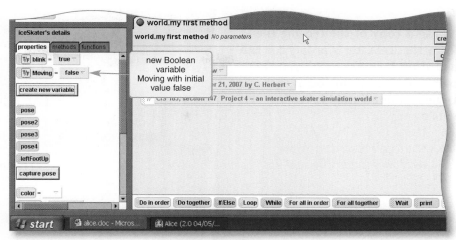

**FIGURE 4-25**

Now the world has a Boolean variable to keep track of whether or not the iceSkater should be moving. The tile on the iceSkater's **properties** tab is labeled simply Moving, but the full name of the new property, which is stored in the variable, is iceSkater.Moving. Next, you will create an event to move the skater forward whenever this variable is true, as described above.

## To Create an Event to Move an Object

**1**

• **Click the** create new event **button in the Events area.**

*The menu of new event types appears (Figure 4-26).*

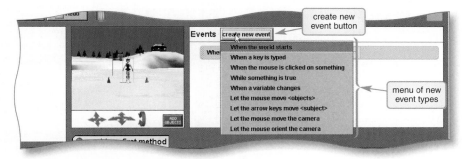

**FIGURE 4-26**

**2**

• **Click** While something is true **on the menu that appears.**

*A blank new event of the Begin, During, and End (BDE) format appears in the Events area (Figure 4-27).*

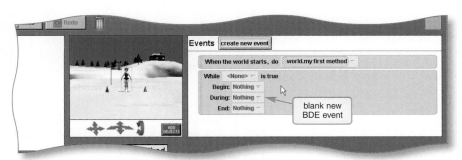

**FIGURE 4-27**

**3**

• **Drag a copy of the** Moving **tile from the** iceSkater's properties **tab and drop it in the new event in place of** <None> **in the event trigger, immediately following** While.

*The event trigger now reads While iceSkater.Moving is true. (Figure 4-28).*

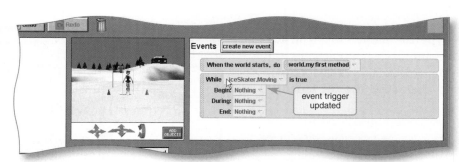

**FIGURE 4-28**

**4**

• **Click the** iceSkater's methods **tab in the Details area, and then drag a copy of the** iceSkater move at speed **method instruction and drop it in the new method in place of the** <Nothing> **following** During:.

*A menu appears, prompting you to select a direction (Figure 4-29).*

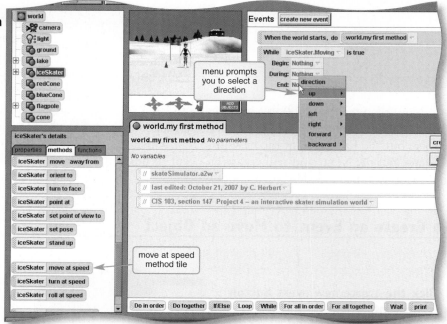

**FIGURE 4-29**

**5**

• **Point to** forward **on the** direction **menu, and then click** 1 meter per second **on the** speed **menu.**

*The During: portion of the new event now reads iceSkater move at speed forward speed = 1 meter per second (Figure 4-30).*

• **Save the world before continuing.**

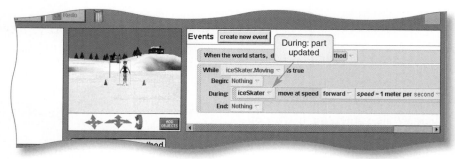

**FIGURE 4-30**

The new event will make the iceSkater move whenever iceSkater.Moving is true, but the speed is fixed at 1 meter per second. Next you will add a numeric variable to hold a speed property for the iceSkater, which will be used to change the iceSkater's speed, and modify the new event to use this property.

## To Create a Numeric Speed Property for an Object

- **If necessary, click the** iceSkater **tile in the Object tree and then click the** properties **tab in the Details area.**
- **Click the** create new variable **button.**
- **In the create new variable dialog box, type the name** speed **in the text box, select** Number **as the type, set** 0 **as the value, and then click the** OK **button.**

*A new Number variable named speed appears on the properties tab with an initial value of 0 (Figure 4-31).*

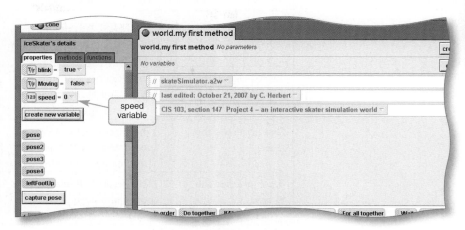

**FIGURE 4-31**

## 2

- **Drag a copy of the** speed **property tile from the** properties **tab and drop it in the new event in place of** speed = 1 meter per second.

*The During: portion of the new event now reads iceSkater move at speed forward speed = speed meters per second. Notice that only the name, speed, appears—not the complex name iceSkater.speed. This is because the instruction in which it appears only affects the iceSkater (Figure 4-32).*

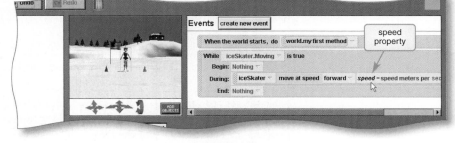

**FIGURE 4-32**

- **Save the world before continuing.**

Next, you will create the events for the iceSkater. This world will not have events that simply stop and start the skater or change her speed, but a series of four events to select the skater's pose that will also change the skater's speed. These events will stop the skater if the 1 key is pressed, and start the skater at a specific speed when the 2, 3, or 4 key is pressed. The events will also change her pose.

The R key will cause the skater to perform her set routine, and the C key will turn the camera. Another event will automatically turn the skater toward the invisible cone at the skater's starting position if she gets too close to the edge of the frozen lake. Table 4-2 shows what the triggers are and what the event handlers will do for these events:

## Table 4-2  Skate Simulator Events

| EVENT TRIGGER | VISIBLE RESULTS | TASKS FOR THE EVENT HANDLER |
|---|---|---|
| User presses the 1 key. | The skater will change to pose and stop moving. | Set pose to pose. Set Moving to false. Set speed to 0 meters per second. |
| User presses the 2 key. | The skater will change to pose2 and begin moving ½ meter per second. | Set pose to pose2. Set Moving to true. Set speed to ½ meter per second. |
| User presses the 3 key. | The skater will change to pose3 and begin moving 1 meter per second. | Set pose to pose3. Set Moving to true. Set speed to 1 meter per second. |
| User presses the 4 key. | The skater will change to pose4 and begin moving 2 meters per second. | Set pose to pose4. Set Moving to true. Set speed to 2 meters per second. |
| User presses the ← key. | The skater will turn left while the key is held down. | The skater will turn at speed left .5 revolutions per second. |
| User presses the → key. | The skater will turn right while the key is held down. | The skater will turn at speed right .5 revolutions per second. |
| User presses the R key. | The skater will perform her set routine. | The skater should stop, turn to face the invisible cone, move to the invisible cone, turn to face the camera, and then perform her routine. |
| User presses the C key. | The camera will turn to face the skater. | The camera should turn to face the skater. |
| Skater gets too far away from the center of the ice (skater's distance to cone exceeds 25 meters). | The skater will automatically turn back toward the center of the ice. | The skater should turn to face the invisible cone. |

Notice that some of the events described in Table 4-2 must do several things. For example, if someone presses the 1 key, then the event must change the values for the pose, Moving, and speed properties of the iceSkater. The iceSkater.Moving event that you previously created used a primitive instruction, iceSkater.move at speed, as its event handler, but you will need to create a new method to be used as the event handler for the 1 event, and for any other events that do more than one thing.

Also notice the pattern for what the first four events must do: In each case, the pose, Moving, and speed properties must be changed. You could create a separate event handler method for each of these four events, but this pattern means that a single method with three parameters can serve as the event handler for all four methods. Your new pose events will each call that method, and pass the new values for the pose, Moving, and speed properties to the method as parameters. The new method will be called setPoseAndSpeed, and will have three method parameters: newPose, newMoving, and newSpeed.

The new method is shown in Figure 4-33. Here is an example of how it will work: If someone presses the 3 key, the setPoseAndSpeed method will be called with the values newPose = pose3, newMoving = true, and newSpeed = 1 meters per second. The three instructions inside the method will then use these values to set the three properties to their appropriate values.

You may recall from the discussion of modular development in Project 2 that methods that will be used as event handlers need to be created before the events that will use them. First, you will create the new **setPoseAndSpeed** method, and then you will create the events which trigger that method.

**FIGURE 4-33**

## To Create a Method to Change the iceSkater's pose, Moving, and Speed Properties

**1**

• **Click the** iceSkater **tile in the Object tree and the** methods **tab in the Details area to make sure that the iceSkater's methods are visible.**

• **Click the** create new method **button, enter the name** setPoseAndSpeed **in the dialog box that appears, and then click the** OK **button.**

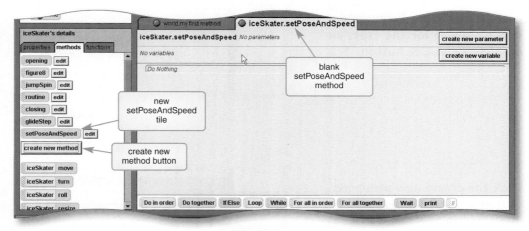

**FIGURE 4-34**

*A new setPoseAndSpeed tile appears on the properties tab. A blank setPoseAndSpeed method appears in the Editor area (Figure 4-34).*

**2**

• **Click the** create new parameter **button in the** setPoseAndSpeed **method in the Editor area.**

*The Create New Parameter dialog box appears (Figure 4-35).*

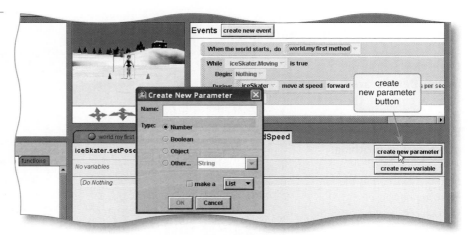

**FIGURE 4-35**

**3**

• **Type** newPose **in the Name field, select Other, select** Pose **from the list box, and then click the** OK **button.**

*A new pose parameter named newPose appears in the method header (Figure 4-36).*

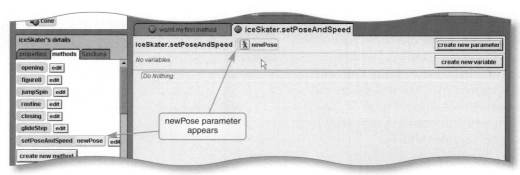

**FIGURE 4-36**

**4**

• **Click the** create new parameter **button again, but this time type** newMoving **in the Name field, select** Boolean **for the type, and then click the** OK **button.**

*A new Boolean parameter with the name newMoving appears in the method header (Figure 4-37).*

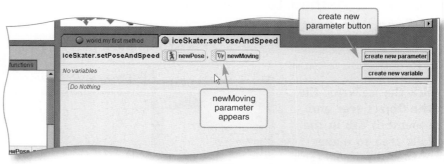

**FIGURE 4-37**

**5**

**Click the** create new parameter **button a third time, type** newSpeed **in the Name field, select** Number **for the type, and then click the** OK **button.**

*A new Number parameter with the name newSpeed appears in the method header (Figure 4-38).*

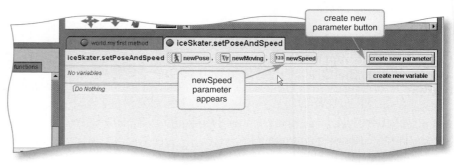

**FIGURE 4-38**

**6**

**Click the** properties **tab in the Details area, then drag a copy of the** pose **property tile and drop it in the new method in place of** Do Nothing.

*A new instruction of the form iceSkater set pose iceSkater.pose appears in the method (Figure 4-39).*

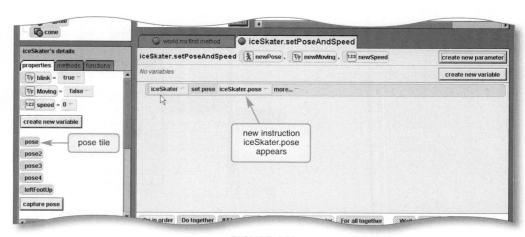

**FIGURE 4-39**

**7**

• **Click the** iceSkater.pose **parameter box in the instruction** iceSkater set pose iceSkater.pose, **point to** expressions, **and then click** newPose.

*The instruction now reads: iceSkater set pose newPose (Figure 4-40).*

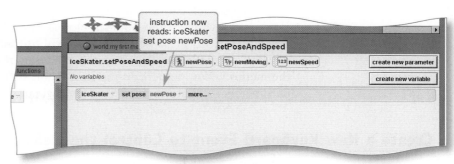

**FIGURE 4-40**

**8**

• **Drag a copy of the** Moving **property tile from the Details area and drop it in the new method below the** iceSkater set pose newPose **instruction. Point to** set value, **point to** expressions, **and then click** newMoving **on the menus that appear.**

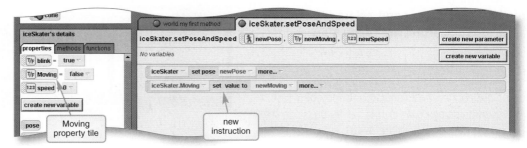

**FIGURE 4-41**

*A new instruction of the form iceSkater.Moving set value to newMoving appears in the method. Notice how this is slightly different from the set pose instruction (Figure 4-41).*

**9**

• **Drag a copy of the** speed **property tile from the Details area and drop it in the new method below the** iceSkater.Moving set value to newMoving **instruction. Select** set value, expressions, **and** newSpeed **on the menus that appear.**

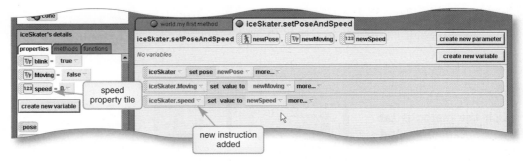

**FIGURE 4-42**

*A new instruction of the form iceSkater.speed set value to newSpeed appears in the method (Figure 4-42). The setPoseAndSpeed method is now complete.*

• **Save the world before continuing.**

You now have an event handler to change the iceSkater's pose and speed. It also changes the value of the Boolean Moving variable. Next you will create the four events described in Table 4-2, which will use setPoseAndSpeed as their handlers. Each will call the setPoseAndSpeed method, passing the values of pose, speed, and Moving to the method. You will create the first event, then copy that event and change its parameters to make each of the other events.

## To Create a New Keyboard Event to Control the iceSkater

**1**

• **Click the** create new event **button in the Events area, and select** When a key is typed **from the menu that appears.**

*A new When any key is typed, do Nothing event appears in the Event area. It may be necessary to scroll down in the Events area to see the new event (Figure 4-43).*

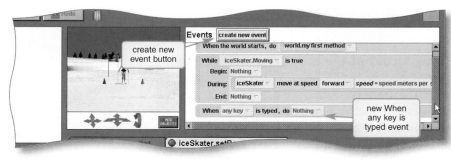

FIGURE 4-43

**2**

• **Click the** any key **parameter in the new event, and then select** numbers **and 1 on the menus that appear.**

*The new event now reads When 1 is typed, do Nothing (Figure 4-44).*

FIGURE 4-44

**3**

• **Click the** methods **tab in the Details area and drag a copy of the** iceSkater's setPoseAndSpeed **tile from the** methods **tab and drop it in the new event in place of** Nothing **following the word** do.

*A newPose menu appears asking you for the value of the method's newPose parameter (Figure 4-45).*

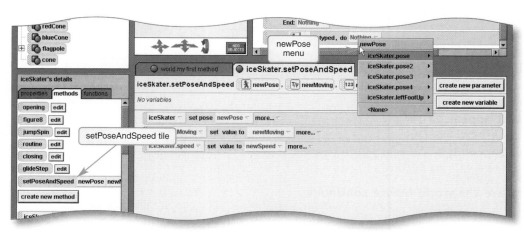

FIGURE 4-45

**4**

- **Point to** iceSkater.pose **on the** newPose **menu.**

- **Point to** false **on the** newMoving **menu.**

- **Click** 0 **on the** newSpeed **menu to set its value to** 0.

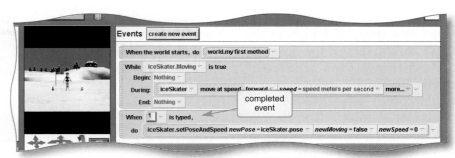

**FIGURE 4-46**

*The event is now complete and reads When 1 is typed, do iceSkater.setPoseAndSpeed newPose = iceSkater.pose newMoving = false newSpeed = 0 (Figure 4-46). It may be necessary to scroll through the Events area to see the details of the new event. The Events area has been enlarged in Figure 4-46 so that you can see the entire event.*

- **Save the world before continuing.**

Now you will copy the event to the Clipboard, then copy it back from the Clipboard and change its parameters to form a new event for the number 2 key. You will repeat this step to create controls for the number 3 and number 4 keys.

> **More About**
>
> **Resizing Areas of the Alice Interface**
>
> Different areas of the Alice interface can be resized by clicking and dragging the blue borders between them. For example, the Events area can be enlarged while you are creating new events so that you can see more of their details at one time.

## To Create New Keyboard Events from an Existing Keyboard Event

**1**

- **Drag the** When 1 is typed, do iceSkater.setPoseAndSpeed newPose = iceSkater.pose newMoving = false newSpeed = 0 **event from the Events area and drop it on the Clipboard, then drag the Clipboard and drop its contents in the Events area below the existing events.**

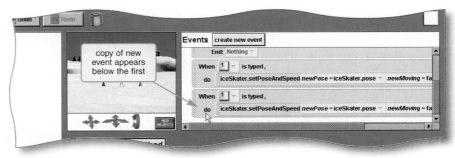

**FIGURE 4-47**

*A copy of the new event appears below the first. It may be necessary to scroll down in the Events area to see the copy (Figure 4-47).*

**2**

- **Click the** 1 **parameter in the bottom copy of the event, point to** numbers, **and then click** 2.

*The new event now reads When 2 is typed, do iceSkater.setPoseAndSpeed newPose = iceSkater.pose newMoving = false newSpeed = 0 (Figure 4-48).*

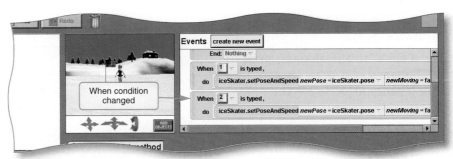

**FIGURE 4-48**

**3**

• **One at a time, click each of the three parameters in the new event tile and change them as follows: change** newPose = iceSkater.pose **to** newPose = iceSkater.pose2, **change** newMoving = false **to** newMoving = true, **and change** newSpeed = 0 **to** newSpeed = 0.5.

**FIGURE 4-49**

*The new event now reads When 2 is typed, do iceSkater.setPoseAndSpeed newPose = iceSkater.pose2 newMoving = true newSpeed = 0.5. It may be necessary to scroll through the Events area to see all the details of the event (Figure 4-49).*

**4**

• **Drag the Clipboard icon and drop its contents in the Events area, below the existing events.**

*Another copy of the When 1 is typed, do iceSkater.setPoseAndSpeed newPose = iceSkater.pose newMoving = false newSpeed = 0 event appears below the existing events. It may be necessary to scroll down in the Events area to see the copy (Figure 4-50).*

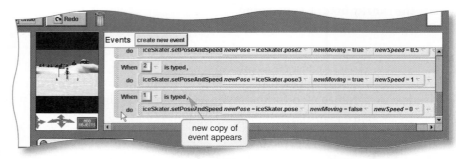

**FIGURE 4-50**

**5**

• **Click each of the parameters in the new event and change them as follows: change** 1 **to** 3, **change** newPose = iceSkater.pose **to** newPose = iceSkater.pose3, **change** newMoving = false **to** newMoving = true, **and change** newSpeed = 0 **to** newSpeed = 1.

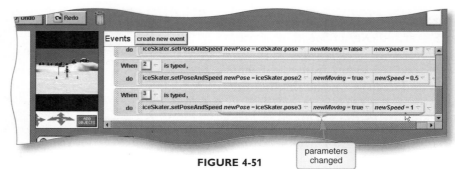

**FIGURE 4-51**

*The new event now reads When 3 is typed, do iceSkater.setPoseAndSpeed newPose = iceSkater.pose3 newMoving = true newSpeed = 1. The Events area has been enlarged so that you can see the entire event (Figure 4-51).*

**6**

• **For a third and final time, drag the Clipboard and drop its contents in the Events area below the existing events.**

*Another copy of the When 1 is typed, do iceSkater.setPoseAndSpeed newPose = iceSkater.pose newMoving = false newSpeed = 0 event appears below the existing events. It may be necessary to scroll down in the Events area to see the copy (Figure 4-52).*

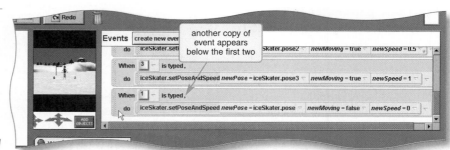

**FIGURE 4-52**

**7**

* **Click each of the parameters in the new event and change them as follows: change** 1 **following the word** When **to 4, change** newPose = iceSkater.pose **to** newPose = iceSkater.pose4, **change** newMoving = false **to** newMoving = true, **and change** newSpeed = 0 **to** newSpeed = 2.

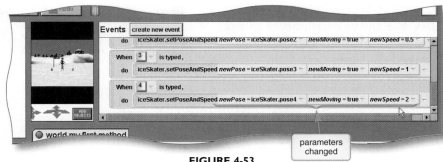

FIGURE 4-53

*The new event now reads When 4 is typed, do iceSkater.setPoseAndSpeed newPose = iceSkater.pose4 newMoving = true newSpeed = 2. All four events that use the setPoseAndSpeed method as their handler are now in place. It will be necessary to scroll up in the Events area to see them all (Figure 4-53).*

* **Save the world again before continuing.**

Next, you will create the two events to turn the skater. Each of these can use the primitive method turn at speed as an event handler.

## To Create Keyboard Events to Turn an Object

**1**

* **Click the** create new event **button in the Events area, and select** When a key is typed **from the menu that appears.**

*A new When any key is typed, do Nothing event appears in the Events area (Figure 4-54). It may be necessary to scroll down in the Events area to see it.*

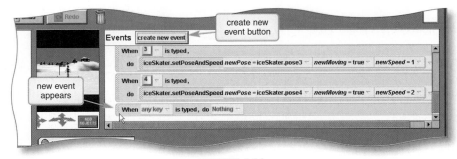

FIGURE 4-54

**2**

* **Right-click the new event tile, point to** change to, **and then click** While a key is pressed.

*The new event is now in the BDE format and reads While any key is pressed instead of When a key is typed (Figure 4-55). It may be necessary to scroll down again in the Events area to see the modified event.*

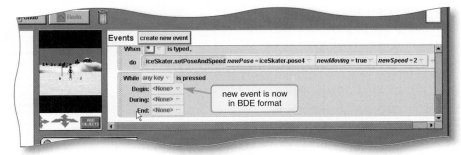

FIGURE 4-55

**3**

• **Click the** any key **parameter in the new event, and then click** Left **on the menu that appears.**

*The trigger for the new event now reads While ← is pressed (Figure 4-56).*

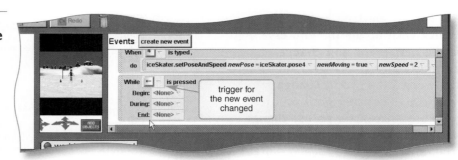

**FIGURE 4-56**

**4**

• **Click** iceSkater **in the Object tree and, if necessary, click the** methods **tab. Drag a copy of the** iceSkater turn at speed **instruction tile from the** methods **tab and drop it in the new event in place of** None **following** During:. **Point to** left **on the** direction **menu, and then click** 0.5 revolutions per second **on the** speed **menu.**

*The new event is complete, with an event handler following During: that reads iceSkater turn at speed left speed = 0.5 revolutions per second (Figure 4-57).*

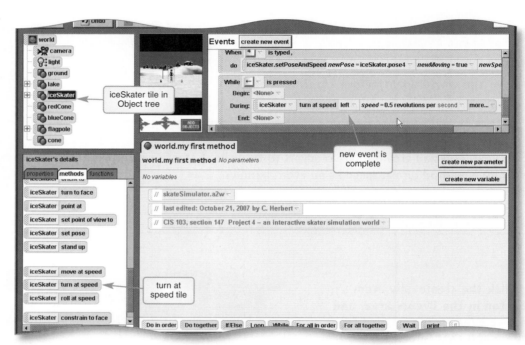

**FIGURE 4-57**

**5**

• **Drag a copy of the new event and drop it on the Clipboard, then drag the Clipboard and drop its contents in the Events area below the new event.**

*A copy of the While ← is pressed event appears in the Event area. It may be necessary to scroll down in the Events area to see it (Figure 4-58).*

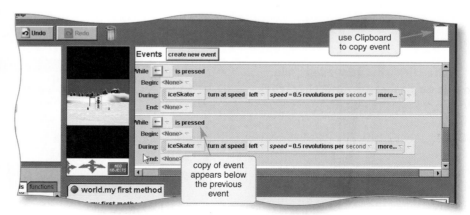

**FIGURE 4-58**

**6**

• **Click the ← in the new event and click** Right **on the menu that appears.**

*The trigger for the new event now reads While → is pressed (Figure 4-59).*

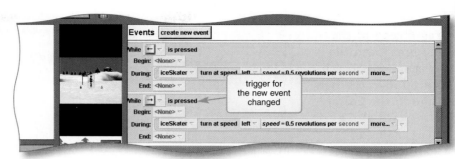

**FIGURE 4-59**

**7**

• **Click the** left **parameter in the** iceSkater turn at speed left speed = 0.5 revolutions per second **instruction in the new event and click** right **on the menu that appears.**

*The new event is complete, with an event handler following During: that reads iceSkater turn at speed right speed = 0.5 revolutions per second (Figure 4-60).*

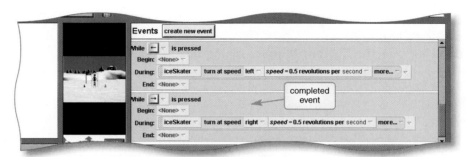

**FIGURE 4-60**

• **Save the world before continuing.**

Next, you will add an event to make the skater perform her set routine whenever the user presses the R key. She will need to go back to her original starting position, which you marked earlier with an invisible cone, then she will stop and turn to face the camera before proceeding. A new event handler method called startRoutine will take care of these things and then call the routine method. You will create this method, then create the event trigger that calls the method when the R key is pressed.

## To Create an Event Handler Method to Start the Skater's Set Routine

**1**

**Click the** create new method **button on the** methods **tab, type** startRoutine **in the New Method dialog box, and then click the** OK **button.**

*A new method named startRoutine appears in the Editor area. A tile for the method appears on the methods tab (Figure 4-61).*

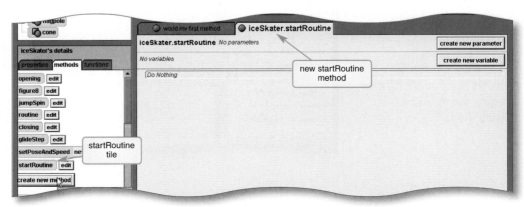

**FIGURE 4-61**

**2**

• **Drag a copy of the** setPoseAndSpeed **tile from the** methods **tab and drop it in the new method in the Editor area in place of** Do Nothing. **Point to** iceSkater.pose **on the** newPose **menu, point to** false **on the** NewMoving **menu, and select** 0 **on the** newSpeed **menu by clicking** Other **and entering** 0 **in the Custom Number dialog box.**

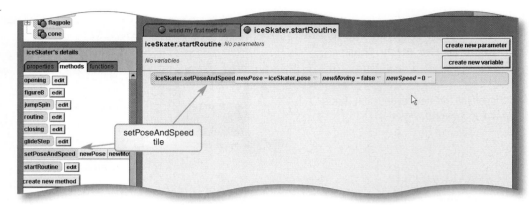

**FIGURE 4-62**

*A new iceSkater.setPoseAndSpeed newPose = iceSkater.pose newMoving = false newSpeed = 0 instruction tile appears in the startRoutine method in the Editor area (Figure 4-62).*

**3**

• **Drag a copy of the** iceSkater **turn to face tile from the** methods **tab, drop it in the new method below the first instruction, and then click** cone **on the target menu.**

*An iceSkater turn to face cone instruction appears as the second instruction in the new method (Figure 4-63).*

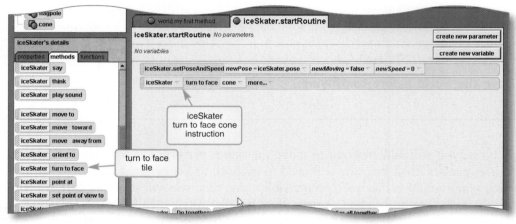

**FIGURE 4-63**

**4**

• **Drag a** Do together **tile from the bottom of the Editor area and drop it in the new method below the first two instructions.**

*A blank Do together tile appears in the method, below the first two instructions (Figure 4-64).*

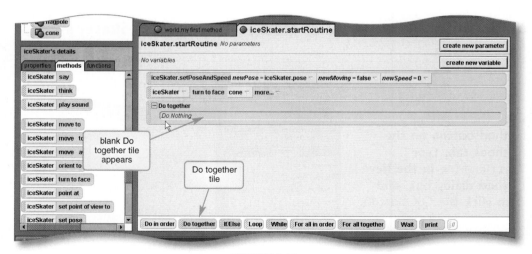

**FIGURE 4-64**

**5**

- **Click the** properties **tab in the Details area, then drag a copy of the** pose3 **tile from the** properties **tab and drop it in the** Do together **tile in place of** Do Nothing.

*An iceSkater set pose iceSkater.pose3 tile appears in the Do together tile (Figure 4-65).*

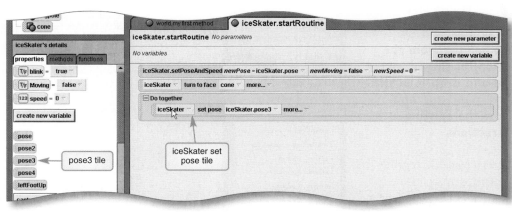

**FIGURE 4-65**

**6**

- **Click the** methods **tab in the Details area, drag a copy of the** iceSkater move to **tile from the** methods **tab, drop it in the** Do together **tile below the** iceSkater set pose **instruction, and then click** cone **on the** asSeenBy **menu.**

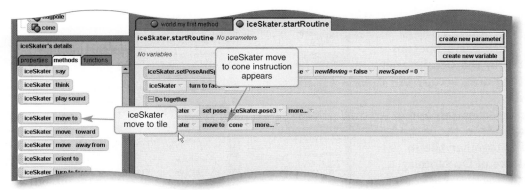

**FIGURE 4-66**

*An iceSkater move to cone instruction appears inside the Do together tile, below the iceSkater set pose instruction (Figure 4-66).*

**7**

- **Click the word** more... **in the** iceSkater move to cone **instruction and change the** duration **to 2 seconds.**

*The instruction now reads: iceSkater move to cone duration = 2 seconds (Figure 4-67).*

**FIGURE 4-67**

**8**

• **Drag a second** Do together **tile from the bottom of the Editor area and drop it in the** startRoutine **method, below the existing instructions.**

*A second blank Do together tile appears in the method, below the existing instructions (Figure 4-68).*

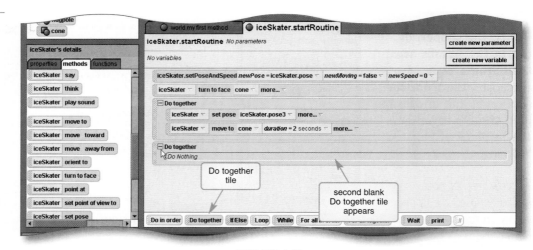

**FIGURE 4-68**

**9**

• **Click the** properties **tab in the Details area, then drag a copy of the** pose **tile from the** properties **tab and drop it in the second** Do together **tile in place of** Do Nothing.

*An iceSkater set pose iceSkater.pose tile appears in the Do together tile (Figure 4-69).*

**FIGURE 4-69**

**10**

• **Click the** methods **tab in the Details area, drag a copy of the** iceSkater turn to face **tile from the** methods **tab, drop it in the second** Do together **tile below the** iceSkater set pose **instruction, and then click** camera **on the target menu.**

*An iceSkater turn to face camera instruction appears as the second instruction in the Do together tile (Figure 4-70).*

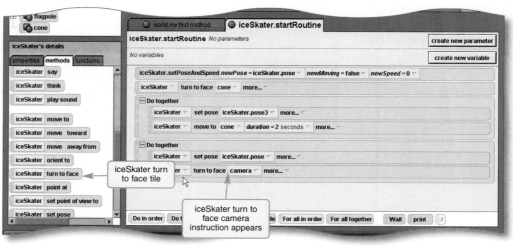

**FIGURE 4-70**

**11**

• **Drag a copy of the** routine **tile from the** methods **tab and drop it in the new method, below the existing instructions.**

*An iceSkater.routine instruction tile appears as the last instruction in the new method (Figure 4-71). The new method is now complete.*

• **Save the world before continuing.**

**FIGURE 4-71**

Now that the event handler method to start the ice skater's routine is in place, you will create the event trigger that calls the method when the R key is pressed.

## To Create an Event Trigger to Start the Skater's Set Routine

**1**

• **Click the** create new event **button in the Events area and select** When a key is typed **from the menu that appears.**

*A new When any key is typed, do Nothing event appears in the Event area (Figure 4-72). It may be necessary to scroll down in the Events area to see it.*

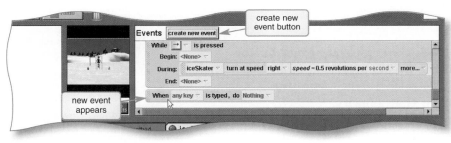

**FIGURE 4-72**

**2**

• **Click the** any key **parameter in the new event, point to** letters, **and then click** R **on the menu that appears.**

*The trigger for the new event now reads When R is typed, do Nothing (Figure 4-73).*

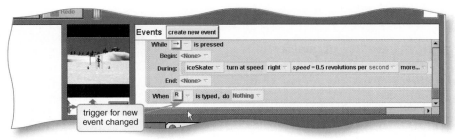

**FIGURE 4-73**

Alice 2.0

**3**

• **Drag a copy of the** startRoutine **instruction tile from the** methods **tab and drop it in the** When R is typed **event in place of** Nothing.

*The event now reads When R is typed, do iceSkater.startRoutine (Figure 4-74).*

• **Save the world before continuing.**

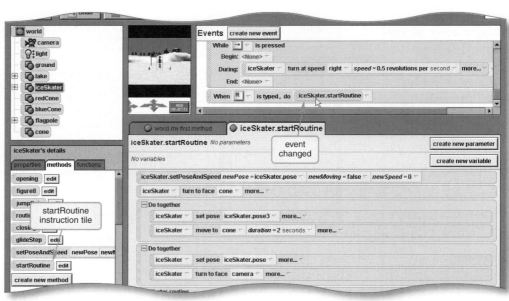

**FIGURE 4-74**

## To Create a Keyboard Event to Turn the Camera to Face the Skater

**1**

• **Click the** create new event **button in the Events area, and select** When a key is typed **from the menu that appears.**

*A new When any key is typed, do Nothing event appears in the Event area (Figure 4-75). It may be necessary to scroll down in the Events area to see it.*

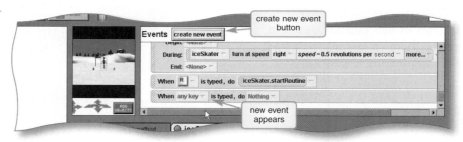

**FIGURE 4-75**

**2**

• **Click the** any key **parameter in the new event, and select** letters **and then** C **from the menus that appear.**

*The trigger for the new event now reads When C is typed, do Nothing (Figure 4-76).*

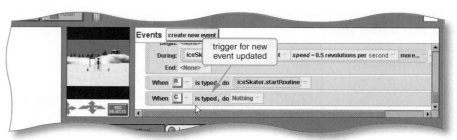

**FIGURE 4-76**

**3**

• **Click the** camera **tile in the Object tree, drag a copy of the** camera turn to face **instruction tile from the** methods **tab and drop it in the** When C is typed **event in place of** Nothing. **Then point to** iceSkater **on the** target **menu and click** the entire iceSkater.

*The event now reads When C is typed, do camera turn to face iceSkater (Figure 4-77).*

• **Save the world before continuing.**

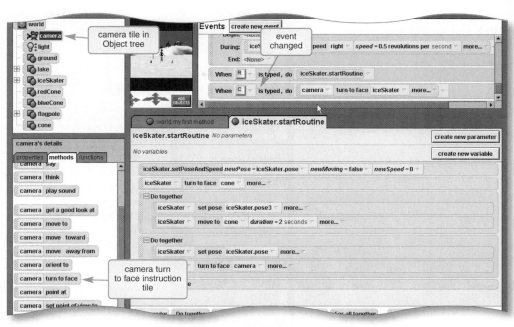

**FIGURE 4-77**

---

The last event that you need to create will turn the ice skater back toward the invisible cone whenever she gets more than 25 meters away from it. This is needed to keep her from skating off the ice and into the snow banks that surround the frozen lake.

## To Create an Event to Keep the Skater from Skating Off the Ice

**1**

• **Click the** create new event **button in the Events area, and click** While something is true **on the menu that appears.**

*A new While <None> is true event with a BDE format appears in the Events area (Figure 4-78). It may be necessary to scroll down in the Events area to see it.*

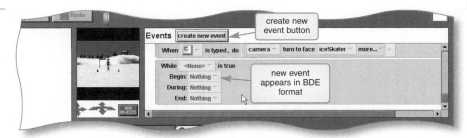

**FIGURE 4-78**

**2**

• **Click the** world **tile in the Object tree, and then click the** functions **tab in the Details area.**

*The world-level functions are now visible in the Details area (Figure 4-79).*

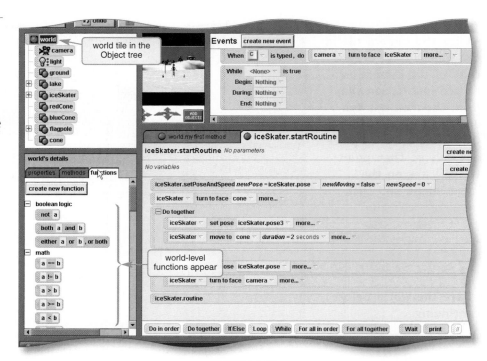

**FIGURE 4-79**

**3**

• **Drag a copy of the a > b function and drop it in the new event in place of** <None>. **Point to 1 on the a menu, click** other **on the b menu, and then enter 25 in the Custom Number dialog box.**

*The trigger for the new event now reads While 1 > 25 is true (Figure 4-80).*

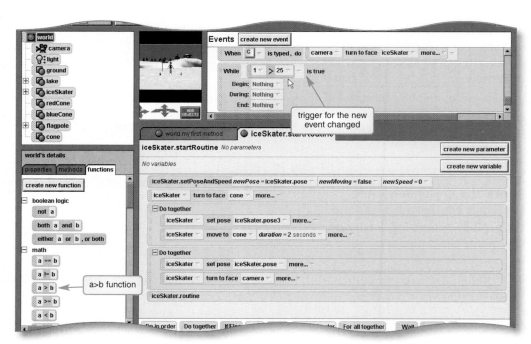

**FIGURE 4-80**

**4**

• **Click the** iceSkater **tile in the Object tree, drag a copy of the** iceSkater distance to **function tile from the** functions **tab, drop it in the new event trigger in place of** 1, **and then click** cone **on the** object **menu.**

*The trigger for the new event now reads While iceSkater distance to cone > 25 is true (Figure 4-81).*

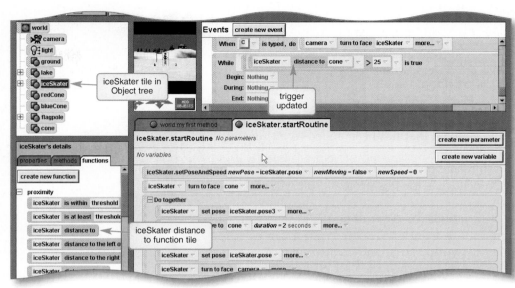

FIGURE 4-81

**5**

• **Click the** methods **tab in the Details area, drag a copy of the** iceSkater turn to face **tile from the** methods **tab, drop it in the new method in place of** Nothing **following the word** During:, **and then click** cone **on the** target **menu.**

*An iceSkater turn to face cone instruction appears as the event handler following the word During (Figure 4-82). The event is now complete.*

• **Save the world before continuing.**

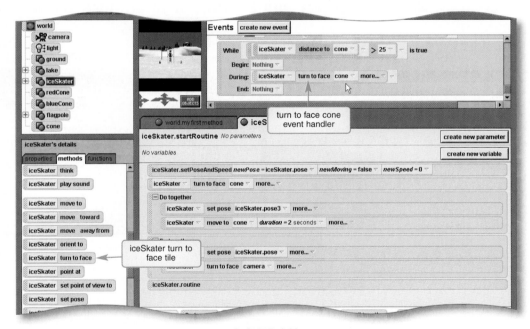

FIGURE 4-82

Everything works in the new world, but it might be nice to give the user a set of instructions to read when the world first starts. A technique similar to the one used in the flight simulator example world will work well here. The instructions for the flight simulator are on a billboard.

A billboard is a picture file that has been added to an Alice world as a flat two-dimensional object with length and width, but no depth. You can see the image on both the front and back of the billboard. Billboards are objects with properties and methods just like other objects. You can make them move, turn, roll, and so on, and you can create new methods for them as well. Figure 4-83 shows a picture of the Grand Canyon that has been added to an Alice world as a billboard.

An image file named controls.jpg is included with the student files for this project. You will add the file to the world as a billboard object that shows the user the instructions for controlling the skater. You will position it in front of the camera so it can be read when the world starts, and create one more event to make it invisible when the user clicks on it to begin the skate simulator.

**FIGURE 4-83**

## To Create a Billboard Object and Position It in an Alice World

**1**

• **Click** File **on the menu bar and then click** Make Billboard **on the File menu.**

*The Import dialog box appears (Figure 4-84).*

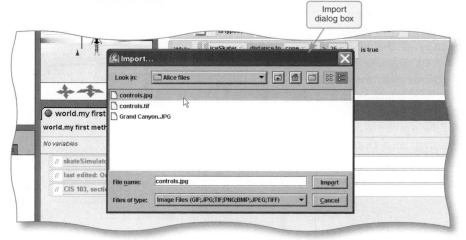

**FIGURE 4-84**

**2**

• **Navigate to the folder that contains the controls.jpg file, click the file name, and then click the** Import **button.**

*The picture appears in the world as a billboard object named controls. A tile named controls appears in the Object tree (Figure 4-85).*

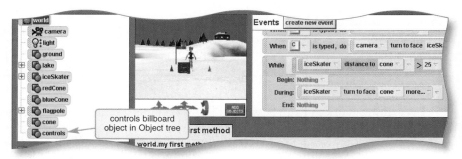

**FIGURE 4-85**

**3**

• **Click the** ADD OBJECTS **button to enter Scene Editor mode.**

*Alice enters Scene Editor mode (Figure 4-86).*

**FIGURE 4-86**

**4**

• **Using the object manipulation tools on the right side of the interface, position the billboard so that it almost fills the World window and faces the camera. You can use the** pointer **tool to move the billboard closer to the camera, the** vertical **tool to move the billboard up and down, and the** rotate **and** turn **tools to turn the billboard so that it is easier to read.**

*The billboard should almost fill the World window and face the camera as in Figure 4-87, although your positioning of the billboard may be slightly different.*

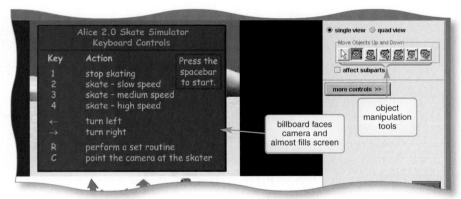

**FIGURE 4-87**

• **Click the** controls **tile in the Object tree, click the** properties **tab in the Details area, and then change the billboard's** opacity **parameter to 0.9 (90%).**

*The billboard becomes slightly transparent (Figure 4-88).*

• **Click the** DONE **button to exit Scene Editor mode and then save the world before continuing.**

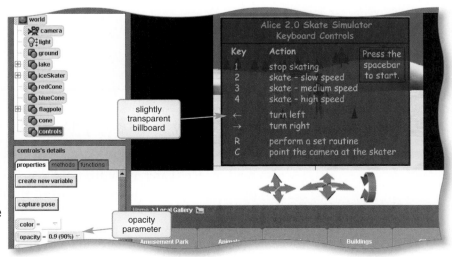

**FIGURE 4-88**

You can now create an event to make the billboard disappear.

## To Create an Event to Make the controls Billboard Disappear

**1**

• **Click the** create new event **button in the Events area, and click** When a key is typed **on the menu that appears.**

*A new When any key is typed, do Nothing event appears in the Event area (Figure 4-89). It may be necessary to scroll down in the Events area to see it.*

**FIGURE 4-89**

**2**

• **Click the** any key **parameter in the new event, and click** Space **on the menu that appears.**

*The trigger for the new event now reads When Space is typed, do Nothing (Figure 4-90).*

**FIGURE 4-90**

**3**

• **Drag a copy of the** controls **object** opacity **property from the** properties **tab, drop it in the** When Space is typed **event in place of** Nothing, **and then click** 0(0%) **on the** value **menu that appears.**

*The new event now reads When Space is typed, do controls set opacity to 0 (0%) (Figure 4-91).*

• **Save the world before continuing.**

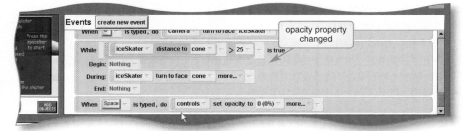

**FIGURE 4-91**

Your new skate simulator world is complete. You should now play the world to see if it works according to the instructions that appear when the world starts. You should try all of the keyboard controls to see that they work properly, and should also send the ice skater away from the center of the ice to see if she turns around automatically as she is supposed to when she gets more than 25 meters away from the invisible cone. If it does not work as expected, then you should isolate the errors and fix them.

Your new simulator should be fun and interesting to use. You should note that the world does not have any collision detection built into it, since this is beyond the scope of this project. This means that the iceSkater will skate through other objects, such as the red and blue cones or the flagpole, instead of bouncing off of them or skating around them.

You may wish to develop this world further on your own, such as adding methods and events for more keyboard controls. The iceSkater.opening and iceSkater.closing methods are still part of this world, although they are not currently in use. If you do decide to continue developing the simulator, then remember to save the new world with a different name so that you will not overwrite the current world.

## Project Summary

In this project you learned about event driven programming. You learned that events can be used to add user interaction to computer software, and you added several events to the ice skater world from the previous chapter.

You learned that events are composed of an event trigger, an event listener, and an event handler. You learned that an event listener is a combination of hardware and software that continuously checks the computer system for an event trigger, which can be any activity or condition selected by the programmer, such as someone pressing the ENTER key. An event handler is a method that is activated when the event trigger occurs.

You learned that Alice has facilities for nine different event types. You first looked at existing events in the lakeSkater world that comes with Alice to see how they work, and then created several keyboard events to provide user controls for your ice skater world.

You also learned how to create a billboard in Alice from an existing graphic image, then used a billboard to provide user instructions for the interactive version of the ice skater world. Finally, you created an event to allow the user to make the billboard disappear.

## What You Should Know

Having completed this project, you should be able to:

1. Start the Flight Simulator World (AL 188)
2. Determine How the World's User Controls Work (AL 189)
3. Play the Flight Simulator (AL 191)
4. View the Event Types Available in Alice (AL 192)
5. Add an Invisible Cone to an Alice World to Mark a Specific Location (AL 195)
6. Create a Boolean Property for an Object (AL 198)
7. Create an Event to Move an Object (AL 199)
8. Create a Numeric Property for an Object (AL 201)
9. Create a Method to Change the iceSkater's pose, Moving, and speed Properties (AL 203)
10. Create a New Keyboard Event to Control the iceSkater (AL 206)
11. Create New Keyboard Events from an Existing Keyboard Event (AL 207)
12. Create Keyboard Events to Turn an Object (AL 209)
13. Create an Event Handler Method to Start the Skater's Set Routine (AL 211)
14. Create an Event Trigger to Start the Skater's Set Routine (AL 215)
15. Create a Keyboard Event to Turn the Camera to Face the Skater (AL 216)
16. Create an Event to Keep the Skater from Skating Off the Ice (AL 217)
17. Create a Billboard Object and Position It in an Alice World (AL 220)
18. Create an Event to Make a Billboard Disappear (AL 222)

## 1 The Three Dancing Penguins

The file, Apply 4 penguin dance.a2w, contains an Alice world with three dancing penguins, similar to the penguin dance you created in Project 1 of In the Lab 2-1. The three penguins are named Pamela, Peter, and Paul and each have their own routine method. There are also world-level methods named world.routine and world.exit. Your task is to add events to the world to create the following keyboard controls:

> 1 – Pamela Penguin dances (Pamela.routine)
> 2 – Peter Penguin dances (Peter.routine)
> 3 – Paul Penguin dances (Paul.routine)
> SPACEBAR – all three penguins dance ( world.routine)
> ENTER – all three penguins exit (world.exit)

**Instructions:** Open the file, Apply 4 penguin dance.a2w, from the Data Files for Students. See the inside back cover of this book for instructions for downloading the Data Files for Students, or see your instructor for information about accessing the files required in this book. Play the world and you will see that a hidden menu (Figure 4-92) appears after the penguins introduce themselves. In addition to the controls listed above, you will also add a keyboard control to hide the menu again.

**FIGURE 4-92**

First, create an event to start Pamela Penguin's routine.

1. Click the create new event button in the Events area and then select When a key is typed from the menu that appears. A new When any key is typed, do Nothing tile will appear in the Events area.
2. Click the any key parameter in the new event tile, point to numbers on the menu that appears, and then select 1.

# Apply Your Knowledge

3. Click the Pamela tile in the Object tree and the methods tab in the Details area, so that the methods for the Pamela object are now visible in the Details area. Notice that one of Pamela's methods is routine.

4. Drag a copy of the routine method from the Details area and drop it in the new event tile in place of Nothing, following the word do.

5. The new event is now complete. Save the world with the name, Apply 4 penguin dance interactive.a2w, then test the new control by playing the world and then pressing the 1 key.

Next, create an event to start Peter Penguin's routine.

1. Click the create new event button in the Events area and then select When a key is typed from the menu that appears. A new When any key is typed, do Nothing tile will appear in the Events area.

2. Click the any key parameter in the new event tile, then point to numbers on the menu that appears and select 2.

3. Click the Peter tile in the Object tree and the methods tab in the Details area, so that the methods for the Peter object are now visible in the Details area. Notice that Peter also has a routine method.

4. Drag a copy of the routine method from the methods tab and drop it in the new event tile in place of Nothing, following the word do.

5. The event to start Peter's routine is now complete. Save the world again, then test the new event by playing the world and then pressing the 2 key.

Now create an event to start Paul Penguin's routine, but instead of starting with a new event, build it by modifying the event for Peter's routine.

1. Drag the last event in the Event area, which reads When 2 is typed, do Peter.routine, and drop a copy of it on the Clipboard.

2. Drag the contents of the Clipboard and drop it in the Events area below the last event.

3. Click the 2 parameter in the bottom copy of the last event, point to numbers on the menu that appears, and then select 3.

4. Click Peter.routine following the word do in the bottom copy of the last event, point to Paul on the menu that appears, and then select routine.

5. The event to start Paul's routine is now complete. Save the world again, then test the new control by playing the world and pressing the 3 key.

Next, add a control to make all three penguins dance by using world.routine as the handler for a new event.

1. Click the create new event button in the Events area and then select When a key is typed from the menu that appears. A new When any key is typed, do Nothing tile will appear at the bottom of the Events area.

2. Click the any key parameter in the new event tile, then select Space from the menu that appears.

3. Click the world tile in the Object tree so that the world-level methods are now visible in the Details area.

4. Drag a copy of the routine method from the methods tab and drop it in the new event tile in place of Nothing, following the word do.

5. The new event is now complete. Save the world again, then test the new control by playing the world and then pressing SPACEBAR.

Build an event to invoke the world.exit routine by copying the spacebar event that you just built and modifying it.

1. Drag a copy of the event tile that reads When Space is typed, do world.routine and drop it on the Clipboard, then drag the content of the Clipboard and drop it in the Events area.

2. Click the Space parameter tile in the new copy of the event tile, then select Enter from the menu that appears.

*(continued)*

## The Three Dancing Penguins *(continued)*

3. Drag a copy of the exit method from the methods tab and drop it in the new event tile in place of world.routine, following the word do.
4. The new event is now complete. Save the world again, then test the new control by playing the world and pressing the ENTER key.

The last event that you need to create is the event to hide the menu when the H key is pressed.

1. Click the create new event button in the Events area and then select When a key is typed from the menu that appears. A new When any key is typed, do Nothing tile will appear at the bottom of the Events area.
2. Click the any key parameter in the new event tile, point to letters on the menu that appears, then select H.
3. Click the menu tile in the Object tree, then click the properties tab in the Details area so that the menu's properties are now visible in the Details area.
4. Drag a copy of the opacity tile from the properties tab and drop it in the new event in place of Nothing, following the word do. Select 0 (0%: invisible) from the menu that appears.
5. All of the events for the interactive version of the Penguin dance world are now complete. Save the world again, and then test the events by playing the world and trying the various controls.

## 1 Building a Simple Flight Simulator

In this exercise, you will build a simple flight simulator. You will start with a water world, add a seaplane to the world, build events to allow the user to control the plane, and then add other objects to the world to make it look more interesting. You will create the following keyboard controls for the seaplane:

↑ – turn the plane forward (nose down)
↓ – turn the plane backward (nose up)
← – turn left
→ – turn right

You will also modify world.my first method to keep the plane in motion with its propeller spinning, and create an event to activate this method while the world is playing. When you are finished, you will have a world that functions as a simple flight simulator, and that you can further develop on your own into a more sophisticated flight simulator or game.

**Instructions:** First, start a new Alice world and add a seaplane.

1. Open Alice and begin a new world with the water template.
2. Click the ADD OBJECTS button to enter Scene Editor mode, then open the Vehicles folder in the Local Object gallery.
3. Click the Seaplane Class tile and then click the Add instance to world button to add a seaplane to the world.
4. Turn the seaplane so that it is facing away from the camera and slightly to the right, then reposition the camera using the blue camera control arrows so that the view in the World window looks similar to Figure 4-93.

In the Lab

**FIGURE 4-93**

5. Click the **DONE** button to return to the standard Alice interface and then save the world with the filename, Lab 4-1 flight simulator.a2w, before continuing.

Next, you add four events to steer the plane. Begin by creating an event to turn the plane forward, which will turn its nose downward. You will then copy and modify this event to create the three other steering events.

1. Click the **create new event button** in the Events area and then select **when a key is typed** from the menu that appears. A new **When any key is typed, do Nothing** tile will appear at the bottom of the Events area.
2. Right-click the new event tile, point to **change to** on the menu that appears, then select **While a key is pressed**.
3. Click the **any key** parameter in the new event tile and then select **Up** from the menu that appears.
4. Click the **seaplane** tile in the Object tree and the **methods** tab in the Details area, then drag a copy of the **seaplane turn at speed** tile and drop it in the new event following **During:**. Select **forward** and **.25 revolutions per second** from the menus that appear.

Now copy the event to the Clipboard and, one at a time, build the three remaining turn controls from the copy.

1. Drag a copy of the new event from the Events area and drop it on the Clipboard.
2. Drag the content of the Clipboard and drop it in the Events area, below the existing events.
3. Click ↑ in the new copy of the event, then select **D** from the menu that appears.
4. Click the **forward** parameter in the **turn at speed** instruction in the event handler of the new copy of the event, and select **backward** from the menu that appears.
5. Again, drag a copy of the contents of the Clipboard into the Events area. In this copy, change ↑ to **Left** and change the **forward** parameter to **left**.

*(continued)*

## Building a Simple Flight Simulator *(continued)*

6. Once more, drag the contents of the Clipboard into the Events area. In this copy, change ↑ to Right and the forward parameter to right.

7. The four turn events are now complete. Save the world again, and then play the world to test the events. The plane should turn in place in response to your keystrokes, but it should not yet move. If it does not respond correctly, then carefully retrace the steps above to find and correct the error.

Next, you will add an event to make the plane move and the propeller spin. Instructions to do both of these actions will be in world.my first method. Also, modify the default event so that world.my first method continues to run while the world plays, and does not run only once when the world starts.

1. Drag a copy of the Do together tile from the bottom of the Editor area and drop it in world.my first method in place of Do Nothing.

2. Drag a copy of the seaplane move at speed tile from the methods tab and drop it in the Do together tile in place of Do Nothing. Select forward and 10 meters per second from the menus that appear.

3. Click the plus sign next to the seaplane tile in the Object tree, and then click the propeller tile to select the propeller.

4. Drag a copy of the propeller roll at speed tile from the methods tab and drop it in the Do together tile, below the seaplane move at speed tile. When the menu appears, point to right, then click other and use the Custom Number dialog box to enter 10 as the number of revolutions per second.

5. Right-click the When the world starts default event tile in the Events area. When the menu appears, point to change to, then select While the world is running.

6. Click the world tile in the Object tree. Drag a copy of the my first method tile and drop it in place of None in the While the world is running tile in the Events area, following the word During:.

7. The changes to the default event and world.my first method are now complete. Save the world again and then play the world. This time, the turn controls should work and the plane should move with the propeller spinning.

You can now fly the plane, but you can easily fly it off camera and lose track of where it is. Next, add mouse events to the world to control the camera: one to allow the user to move the camera, and one to point the camera at the plane. These will allow you to follow the plane as it flies around, and to find the plane if it moves off camera.

1. Click the create new event button in the Events area and select Let the mouse move the camera. This is a built-in event type; you do not need to do anything else to create the complete event.

2. Click the create new event button and select When the mouse is clicked on something from the menu. Scroll to the bottom of the Events area to see the new event tile.

3. Click the camera tile in the Object tree, then drag a copy of the camera point at instruction tile and drop it in the new event in place of Nothing, following the word do. When the menu appears, select seaplane. The new event now reads When the mouse is clicked on anything, do camera point at seaplane. Save the world before continuing.

# In the Lab

Your two new events are complete and ready to be tested. While the world is playing, click and drag the mouse pointer forward, backward, left, and right in the playing world window to move the camera. You can pan left and right and zoom in and out. Simply click the mouse without dragging it to point the camera at the plane. These controls will work while the keyboard controls are being used to fly the plane. One person can operate both the mouse and the keyboard using two hands, or two people can work together — one flying the plane and the other operating the camera.

Your final task in this exercise is to populate the world with several objects to make the scene more interesting, as in Figure 4-94. For example, you could place a lighthouse in the distance, and then fly the plane around the lighthouse. Several folders, particularly the Vehicles folder and the Beach folder, contain objects that you can place in the water to make your world more interesting as you fly the plane. The Environments folder contains two different islands. Once you have created a world you like, save the world.

**FIGURE 4-94**

Also, remember that you can use the Take Picture button while the world is playing to capture an image of the plane in your virtual world. Perhaps you can fly the plane near some of the objects you add to the world and capture it in an interesting position while the world is playing.

Alice 2.0

# In the Lab

## 2 An Interactive Ballerina World

The file, Lab 4-2 ballerina practice.a2w, contains a number of objects and methods for an interactive ballerina world. Your task is to add the necessary events so that the world will function properly.

The world contains five ballerinas—Ava, Bronwyn, Cathy, Debbie, and Evelyn—and has a world-level object property named currentBallerina. When the user clicks on a ballerina, currentBallerina should be set to that ballerina. There are also four movement buttons in the world—left, right, bow, and spin—as shown in Figure 4-95. When the user clicks a movement button, the current ballerina should perform the corresponding action. The four buttons were drawn using Microsoft Visio, saved as jpeg files, then added to the world as individual billboard objects.

**FIGURE 4-95**

The world needs nine new events to function properly—one mouse event for each of the five ballerinas, and one mouse event for each of the four buttons, as described in the following list:

- When the mouse is clicked on Ava, do world.currentBallerina set value to Ava.
- When the mouse is clicked on Bronwyn, do world.currentBallerina set value to Bronwyn.
- When the mouse is clicked on Cathy, do world.currentBallerina set value to Cathy.
- When the mouse is clicked on Debbie, do world.currentBallerina set value to Debbie.
- When the mouse is clicked on Evelyn, do world.currentBallerina set value to Evelyn.
- When the mouse is clicked on bowButton, do world.bow who = world.currentBallerina.
- When the mouse is clicked on spinButton, do world.spin who = world.currentBallerina.
- When the mouse is clicked on leftButton, do world.jumpMove who = world.currentBallerina direction = left.
- When the mouse is clicked on rightButton, do world.jumpMove who = world.currentBallerina direction = right.

Open the file, Lab 4-2 ballerina practice.a2w, from the Data Files for Students. See the inside back cover of this book for instructions for downloading the Data Files for Students, or see your instructor for information about accessing the files required in this book.

Examine the world and you will see that it contains two events in the Events area. One event calls a method that will highlight a button whenever the mouse is clicked on it. It does this by changing the opacity of all of the buttons to 50%, then changing the opacity of the object under the cursor to 100%. If the object is a button, then that button will be solid while the rest will be semitransparent. If the object is not a button, then it will

already be solid and no change will be visible. The other event is the default event, which calls world.my first method as its event handler when the world starts. world.my first method causes the ballerinas to jump together, and then scrolls instructions across the screen.

**Instructions:** First, add the event to select the ballerina Ava.

1. Click the **create new event** button in the Events area and then select **When the mouse is clicked on something** from the menu that appears. A new **When mouse is clicked on anything, do Nothing** tile will appear in the Events area, below the existing events.
2. Click the **anything** parameter in the new event, then select **Ava, the entire Ava** from the menus that appear.
3. Select the **world** tile in the Object tree, click the **properties** tab in the Details area, then drag a copy of the **currentBallerina** tile from the **properties** tab and drop it in the new event in place of the word **Nothing**. When the first menu appears, point to the top item, **set value**, then click **Ava, the entire Ava**.

The first ballerina event is in place and should read **When the mouse is clicked on Ava, do world.currentBallerina set value to Ava**. Next, you will create the five remaining ballerina events from a copy of the Ava event.

1. Drag a copy of the **Ava** event that you just created from the Events area to the Clipboard.
2. Drag the content of the Clipboard and drop it in the Events area, below the existing events.
3. Scroll down to the bottom of the Events area to see the new copy of the **Ava** event. The name **Ava** appears twice as parameters in this event. Click each of the two parameters in the new copy of the **Ava** event and change them to **Bronwyn, the entire Bronwyn**.
4. The new **Bronwyn** event is in place. Repeat the last two steps for each of the remaining three ballerinas: **Cathy**, **Debbie**, and **Evelyn**.

Events are now in place to allow the user to select any of the five ballerinas. Next, you will build the four events to make the movement buttons work. You will work from the bottom up, starting with the Spin button.

1. Click the **create new event** button in the Events area and then select **When the mouse is clicked on something** from the menu that appears. A new **When mouse is clicked on anything, do Nothing** tile will appear in the Events area, below the existing events.
2. Scroll to the bottom of the Events area. Click the **anything** parameter in the new event, then select **spinButton** from the menu that appears.
3. Click the **methods** tab in the Details area so that you can see the world-level methods.
4. Drag a copy of the **spin who** tile from the **methods** tab and drop it in the new event in place of **Nothing**, following the word **do**.
5. When the menu appears, point to **expressions** near the bottom of the menu, then click **world.currentBallerina**.

The Spin button's event is now in place. Next, create the **Bow** button event.

1. Click the **create new event** button in the Events area and then select **When the mouse is clicked on something** from the menu that appears. A new **When mouse is clicked on anything, do Nothing** tile will appear in the Events area, below the existing events.
2. Scroll to the bottom of the Events area. Click the **anything** parameter in the new event, then select **bowButton** from the menu that appears.
3. Drag a copy of the **bow who** tile from the **methods** tab and drop it in the new event in place of **Nothing**, following the word **do**.
4. When the menu appears, point to **expressions** near the bottom of the menu, then click **world.currentBallerina**.

*(continued)*

**In the Lab**

## An Interactive Ballerina World *(continued)*

Now create the event for the left button. The menus you will encounter are a little more complicated than the menus you used to create the spin and bow instructions.

1. Click the create new event button in the Events area and then select When the mouse is clicked on something from the menu that appears. A new When mouse is clicked on anything, do Nothing tile will appear in the Events area, below the existing events.
2. Scroll to the bottom of the Events area. Click the anything parameter in the new event, then select leftButton from the menu that appears.
3. Drag a copy of the jumpMove who direction tile from the methods tab and drop it in the new event in place of Nothing, following the word do. Notice that this tile has two parameters, who and direction.
4. When the who menu appears, point to expressions near the bottom of the menu, then point to world.currentBallerina. When the direction menu appears, click left.

The last event you will create is the event for the right button.

1. Click the create new event button in the Events area and then select When the mouse is clicked on something from the menu that appears. A new When mouse is clicked on anything, do Nothing tile will appear in the Events area, below the existing events.
2. Scroll to the bottom of the Events area. Click the anything parameter in the new event, then select rightButton from the menu that appears.
3. Drag a copy of the jumpMove who direction tile from the methods tab and drop it in the new event in place of Nothing, following the word do. Notice that this tile has two parameters, who and direction.
4. When the who menu appears, point to expressions near the bottom of the menu, then point to world.currentBallerina. When the direction menu appears, click right.

All of your events are now in place. Save the world with the name, Lab 4-2 ballerina interactive.a2w, then play the world and try the controls. As the instructions indicate, first you should select a ballerina, then use the four movement buttons to make the ballerina move.

## 3 Creating New Controls for an Amusement Park

In this exercise, you will work with a variation of the amusement park example world that is included with the Alice software. You will create keyboard controls that allow the user to move through the amusement park and look around, along with a mouse event to start the different rides in the park. You will create six camera control events for the world, as follows:

↑ – move the camera forward
↓ – move the camera backward
← – turn the camera left
→ – turn the camera right
F – tilt the camera forward
B – tilt the camera backward

You will be able to move around in the amusement park and look at the various rides. The park has six amusement park rides and the rides have methods to animate them. In addition to the camera movement events, you will create six events to allow the user to start each ride by clicking the mouse pointer on the ride.

**Instructions:** Open the file, Lab 4-3 amusement park.a2w, from the Data Files for Students. See the inside back cover of this book for instructions for downloading the Data Files for Students, or see your instructor for information about accessing the files required in this book.

The world currently has no events. Create each of the following six keyboard camera-control events in the Events area:

While Left is pressed
Begin:          <None>
During:        Camera turn at speed left speed = 0.1 revolutions per second
End:            <None>

While Right is pressed
Begin:          <None>
During:        Camera turn at speed right speed = 0.1 revolutions per second
End:            <None>

While Up is pressed
Begin:          <None>
During:        Camera move at speed forward speed = 5 meters per second
End:            <None>

While Down is pressed
Begin:          <None>
During:        Camera move at speed backward speed = 5 meters per second
End:            <None>

While F is pressed
Begin:          <None>
During:        Camera turn at speed forward speed = 0.1 revolutions per second
End:            <None>

While B is pressed
Begin:          <None>
During:        Camera turn at speed backward speed = 0.1 revolutions per second
End:            <None>

To create the camera-control events, start by clicking the create new event button in the Events area and selecting When a key is typed. This will create a new event of the type When any key is typed, do Nothing. You will need to right-click the new event tile, point to change to on the menu that appears, then click While a key is pressed. Then you can change the parameters to create the first event listed above, for the left arrow key. After this event is finished, you can copy it and modify the parameters in the copy to form the second event. Repeat this process of copying and modifying the event to create the remaining camera-control events. Save your world with the name, Lab 4-3 amusement park interactive.a2w, before continuing.

You can test the camera-control events by playing the world and manipulating the camera. You will see the world from the camera's point of view as it moves, so it will appear as if you are flying around the amusement park.

*(continued)*

## Creating New Controls for an Amusement Park *(continued)*

When the camera-control events are finished, you can create the six mouse events that will allow the user to start the rides, as follows:

When [mouse] is clicked on Octopus
Do: World.octoAnimationLoop

When [mouse] is clicked on Skyride
Do: World.skyrideAnimation

When [mouse] is clicked on Teacups
Do: World.teacupBaseAnimationLoop

When [mouse] is clicked on FerrisWheel
Do: World.ferrisAnimation

When [mouse] is clicked on Carousel
Do: World.carouselAnimationLoop

When [mouse] is clicked on Swings
Do: World.swingsAnimation

You can start to create the mouse events by clicking the create new event button in the Events area and selecting When the mouse is clicked on something. This will create a new event of the type When [mouse] is clicked on anything, do Nothing. Click the anything parameter, and select Octopus, the entire Octopus from the menus that appear. Next, drag a copy of the octoAnimationLoop tile from the world's methods tab and drop it in the new event in place of Nothing. After this event is completed, you can copy it and modify the parameters in the copy to form the second event. Repeat this process of copying and modifying the event to create the remaining mouse events. When you are finished, you can play the world and test the new controls by finding and clicking the six animated rides.

Save your world with the name, Lab 4-3 amusement park interactive.a2w, when you are sure that it works as specified.

1 The file, Case 4-1 fan dancer.a2w, has a version of the Fan Dancer world used in earlier exercises. The dancer has four different poses and a method to make her bow. Your task is to create an interactive world in which the user makes the dancer perform different movements by using the keyboard controls. You should start by examining the world to see what the four poses are, creating an outline of the user controls and movements you wish to add to the world, then building the world you have described. When you are finished, save your world with the name, Case 4-1 fan dancer interactive.a2w.

# Cases and Places

**2** Many amusement parks have a shooting gallery in which various objects react if the user shoots them. For example, the dial on a clock might spin if the shooter hits the clock. Your task in this exercise is to build something similar in Alice, but instead of a shooting gallery, the user will move around in a world and click different objects to see their behaviors. You should decide on a theme for your world, then build the world and populate it with a variety of objects. You should create methods that provide a behavior for each object, along with events to trigger the behavior if the user clicks on the object. You should also provide some way for the user to move the camera around in the world. When you are finished, save your world with the name, Case 4-2 gallery.a2w.

**3** Start a new Alice world with a grass template, then create a new character for the world using the **hebuilder** or **shebuilder** in the Alice object gallery's **People** folder. Examine the character's methods and then build a set of event-driven controls that will allow the user to manipulate the character using those methods and others that you may wish to build. When you are finished, you should have a world with a character that the user may manipulate like an animated puppet, causing it to stand, sit, walk, run, turn, or show a variety of emotions, such as anger, happiness, or confusion. You may add other objects to your world as you wish, but your focus should be on creating events to animate the puppet. When you are finished, save your world with the name, Case 4-3 puppet.a2w

# Learning Exercises

**1** **Online Research** The Web site Webopedia.com is a good place to start if you would like to learn more about computer terminology and concepts. Visit www.webopedia.com and search for more information about the term "interrupt". How is a computer system interrupt related to event-driven programming?

**2** The blue camera-control arrows that appear below the world window in the standard Alice interface and in Scene Editor mode allow the user to move the camera in a variety of ways. List and describe a set of events that will provide the same capability while an Alice world is playing.

*(continued)*

# Learning Exercises

**3** **Describing Alice Programming Tasks** Briefly describe how to complete each of the following tasks in Alice:

    a.  view the event types available in Alice

    b.  create a keyboard event to move an object

    c.  create a keyboard event to change an object's pose

    d.  create a mouse event to change an object's pose when the user clicks the object

    e.  create a new keyboard event from an existing keyboard event

    f.  use an existing method as an event handler for a new keyboard event

    g.  use an existing method as an event handler for a new mouse event

# Index

Page numbers in **bold** indicate where a key term is defined in the text.